Portuguese and Amsterdam's Sephardic Merchants in the Tobacco Trade

Tierra Firme and Hispaniola in the Early Seventeenth Century

Yda Schreuder

ANTHEM PRESS

Anthem Press
An imprint of Wimbledon Publishing Company
www.anthempress.com

This edition first published in UK and USA 2025
by ANTHEM PRESS
75–76 Blackfriars Road, London SE1 8HA, UK
or PO Box 9779, London SW19 7ZG, UK
and
244 Madison Ave #116, New York, NY 10016, USA

First published in the UK and USA by Anthem Press in 2023

© 2025 Yda Schreuder

The author asserts the moral right to be identified as the author of this work.

All rights reserved. Without limiting the rights under copyright reserved above,
no part of this publication may be reproduced, stored or introduced
into a retrieval system, or transmitted, in any form or by any means
(electronic, mechanical, photocopying, recording or otherwise),
without the prior written permission of both the copyright
owner and the above publisher of this book.

British Library Cataloguing-in-Publication Data
A catalogue record for this book is available from the British Library.

Library of Congress Control Number: 2024950674
A catalog record for this book has been requested.

ISBN-13: 978-1-83999-474-6 (Pbk)
ISBN-10: 1-83999-474-6 (Pbk)

This title is also available as an e-book.

CONTENTS

List of Figures   v

Preface   vi

1. Portuguese and Amsterdam Sephardic Merchants in the Tobacco Trade in the Early Seventeenth Century   1
   1.1 Introduction   1
   1.2 Amsterdam's Colonial Staple Market and Sephardic Merchants   8
   1.3 Portuguese and Amsterdam's Sephardic Merchants and the Eighty Years' War   16
   1.4 The Portuguese Nation and the Illegal Tobacco Trade   20
   1.5 Evidence from the Amsterdam Notary Public Records   27

2. The Contraband Tobacco Trade with Spanish America: *Tierra Firme* and Hispaniola   33
   2.1 Trade and Navigation between Spain and Its Colonies   33
   2.2 The Engel Sluiter Historical Documents Collection   39
   2.3 Engel Sluiter's Analysis of the Documents Collection   44
   2.4 Tobacco Monopolies and Tariff Systems   54

3. Portuguese Merchants and the Tobacco Trade with *Tierra Firme*   63
   3.1 Contraband and Trade Rivalry in the Eighty Years' War   63
   3.2 Salt Winning, Pearl Fishing, and Tobacco Smuggling at *Tierra Firme*   70
   3.3 The Canary Island Connection   77
   3.4 Depopulation and Prohibition of Tobacco Cultivation   80
   3.5 Smuggling as a Way of Life on Trinidad Island   82
   3.6 Unintended Consequences   85
   3.7 Summary and Conclusion   92

4. Portuguese Merchants and the Tobacco Trade with Hispaniola   99
   4.1 Political, Economic, and Geographical Context   99
   4.2 Portuguese Resident Merchants and Foreign Intruders   105

	4.3	Bribery and Corruption among Officials and Administrators	110
	4.4	Depopulation and Evacuation Ordered and Dismissed	116
	4.5	Portuguese Resident Merchants and the "Nation"	121
	4.6	Summary and Conclusion	123
5.	Conclusion	127
	5.1	Introduction	127
	5.2	The "Vast Machine" of the Portuguese Nation	131
	5.3	Conclusion	145

Bibliographic Notes — 147

Index — 151

LIST OF FIGURES

1.1	The North Atlantic World, ca. 1630	5
2.1	Spanish provinces, audiencias, and captaincies general in the Caribbean and Gulf of Mexico in the sixteenth to seventeenth centuries	42
3.1	Historical Map of Terra Firma, Guiana and the Antilles Islands ca. 1732	69
4.1	The Island of Santo Domingo or Hispaniola ca. 1723	103

PREFACE

The story of the tobacco trade in the Atlantic world in the late sixteenth and early seventeenth centuries is a story of entanglement among different merchant groups embedded in trans-imperial connections which transcended political or state boundaries and ethnic associations. The different participants in trade included European colonial settlers, native and indigenous people, run-away slaves, and merchants of various kinds and backgrounds and formed part of a network of contact that had developed over time engaged in tobacco cultivation, trade, and smuggling. In the story, I will focus on Portuguese merchants who straddled the Portuguese, Spanish, and North European maritime Atlantic world and Sephardic or Portuguese Jewish merchants who traded on behalf of the Dutch after they resumed Jewish identity with residency in the Dutch Republic. In some instances, the Sephardic merchants were the key link facilitating Dutch trade in particular in Amsterdam. A good example is Simon de Herrera, a Portuguese Jew who had connections and associations with both English and Dutch merchants and smugglers. He was captured in Hispaniola by the Spanish in 1596 and during the court case against him following his arrest it was discovered that he held documents which implicated him with Dutch interests and contacts as he was offered safe passage to Holland or Zeeland in the Dutch Republic. Being Jewish and charged with trading for the Dutch he became a target for the Inquisition. The Dutch were at war with Spain at the time which did not improve his chances to be let free. He was taken for trial in Mexico and executed in 1604. Herrera had likely been a factor or agent for a Dutch merchant who traded illegally with the Portuguese and Spanish in the Caribbean. Hispaniola had by then become a regular transfer point for Dutch, English, and French privateers engaged in the tobacco trade.

Contraband trade and war is all too familiar in the sixteenth and seventeenth centuries. In the case of the Dutch Republic, it were the circumstances dictated by the Eighty Years' War with Habsburg Spain that explain how trade or exchange was conducted. For the most part, battles were fought at sea and commercial rivalry dictated the relationships between Spain and the Dutch Republic in which Portuguese and Sephardic merchants played a role of some importance. The main source of information on Spanish–Dutch commercial rivalry and smuggling of tobacco is the Engel Sluiter Historical Documents Collection described in detail in Chapter 2. The records in the collection are copies of documents dating back to the 1590s and include records for specific regions of Spanish America and Portuguese Brazil where tobacco smuggling occurred and where Portuguese merchants were active in trade. The records illustrate the extent to which Spanish officials were prepared to combat Dutch merchant trade or engage in bribery and in manipulating the local populations to participate in illegal exchange. The historical documents collection derived mostly from reports made by Spanish officials which revealed a close-knit relationship between smugglers and their go-betweens, the Portuguese merchants, resident along the coast of *Tierra Firme* and the islands in the Caribbean on whom the Spanish officials depended for needed supplies and income. This tale of intrigue was in direct relation to the profit interests of Dutch, French, and English private merchants and smugglers connected to the European tobacco markets.

The book presents a historical-geographic perspective with a focus on Amsterdam in the late sixteenth and early seventeenth centuries. During that time, known in Dutch history as the Golden Age, Amsterdam was the center of colonial trade for the Northwest European market and developed, besides sugar refining, also processing industries for other colonial staples like tobacco. As the trade in Atlantic colonial staples originated within the Spanish-Portuguese realm, the Dutch, French, and English privateers were interlopers and thus were associated with smuggling and contraband trade. This was the case also in the sugar trade until the Dutch captured territory in the sugar producing regions of Portuguese Brazil where tobacco was likely traded alongside sugar when the Dutch held sway from 1630 to 1654. In the book, I focus on the tobacco contraband trade along the coast of Guiana and Venezuela (*Tierra Firme*) and the Caribbean islands of Hispaniola. Here, originally, trade and smuggling was incidental as the prevailing winds and currents dictated the routes mariners sailed and indigenous populations made contact with merchants coming ashore. Tobacco growing occurred in many parts of the region and had its origin in trade among indigenous populations and run-away slaves or Maroons. And, thus, as Spanish or Portuguese territorial control was recognized, though not always enforced, illegal trade or smuggling prevailed among the various groups that participated in the cultivation and exchange of tobacco in which Portuguese merchants played a crucial role.

The research for this book has been conducted over several years and started when I was still working on the sugar trade book. As I investigated the role

Amsterdam Sephardic merchants played in the Atlantic sugar trade, I realized that often the tobacco trade had preceded the sugar trade as was the case in Barbados for instance. I knew that the geographical coincidence or sequence of events deserved more research attention but I was not in a position to pursue the topic further for a long while. The source materials I had used for the sugar trade book included the Archives of Notary Publics in the Netherlands which did not reveal a great deal about the tobacco trade and suggested that the trade was of a different kind. Illegal, perhaps ..., and thus evidence was not found in public records. Whereas sugar plantations and the sugar trade formed part of the European colonial plantation economy, tobacco cultivation and trade was not. Tobacco was indigenous to the Americas. Sugar cultivation and trade had originated in India and via Egypt and the Mediterranean region had been transplanted to the islands of the West Coast of Africa and then Portuguese Brazil and, still later, several Caribbean islands including Barbados and Jamaica among the British colonies. The westward expansion of both cultivation and trade of sugar was characteristic of the European sugar trade complex. Tobacco cultivation and trade went in the opposite direction, from the Americas to Europe with indigenous groups as originators. This was a fascinating aspect of the tobacco trade and raised all kinds of questions. Were the European merchants engaged in the tobacco trade members of the same merchant networks that supported the sugar trade or were they different merchant groups engaged in a different kind of exchange? I already knew that Amsterdam's Sephardic merchants participated in the tobacco trade but I did not know if they originated from the same merchant families who participated in the sugar trade. I suspected that Portuguese merchants played a role of some significance but how and via which channels was not clear. In any event, I knew that I had to find a different tool for research and a different research strategy, the source of which I found in the Engel Sluiter Historical Documents Collection.

The Engel Sluiter Historical Documents Collection contains historical documents from archives throughout Europe and Latin America and are kept at Bancroft Library at the University of California, Berkeley. They were a rare find and formed the basis for the research of the book. The documents collected include government records, fiscal and business accounts, and reports on military matters. The main theme of Sluiter's Historical Documents Collection is Dutch–Iberian trade rivalry at the time of the Eighty Years' War from 1568 to 1648. The documents also include Dutch, English, French, Spanish, and Portuguese voyages to the New World in rivalry with each other in search of gold, silver, and other goods to trade. Many of the records were filed with the Archives of the Indies in Seville. The documents in the collection relate mainly to Dutch, Spanish, and

Portuguese affairs in Europe and in the overseas Spanish and Portuguese possessions but include references to English and French accounts of affairs with Spain as well. The majority of the documents are in Spanish, transcribed, translated in English, and provided with notes by Engel Sluiter himself. I am sure that if I had traveled to Seville, Lisbon, London, or returned for more research at the City Archives of Amsterdam, I would have found more material and I am sure that there is more to the story than I present here. I can only hope that some ambitious graduate student will continue the research but for now this is all I can present to you, the reader and scholar interested in the topic area. The New Netherland Institute in Albany, NY, provided welcome and generous support for the project when I was awarded the Charles W. Wendell Research Grant in 2019. Julie van den Hout completed an inventory of the collection of documents at Bancroft Library in 2016 and without the help of the index she provided, the research would likely not have occurred.

Historical research is for the most part a solitary enterprise. A very exciting enterprise, with very little financial reward for most of us, but with the reward of knowing that you contributed to an interesting or worthwhile topic of inquiry. I have been part of a community of historians and geographers for most of my academic career and have been recognized by a small group of specialists all of whom I like to thank for their critical reading of my work, including two anonymous reviewers. During my scholarly journey there have been several people who have encouraged me and spurred me on to continue with the project. There are three people in particular I would like to recognize here. First of all, my dear friend and colleague, Peter Rees, with whom I have explored the intellectual landscape of historical geography from the start of my career at the University of Delaware and who has served as my mentor. Secondly, Wim Klooster, who has followed my pursuits of studying Atlantic history and has introduced me to and included me in the company of scholars of Sephardic Jewish history. His writings and thoughts have been inspirational over the past decade. Finally, I would like to thank my editor at Anthem Press, Jebaslin Hephzibah. His professional and encouraging approach was unceasing. Without his support and good natured insistence to receive the manuscript in good order, this book would not have been completed. My decision to move to Colorado and the actual move interfered with my research and writing and also meant that I had to leave one of the greatest research institutions on the East Coast, the Hagley Museum and Library, where I had been conducting research and found a quiet place to write for the better part of thirty years. I miss the contact with my colleagues and staff there and will always have fond memories of the discussions, debates, and seminars we held.

Chapter 1

PORTUGUESE AND AMSTERDAM SEPHARDIC MERCHANTS IN THE TOBACCO TRADE IN THE EARLY SEVENTEENTH CENTURY

1.1 Introduction

According to Simon Schama in *The Embarrassment of Riches* (1987): "... The smell of the Dutch Republic was the smell of tobacco."[1] Describing the Dutch Golden Age, he referred to accounts by visitors to the Netherlands who were struck by the omnipresence of tobacco smoke in inns and towing barges and the common sight of men and women smoking in public. I am not sure if this was a general situation at the time, but it was certainly true that in depictions of hearth and home in Dutch paintings of the seventeenth century, tobacco pipes and smoking were prominent features. Tobacco consumption in Europe in the seventeenth century experienced a remarkable growth and provided substantial profits for merchants engaged in the tobacco trade. Yet, we know very little about its very beginnings and, in fact, you could say that compared to the sugar trade, the tobacco trade is *terra incognita*. In part, this is because the tobacco trade was contraband trade in the early seventeenth century when Portuguese and Sephardic merchants became engaged in exchange with the coastal regions of South America and the Caribbean islands under Spanish and Portuguese rule where Dutch merchants including Amsterdam's Sephardic merchants were considered "interlopers"; foreign merchants with no license to trade.[2] Furthermore, they were considered enemy merchants as the Dutch Republic was at war with Habsburg Spain during the Eighty Years'

---

1 Simon Schama, *The Embarrassment of Riches: An Interpretation of Dutch Culture in the Golden Age* (Alfred A. Knopf, New York, 1987), p. 189.
2 The term Sephardic or Sephardim refers to Jews of Spanish or Portuguese descent who had begun to arrive in Amsterdam toward the end of the sixteenth century as Portuguese merchants engaged in the sugar trade and as members of the Portuguese Nation. Many Portuguese merchants were New Christian or *Converso* who were

War (1568–1648).[3] Whereas we know the broad outline of various aspects of the tobacco contraband trade in the later part of the seventeenth century, we know very little about why and when Amsterdam became the European—or you might say—the global marketplace for tobacco or where tobacco was first traded for profit.[4] Here, we need to delve into the history of Amsterdam as a staple market and the role Portuguese and Sephardic merchants played in the Spanish and Portuguese colonial trade. In the sixteenth century, Antwerp in Flanders (the Southern Netherlands) had been the main market place for colonial goods exchanged in Northwestern Europe, but toward the end of the century, Amsterdam replaced Antwerp in that role. The Dutch Republic (the Northern Netherlands), founded in opposition to Habsburg rule, waged a war strategy which included raids, blockades, and trade embargoes by which the Northern Netherlands provinces of Holland and Zeeland laid siege on Antwerp. This severely undermined Antwerp's role in exchange between the Iberian Peninsula and the Baltic region. In a fairly short period of time as a result of blockades and embargoes imposed by the warring parties, the provinces of the Northern Netherlands went from relative obscurity as the poor cousins relative to the more industrial and urbanized Southern Netherlands provinces of Flanders and Brabant to the pinnacle of European commercial success. As Antwerp, the main staple port in the Southern Netherlands, remained aligned with Habsburg Spain during the Eighty Years' War (1568–1648) and suffered repeated attacks and counterattacks and lost its position as staple port in the Iberian–Baltic trade circuit, Amsterdam took over that role and expanded its reach across the Atlantic. Taking advantage of a favorable agricultural base, success in the North Sea herring fisheries, and shipments to and from the Baltic, the Dutch Republic established a

---

granted special privileges to trade in various Atlantic port cities and were often suspected of adhering to Judaism in which case they may be referred to as crypto-Jews. In Amsterdam, many turned to openly practicing Judaism. In the text, I use the term Sephardic usually with reference to merchants, whereas I may refer to Portuguese Jews in more general terms.

3 Portugal formed part of the Spanish Habsburg realm from 1580 to 1640.

4 Significant contributions to our understanding of tobacco cultivation and trade in the Caribbean region include Marcy Norton, *Sacred Gifts, Profane Pleasures: A History of Tobacco and Chocolate in the Atlantic World* (Cornell University Press, Ithaca and London, 2008) and Melissa N. Morris, "Cultivating Colonies: Tobacco and the Upstart Empires, 1580–1640" (PhD dissertation, Columbia University, 2017). Our understanding of illicit trade and contraband trade in the eighteenth century has benefitted from the work by Wim Klooster, *Illicit Riches: Dutch Trade in the Caribbean, 1648–1795* (KITLV Press, Leiden, 1998), Linda M. Rupert, *Creolization and Contraband: Curacao in the Early Modern Atlantic World* (The University of Georgia Press, Athens and London, 2012), and Jesse Cromwell, *The Smugglers' World: Illicit Trade and Atlantic Communities in Eighteenth-Century Venezuela* (University of North Carolina Press, Chapel Hill, 2018).

far-flung maritime empire in the seventeenth century and Amsterdam became the main staple port.[5]

Within a decade after the fall of Antwerp in 1585, scores of mostly Protestant merchants, craftsmen, and shopkeepers from the Southern Netherlands sought the relative security of the Northern Netherlands. Meanwhile, merchants from Spain and Portugal recognizing better opportunities in the Baltic and North Sea trade being based in the Dutch Republic began to relocate to Amsterdam in the province of Holland or trading towns in the province of Zeeland. Subsequently, shipping emerged as a significant sector of the Dutch economy, and the Baltic grain trade became a robust part of the North–South (Iberian–Baltic) trade circuit. Building on the successes of the Baltic trade, Dutch shippers expanded their sphere of influence eastward into Russia and southward into the Portuguese, Mediterranean, and the Levantine markets. By 1600, Dutch merchants had their eyes cast on the American and Asian markets that were then still dominated by Spanish and Portuguese merchants. Not encumbered by high costs of shipping and protective restrictions affecting Spanish and Portuguese merchants in the sixteenth and seventeenth centuries, the Dutch established world primacy in trade. Consequently, merchants from Antwerp, including Portuguese New Christian merchants, also relocated to Zeeland and Holland from Flanders and Brabant and engaged in the Guinea trade with West Africa and the sugar trade with the Atlantic islands of Madeira and São Tomé, and Brazil, which introduced Dutch, including Amsterdam Sephardic merchants to the Atlantic trade, including the tobacco trade.[6]

---

5 The rise to power of the Dutch Republic in the seventeenth-century Atlantic world is presented by Jonathan I. Israel, *Dutch Primacy in World Trade, 1585–1740* (Clarendon Press, Oxford, 1989), and Jan de Vries and Ad van der Woude, *The First Modern Economy: Success, Failure, and Perseverance of the Dutch Economy, 1500–1850* (Cambridge University Press, Cambridge, 1997). The impact of the war has been a point of debate among historians of the Dutch Golden Age of the seventeenth century. Some, like Israel (1989), have argued that the war conditions meant a shift in trade when embargoes damaged trading prospects for Antwerp and allowed the Dutch to expand the Atlantic trade circuits. Others, like de Vries and van der Woude (1997), maintained that commercial structural conditions dictated economic development and provided the edge in favor of Dutch competition. For a detailed analysis, see C. Lesger, *The Rise of the Amsterdam Market and Information Exchange* (Ashgate, Aldershot, UK and Burlington, VT, 2006) and the edited volume by C. Lesger and L. Noordegraaf, *Entrepreneurs and Entrepreneurship in Early Modern Times: Merchants and Industrialists within the Orbit of the Dutch Staple Market* (Hollandse Historische Reeks, the Hague, 1995).

6 For a detailed discussion about the emergence of Amsterdam as the primary European port for the colonial staple trade, in particular sugar, in the late sixteenth and early seventeenth centuries, see my book *Amsterdam's Sephardic Merchants and the Atlantic Sugar Trade in the Seventeenth Century* (Palgrave Macmillan, New York and London, 2019).

During the last decades of the sixteenth century, Dutch merchants still focused their primary attention on Iberia and the nearby Atlantic islands to obtain colonial trade goods, and only a few Dutch ships were making voyages across the Atlantic to the Spanish Caribbean or to Portuguese Brazil. This began to change when the Spanish instituted embargoes on Dutch trade and a general embargo imposed in 1598 completely prohibited trade with Portugal.[7] Shortages of products traditionally obtained at ports along the Portuguese Atlantic coast or at Antwerp, like salt or sugar, became common occurrences. Consequently, Dutch merchants seized the opportunity to explore new sources of salt supplies and sugar cargo and soon fleets of Dutch ships sailed to Spanish America and to West Africa and Portuguese Brazil where they resorted to illegal trade.[8] The Dutch War strategy was to avoid Iberian strongholds while searching for products they needed or traded at Amsterdam, which meant that points of contact along the coast of West Africa and the Western Atlantic became the main destinations (Figure 1.1). These included The South American Caribbean coastal areas including the Amazon and Orinoco delta regions known as *Tierra Firme* in Spanish and in the English geographic literature often referred to as the Wild Coast. Various Caribbean islands like Hispaniola, Cuba, and Puerto Rico were also targeted destinations. In some instances, the Dutch established forts to defend their interests or harass the Spanish, and Amsterdam merchants among them Portuguese New Christian merchants and Sephardic merchants, made contacts with Portuguese merchants who had established themselves in the Spanish and Portuguese possessions.[9]

---

7 In 1580, the unification agreement between Spain and Portugal had taken effect and, as a consequence, Dutch trade with Portugal became more restrictive and more often illegal trade occurred.

8 Israel, *Dutch Primacy* (1989); see also, Christopher Ebert, "Dutch Trade with Brazil before the Dutch West India Company, 1587–1621," in Johannes Postma and Victor Enthoven (eds.), *Riches from Atlantic Commerce: Dutch Transatlantic Trade and Shipping, 1585–1817* (Brill, Leiden, Boston, 2003), pp. 49–75. The first ships sailing to Brazil were reported in 1587. Some trips were contracted in Amsterdam at this time in partnership with Portuguese merchants in Lisbon as correspondents while Dutch skippers often obtained information about trade prospects in Portuguese ports. For the early Dutch explorations and trade in the Caribbean region, see Cornelis Ch. Goslinga, *The Dutch in the Caribbean and on the Wild Coast, 1580–1680* (University of Florida Press, Gainesville, 1971).

9 See Jonathan I. Israel, "Jews and Crypto-Jews in the Atlantic World Systems, 1500–1800," in Richard L. Kagan and Philip D. Morgan (eds.), *Atlantic Diasporas: Jews, New Christians, and Crypto-Jews in the Age of Mercantilism, 1500–1800* (Johns Hopkins University Press, Baltimore, 2009), pp. 3–17. See also, Israel, *Dutch Primacy* (1989), pp. 62–66.

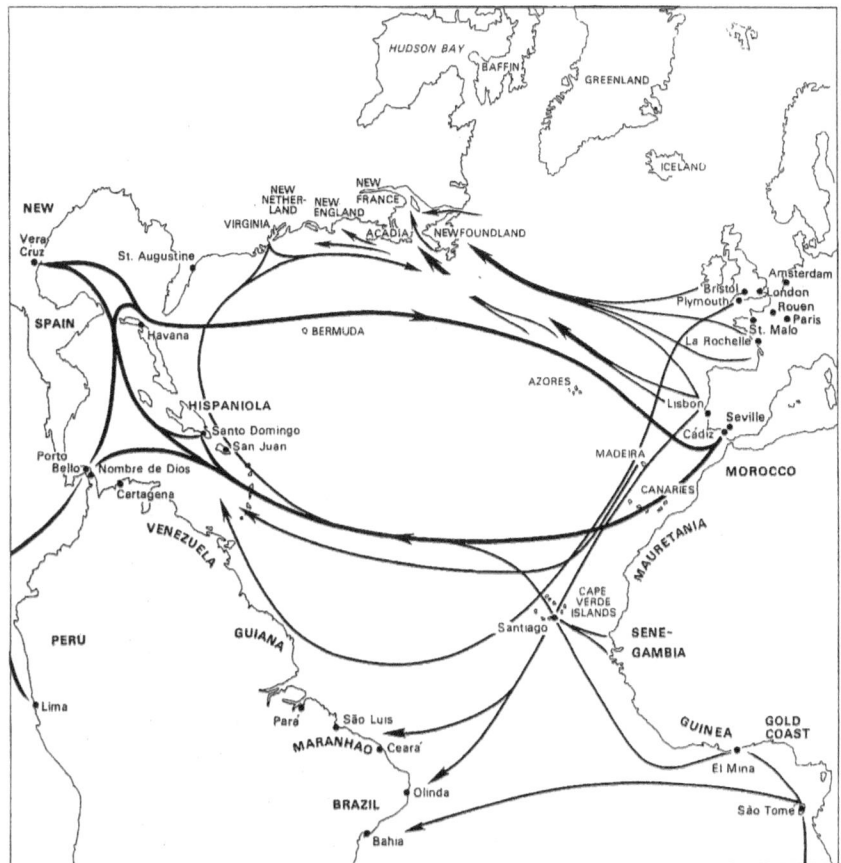

Figure 1.1 The North Atlantic World, ca. 1630.
Zone A: Fisheries to and from the West coast of England, France, Holland, and Portugal to Newfoundland, Acadia, New France, New England, New Netherland, and Virginia.
Zone B: Spanish Maritime with focus on (1) Mexico and Peru gold and silver and (2) Hispaniola (Santo Domingo) as distribution center for supply goods from Europe and return cargo of dyewood, tobacco, and pearls.
Zone C: Portuguese Maritime with connection to (1) West Africa (Cape Verde islands, Senegambia, Guinea, and Sao Tome) ivory, gold, and slaves and (2) Brazil sugar trade and dye wood.

Source: Adapted from D. W. Meinig, The Shaping of America: A Geographical Perspective on 500 Years of History: Volume 1: Atlantic America, 1492–1800 (Yale University Press, New Haven, CT, 1986).

While the search for salt for the herring fishing industry was likely a driving motive in exploring Atlantic and Caribbean coastal areas, along the way and not by accident, merchants from the Dutch Republic also engaged in the sugar trade with Brazil and the contraband tobacco trade with *Tierra Firme* and Hispaniola.[10] Competition between rival merchant groups engaged in trade with Spanish and Portuguese possessions in the Americas in the first years of the seventeenth century was fierce but, by the time the West India Company (WIC) received its charter in 1621, efforts to trade and raid were better coordinated. The WIC carried in its banner attacks on the Spanish fleet in its regular Atlantic crossings and Dutch merchants and mariners soon found raiding directed at the Spanish and Portuguese possessions to be their most profitable activity until the WIC was able to attack and occupy several coastal trading posts and territories, including the province of Pernambuco in Portuguese Brazil in 1630.[11] Sugar became for the time of Dutch occupation of Portuguese territories in Brazil the most lucrative commercial activity, but tobacco obtained through illegal enterprise along the coast of *Tierra Firme* or in exchange with Hispaniola also engaged many Amsterdam merchants. Operating outside of regulated colonial markets, in the backwaters of Spanish America along the coast of South America, the tobacco trade concentrated on La Margarita Island, Cumana and Punta de Araya where salt was won, and Trinidad Island and the Orinoco delta region. Hispaniola, the primary Spanish trading post in the Caribbean became the center where gold, silver, and other colonial products were exchanged for supply goods from Europe in which English, French, and Dutch privateers participated and where contraband, corruption, and bribery were commonplace.

Over time, Amsterdam developed into a thriving staple port, and sugar refining alongside tobacco curing, spinning, and mixing became important industries in the seventeenth century. Between 1600 and 1620, the tobacco varieties from the Spanish territories were the most sought after.

---

10 Goslinga, *The Dutch in the Caribbean* (1971), pp. 141–172. The coastal Spanish possessions referred to as *Tierre Firme* along the coast of South America encompasses the study area centered on La Margarita Island, Cumana and Punta de Araya, and Trinidad Island and the Orinoco Delta region.

11 For a history of the Brazil sugar cultivation and trade, see Stuart B. Schwartz, *Sugar Plantations in the Formation of Brazilian Society, Bahia, 1550–1835* (Cambridge University Press, New York, 1985); Christopher Ebert, *Between Empires: Brazilian Sugar in the Early Atlantic Economy, 1550–1630* (Brill, Leiden, Boston, 2008), and Daniel Strum, *The Sugar Trade: Brazil, Portugal, and the Netherlands 1595–1630* (Stanford University Press, Stanford, CA, 2013).

Later, Virginia and Maryland tobacco varieties gained more popularity. As noted, at the turn of the century, Amsterdam had replaced Antwerp as the Northwest European market for colonial staples and by the early- to mid-seventeenth century, the city had become Europe's primary sugar and tobacco processing and distribution center. From the start, Sephardic merchants played a role of some significance in the sugar and tobacco trade and supplied sugar refineries with raw sugar from Brazil and the spinners and mixers of tobacco leaf with tobacco from *Tierra Firme* and Hispaniola. By 1620, tobacco leaf was also imported from Virginia and Maryland, and in the 1630s, domestic cultivation added to the supply of tobacco available at the Amsterdam market. In the 1670s, between thirty and forty tobacco workshops employed around 4,000 workers.[12] It is estimated that at the end of the seventeenth century, Amsterdam supplied between ten and fifteen million pounds of tobacco for export to Scandinavia, Russia, Poland, Prussia, and the Levant.[13]

The context in which this story unfolds is the Atlantic circuit of trade and connections and the expansion of Europe overseas.[14] Europe's western expansion started with explorations after Columbus' discovery of the Americas in the vanguard of which were mariners from seafaring communities in the Eastern Atlantic; the Portuguese, the Spanish, the Basques, Bretons, English, and Dutch. Most of the time the initial seafarers were predatory and subsisted by raiding and plundering. Indigenous populations at the receiving end were often subjugated into forced labor. Following exploration came conquest and forced imposition of European rule followed by colonization and European settlement. European settlers required food supplies and provisions of clothing, implements, and arms, which usually determined that settlers had to grow crops for export or extract other resources in order to trade. By expanding crop cultivation and mining, additional labor was required

---

12 H. K. Roessingh, "Inlandse Tabak: Expansie en Contractie van een Handelsgewas in de 17e en 18e Eeuw in Nederland" (PhD dissertation, Agricultural University of Wageningen, 1976) and G. A. Brongers, *Nicotiana Tabacum: The History of Tobacco and Tobacco Smoking in the Netherlands* (Publisher unknown, Amsterdam, 1964).

13 Schama, *The Embarrassment of Riches* (1987), p. 194 with reference to Roessingh, *Inlandse Tabak* (1976), pp. 200–201. In comparison, it is estimated that England exported only 1.2 million to the Nordic countries. For the role of Sephardic merchants engaged in the tobacco industry, see Herbert I. Bloom, *The Economic Activity of the Jews of Amsterdam in the Seventeenth and Eighteenth Centuries* (The Bayard Press, Williamsport, PA, 1937), pp. 60–64.

14 Donald W. Meinig, *The Shaping of America: A Geographical Perspective on 500 Years of History*; Volume 1: Atlantic America, 1492–1800 (Yale University Press, New Haven and London, 1986).

and slavery was often instituted. In the process of colonization, the rooting of European culture and exchange systems as well as property rights and rules and regulations were implemented, and indigenous populations were often expelled or driven out of areas where European settlement occurred. The first large-scale colonizing schemes were of Portuguese and Spanish origin followed by Dutch, French, and English initiatives.

It is with this general background as an introduction that I like to start the discussion about the role Portuguese and Amsterdam's Sephardic merchants played in the early phase of tobacco cultivation and trade with a focus on *Tierra Firme* and Hispaniola in the Atlantic-Caribbean region. As the main source of information on contraband tobacco trade, I will analyze documents from the Engel Sluiter Historical Documents Collection, but first a brief discussion about Amsterdam and Amsterdam's Sephardic merchants engaged in the colonial staple trade at the turn of the sixteenth to the seventeenth century.

1.2 Amsterdam's Colonial Staple Market and Sephardic Merchants

Enduring debates have been held about the relationships between the plantation-slave economy and colonial trade in which European capital and technology and African slave labor were combined to generate profit from processing and distribution of tropical staple goods, which contributed to Europe's economic growth in the seventeenth and eighteenth centuries.[15] As the European market in colonial goods expanded, greater efficiency of production, transportation, and trade enhanced imperial competition for access to staple producing colonies. These developments contributed to a geographical expansion of sugar and tobacco cultivation throughout the Caribbean region and manifested itself in the opening up of new markets and an expanding distribution trade. This was particularly the case for sugar production. New sugar colonies developed at a rapid rate replacing older colonies and being overtaken in turn by new sugar frontiers. Sometimes soil depletion and overproduction were the reasons for relocating production to new colonies. In other instances, competition, wars, blockades, embargoes, and protectionist policies contributed to the shifts that occurred often under different imperial regimes which led to

---

15 Eric E. Williams, *Capitalism and Slavery* (University of North Carolina Press, Chapel Hill, 1944); Andre G. Frank, *Dependent Accumulation and Underdevelopment* (Macmillan, London, 1978); Immanuel M. Wallerstein, *The Modern World System* (3 Volumes, Academic Press, New York, 1974–1980).

differential access to commodities, labor, and markets, affecting long-distance trade and the merchant groups engaged in trade across the Atlantic. Under these circumstances, some merchant groups survived and thrived, and proved to be prepared to relocate, migrate, and shift alliances. Other merchants proved to be less resilient or adaptable or had no opportunity to compete under protective measures imposed by the imperial competitor. In the case of sugar, this scenario played itself out several times in the seventeenth and eighteenth centuries in the westward expansion of sugar production and trade; a trade in which Sephardic merchants connected to the Amsterdam market played an important role.[16]

Sephardic merchants were also engaged in the tobacco trade, but here the relationships are less clear. It has been suggested that Dutch merchants and mariners, exploring the coasts of Brazil for profitable trade since the 1580s, sailed as the trade winds dictated and thus inevitably encountered other groups, including indigenous populations along the coast of South America.

Thus, it is likely that the first barter opportunities occurred along the coast in chance encounters. As tobacco smoking became a popular pastime among mariners, smuggling for small gain was easy to engage in, and as tobacco contraband trade initially occurred at a small scale, it was not contractually recorded.[17] Tobacco was known for its healing and regenerative qualities among seafarers, but it was not associated with European trade and it took more than a century after Columbus' discovery of America before tobacco was cultivated and traded as a consumer staple crop for profit. As The Devil's

---

16 Schreuder, *Amsterdam's Sephardic Merchants* (2019). Israel, "Jews and Crypto-Jews in the Atlantic World Systems, 1500–1800," in Kagan and Morgan (eds.), *Atlantic Diasporas* (2009), pp. 3–17 about a more general discussion on the role Jews and crypto-Jews played in the Atlantic trade of the sixteenth and seventeenth centuries and how they aligned and realigned themselves with different mercantile powers. For a more detailed discussion, see Section 1.3.

17 In the literature, we encounter various names describing maritime commercial activities; contraband trade goods are smuggled goods that have been imported or exported illegally; buccaneers are pirates, originally off the Spanish American coasts; and corsairs are privateers operating along the southern coast of the Mediterranean in the sixteenth to eighteenth centuries. Generally speaking, an armed ship owned by private individuals holding a government commission and authorized for use in war, especially in the capture of enemy merchant ships, is referred to as a privateer; piracy refers to the practice of attacking and robbing ships at sea; illicit trade is the production or distribution of goods or services that are considered illegal by law established by one or more trading partners.

Weed, tobacco consumption was hidden and considered an indulgence in European societies as Norton in *Sacred Gifts, Profane Pleasures* (2008) illustrates and it had the stigma of vice.[18] As a crop, tobacco originated in the Americas, and it had been exchanged among indigenous populations in the context of ritual performances and as a way to express tribal unity or to celebrate peace among tribes. In Aztec society, tobacco served to honor the Gods. Sugar, on the other hand, was associated with European trade when it was first introduced as a plantation crop to the Americas, but it had no inherent cultural value among Amerindian populations. Sugar was transplanted by Portuguese and Spanish settlers to Brazil and the Caribbean region after it was first cultivated as a plantation crop in the Mediterranean region and on the Atlantic islands of Madeira and São Tomé and then transplanted to various Caribbean colonies. As the tobacco trade was not engaged in by design but encountered by Europeans when they first explored various routes along the coast of South America and the Caribbean islands, they discovered the use of the plant and the way it was consumed and exchanged in ritual settings among the populations they established contacts with. By the time tobacco was purposely cultivated and traded for profit, it had already had a long history in local exchange among indigenous populations and it had been consumed and indulged in by European merchants and mariners. Norton (2008) documents that tobacco did not enter the European market in significant amounts until the 1590s. Tobacco cultivation for the European market occurred initially along the coastal mainland of South America (*Tierra Firme*), and Trinidad is often mentioned as the first island where tobacco was cultivated for the export trade.[19] At the time, the region was considered a Spanish backwater as all the attention on the part of Spanish conquistadors had been directed to Mexico and Peru in search of gold and

---

18 Norton, *Sacred Gifts* (2008), Chapter 6, pp. 129–140. See also, Stephen Snelders, "Normalisation and Ambivalence: Tobacco in the Seventeenth-Century Dutch Republic," *Cultural and Social History*, published online, September 9, 2021, who traces the origins of tobacco use in the Dutch Republic to seamen and marginal groups associated with port life.

19 Norton, *Sacred Gifts* (2008), Chapter 7, describes how the genesis of the tobacco trade was a multinational, multiethnic business affair in which coastal populations, including Amerindians and Blacks along with Creoles and Portuguese all formed part as they encountered French buccaneers and English and Dutch privateers. She attributes the onset of exchange relations to the different Indian tribes who traded among each other and aligned themselves with foreigners in order to pursue their own interests. Often, textiles, tools, and arms were exchanged for tobacco (pp. 141–161). See also, Morris, "Cultivating Colonies" (2017).

silver. Because of neglect, alliances had formed between tobacco-trading native Amerindian communities and English, French, and Dutch privateers and Portuguese merchants and various local communities consisting of Creoles, Mestizos, and run-away slaves.[20]

Over time, trading networks developed supplying tobacco to an expanding European consumer market in which Sephardic merchants were engaged. Dating back to the first decade of the seventeenth century, reports document how tobacco was traded and distributed via Amsterdam. One report derived from a source of correspondence between an informant and the Court of de' Medici in Tuscany, Italy, describes how Amsterdam merchants managed their trade circuits in the Caribbean. In a letter sent from Amsterdam in December 1605, the informant refers to tobacco and pearls procured by merchants at La Margarita Island (off the coast of *Tierra Firme*) and shipped to Santo Domingo, Hispaniola, and Cuba where merchants procured hides, pearls, exotic woods (ebony), and ginger in addition to tobacco in return for a variety of goods supplied by Dutch merchants, including woolen cloth and silks, iron ware, tools, and weapons. In the report, Amsterdam's Sephardic merchants are referred to specifically in the tobacco distribution trade with the port of Livorno as they distributed colonial goods derived from the Caribbean region.[21] Obviously, Sephardic merchants in the Dutch Republic had begun to play a role of some significance in processing and distributing tobacco for the Northwestern European, Mediterranean, and the Baltic markets.

In *Reluctant Cosmopolitans*, Swetschinski (2002) notes that among Amsterdam's Sephardic residents in the second half of the seventeenth century, a growing number of merchants were engaged in tobacco brokerage and wholesale trade.[22] We also know that many Amsterdam Sephardic

---

20 Marcy Norton and Studnicki-Gizbert in "The Multinational Commodification of Tobacco, 1492–1650: An Iberian Perspective," in Peter C. Mancall (ed.), *The Atlantic World and Virginia, 1550–1624* (University of North Carolina Press, Chapel Hill, 2007), pp. 251–273.

21 For trade between Amsterdam and Livorno Sephardic merchants, see Francesca Trivellato, *The Familiarity of Strangers: The Sephardic Diaspora, Livorno, and Cross-Cultural Trade in the Early Modern Period* (Yale University Press, New Haven, London, 2009) and Corey Tazzara, *The Free Port of Livorno and the Transformation of the Mediterranean World, 1574–1790* (Oxford University Press, Oxford, 2017). Sephardic merchants were offered safe haven by the de' Medici's thanks to decrees issued between 1591 and 1593. Informants from the de' Medici Court were stationed in various European ports and courts to report on trade.

22 Daniel M. Swetschinski, *Reluctant Cosmopolitans: The Portuguese Jews of Seventeenth-century Amsterdam* (The Littman Library of Jewish Civilization, London, Portland, 2000). Table 3.1, p. 103, lists approximately 80 percent of Portuguese Jewish residents

merchants had been engaged in the sugar trade with Brazil which by extension suggests that they may have been engaged in the tobacco trade as well.[23] This raises the question, were they the same merchants or different merchant groups? Unfortunately, archival records do not reveal a clear relationship. Swetschinski (2002) suggests that routes or trade circuits and family contacts or kin networks were often more important in determining which goods came to market than demand in the market at a specific time. If that is the case, then it is likely that sugar merchants were also engaged in the tobacco trade and that co-occurrence was a factor in explaining the development of the Amsterdam tobacco market alongside the sugar market. However, freight contracts documenting the Amsterdam sugar trade do not record tobacco. In fact, evidence of tobacco traded on the Amsterdam exchange or noted in freight contracts is scarce. The first tobacco shipments recorded in the freight records of the Notarial Archives of Amsterdam date from the mid-1590s, but recorded shipments of tobacco occur only intermittently. This does not mean that tobacco was not among the staples found at the Amsterdam market as we assume that tobacco was shipped but escaped notice as mariners and sailors were usually allowed to carry a certain amount of personal goods as they traversed the oceans and as tobacco was an illicit trade good.[24]

---

of Amsterdam (of a total of 560) engaged in commerce of whom about 70 percent (of a total of about 500) are merchants, 31 are brokers, and 4 are tobacco wholesalers. Far fewer are engaged in retail occupations. A total of twenty-seven are listed as shopkeepers of whom about half are tobacconists. Among laborers, thirteen of a total of forty-seven are listed as tobacco workers. Commerce is not well defined in sources of the seventeenth century. Unlicensed brokers in Amsterdam would often call themselves merchants while peddlers could be considered merchants too.

23 Christopher Ebert, "Dutch Trade with Brazil before the Dutch West India Company, 1587–1817," in Johannes Postma and Victor Enthoven (eds.), *Riches from Atlantic commerce: Dutch Transatlantic Trade and Shipping, 1585–1817* (Brill, Leiden, Boston, 2003), Chapter 3, pp. 49–75; pp. 50–51; Schreuder, *Amsterdam's Sephardic Merchants and the Atlantic Sugar Trade* (2019), Chapter 2.

24 The Notarial Archives at the City Archives of Amsterdam contain the Notary Public records which include trade contracts that record merchants by name and vessel and cargo contracted for. In most instances, the records refer to port cities in Europe and specific destinations overseas. The records or protocols may also refer to disputes, partnerships, the price of cargo, and insurance. The records date back to the sixteenth century and demonstrate that during the last quarter of the century, Amsterdam merchants engaged in trade with Northern Europe, the Baltic sea coast, and the Iberian Peninsula, trading bulk goods for spices from East Asia and sugar from Brazil via the Portuguese merchant network which operated in a separate circuit and involved the Portuguese Atlantic Islands, the West Coast of Africa, and Brazil. Norton,

Officially, all the shipments from Spanish America and Portuguese Brazil had to first clear customs in Seville or in Lisbon, but officials and various groups involved in the Atlantic trade lent a willing hand to pass desired products in demand in England, France, and the Dutch Republic to customers on hand in distribution and retail. As tobacco was not an officially recognized trade good, it was consigned in secret to Portuguese and Sephardic merchants in the trading networks.[25] As the Atlantic contraband trade networks developed, Amsterdam's Sephardic merchants became engaged in the tobacco wholesale trade, processing, distribution, as well as retail trade. For most of the first half of the seventeenth century, Portuguese merchants, including Portuguese Jewish (i.e., Sephardic) merchants in Amsterdam, were most often partners or factors of merchants established in the Iberian Peninsula who controlled the network contacts and thus political and military developments during the Eighty Years' War (1568–1648) between the Dutch Republic and the Habsburg Spanish Empire of which Portugal was part at the time, determined the ups and downs of trade with Amsterdam. As blockades and embargoes were imposed and lifted, shipments were often diverted and redirected to and from Hamburg or London and other points of contact in Western Europe or transferred via the Atlantic islands. During the Twelve Years' Truce, in effect from 1609 until 1621, some trade with the Iberian Peninsula was restored, but the staple goods trade with Spanish America and Portuguese Brazil had taken on a course independent of the traditional Iberian trade circuit and had developed on its own by then.

Sacred Gifts (2008), Chapter 7, pp. 141–172; pp. 142–143, dates the first recorded imports of tobacco into Seville, Spain, for 1598. Note the dramatic increase in tobacco imports to Spain (Norton, *Sacred Gifts* Table 7.1, p. 143) for the next ten years during which the Amsterdam colonial goods staple market developed.

25 See Ebert, "Dutch Trade with Brazil," in Postma and Enthoven (eds.), *Riches from Atlantic Commerce* (2003). Many of the networks involving merchants in long-distance trade and local merchants operated both inside and outside of imperial boundaries. As illustrated by recently published research, Portuguese trading networks were mostly self-organizing, cross-cultural, and transnational which transcended official or institutional trade. The networks often engaged European, African, Euro-African, Amerindian, Mestizo, and Creole merchants as free agents. See, for instance, Catia Antunes and Amerila Polonia (eds.), *Beyond Empires: Global, Self-organizing, Cross-imperial Networks, 1500–1800* (Brill, Leiden, 2016) and Zakharow et al. (eds.), *Merchant Colonies in the Early Modern Period* (Routledge, London, New York, 2016). See also, Daviken Studnicki-Gizbert, *A Nation Upon the Ocean Sea: Portugal's Atlantic Diaspora and the Crisis of the Spanish Empire, 1492–1640* (Oxford University Press, Oxford, New York, 2007); Trivellato, *The Familiarity of Strangers* (2009); Jessica Vance Roitman, *The Same but Different: Inter-Cultural Trade and the Sephardic, 1595–1640* (Brill, Leiden, 2011).

In *A Nation Upon the Ocean Sea*, Studnicki-Gizbert (2007) illustrates how the colonial and tobacco contraband trade evolved in the context of the development of the Atlantic trade network engaging merchants of the Portuguese Nation.[26] The Portuguese Nation or the *Nação* consisted of Portuguese merchants and their correspondents or factors resident in various Atlantic ports in Europe, the Mediterranean, West Africa, the Atlantic islands, and Brazil as well as in *Tierra Firme*, and on the Spanish Caribbean islands. Often the members of the Nation were offered special protection and privileges to trade in foreign port cities. As Portuguese merchants were particularly well situated and located in coastal areas of Spanish and Portuguese colonial territories, they became crucial in the trade of several aspiring staple ports. The "Vast Machine" of the Portuguese Nation, as referred to by Studnicki-Gizbert (2007) consisted of mostly New Christian or *Converso* merchants which had established themselves alongside Spanish officials in Spanish America and in Portuguese Brazil as merchant-bankers and as members of a widespread Atlantic merchant network that was engaged in the slave trade, the supply trade, and the trade in colonial staples. Portuguese merchants had been involved in the trans-Atlantic trade for most of the sixteenth century, but after the unification of Portugal and Spain in 1580, they had become much more prevalent in Spanish overseas trade and became engaged with the official Spanish trade, the *Carrera de Indias*.[27] At the same time, French, English, and in particular merchants from the Dutch Republic had begun to prosper in trade as privateers with Spanish America and Portuguese Brazil despite the fact that the Dutch Republic was at war with Spain and Portugal and thus Dutch merchants—among them Amsterdam's Sephardic merchants—were considered enemy conspirators and interlopers. As it was, many of the merchants of the Portuguese Nation operated outside of the *Carrera de Indias* avoiding registration, licenses, and custom duties imposed on the official trade and they were often trading illegally via clandestine routes and often in league with enemy merchants (the Dutch, the English, and from time to time, the French). Officials of the Spanish regime were well aware of the clandestine activities and often referred to members of the Portuguese Nation as foreigners although Portugal was part of the Spanish Habsburg regime after 1580. In due time, members of the Nation became key players of the Spanish mercantile establishment as they

---

26 Studnicki-Gizbert, *A Nation Upon the Ocean Sea* (2007), specifically Chapter 4, pp. 91–121.

27 The *Carrera de Indias*, the official convoy of vessels sailing out of Seville, counted over 200 sailing ships in 1608. In 1618, there were 125, and in 1628, the convoy counted 72. See Studnicki-Gizbert, *A Nation Upon the Ocean Sea* (2007), p. 91, with reference to Pierre Chaunu and Huguette Chauna, *Séville et l'Atlantique*, vol. 1, (1955), p. 330.

bankrolled the treasury of the Habsburg Empire, controlled the monopolies, ran the tax-farming schemes, and facilitated trade via their merchant networks.[28] They also invested in plantations and engaged in the slave trade. In total, the "Vast Machine" operated in a world where rulers opposed each other or were at war with each other and where trade was conducted through a widespread web of illegal activities in which contraband, smuggling, bribery, and fraud were commonplace.[29]

Merchants of the Portuguese Nation devoted most of their energies to the circulation and distribution of goods as they had ready access to materials, markets, enslaved labor provisions, and capital.[30] In the Spanish and Portuguese possessions, they served both the sugar and the tobacco plantations and financed mining operations. In this sphere of commerce, Portuguese merchants distinguished themselves as they formed overlapping networks that linked small retail operations with networks of trans-Atlantic wholesalers, brokers, and distributors. Wholesalers usually had direct ties to merchants of the Portuguese Nation who in turn had their contacts in the Canary islands or the Azores, Spanish America, and Brazil. Kin connections and exchange between Portuguese wholesalers in the Spanish and Portuguese possessions and merchant-bankers in Lisbon and Seville formed the backbone of the networks which incorporated Sephardic merchants in Amsterdam and their success in commerce held the key to immigration of *Converso* merchants from Spain and Portugal to Amsterdam during the early and mid-decades of the seventeenth century.[31]

---

28 Studnicki-Gizbert, *A Nation Upon the Ocean Sea* (2007), Chapter 5, pp. 123–150.
29 Officials in the late-sixteenth century Spanish Caribbean often referred to Portuguese merchants as foreigners although Portugal was officially aligned with Spain after 1580. Loyalty of resident Portuguese merchants was often questioned and association with interlopers from Northwestern Europe referred to as heretics and rebels aligned Portuguese merchants alongside *Luteranos*; English, French, and Dutch merchants. See Brian Hamm, "Between Acceptance and Exclusion: Spanish Responses to Portuguese Immigrants in the Sixteenth-Century Spanish Caribbean," in Ida Altman and David Wheat (eds.), *The Spanish Caribbean and the Atlantic World in the Long Sixteenth Century* (University of Nebraska Press, Lincoln, 2019), pp. 113–135.
30 With respect to the slave trade to Spanish America, see Marc Eagle, "The Early Slave Trade to Spanish America," in Altman and Wheat (eds.), *The Spanish Caribbean* (2019), pp. 139–160.
31 Jonathan I. Israel, "The Economic Contribution of Dutch Sephardi Jewry to Holland's Golden Age, 1595–1713," in Israel, *Empires and Entrepots: The Dutch, the Spanish Monarchy and the Jews, 1585–1713* (The Hambledon Press, London, 1990), pp. 417–447. See also, by the same author: "Sephardic Immigration into the Dutch Republic, 1595–1672," in *Studia Rosenthaliana*, vol. 23, 1989, pp. 45–53. For a brief overview, see Filipa Ribeiro da Silva, "The Portuguese Sephardi of Amsterdam and the Trade with Western Africa, 1580–1660," in *Le Verger V, Bouquet Histoire*, Janvier 2014.

1.3 Portuguese and Amsterdam's Sephardic Merchants and the Eighty Years' War

As noted, Amsterdam had begun to develop its role as colonial staple port in the late sixteenth century. At that time, Portuguese *Converso* merchants were establishing themselves as correspondents or factors for Portuguese merchant houses in Amsterdam. The newly formed Dutch Republic subsequently extended residential and trading rights to Portuguese merchants which included a growing number of Sephardic merchants. These Portuguese Jewish merchants had converted to Judaism in the late sixteenth and early seventeenth centuries at a time when Amsterdam was replacing Antwerp as the gateway to the northwestern European market.[32] At the end of the sixteenth century, Amsterdam's trade was intimately affected by trade with the Iberian Peninsula and was shaped by naval attacks, blockades, and embargoes as part of the war between Habsburg Spain and the Dutch Republic.[33]

The war was fought against Philip II of Spain, the Habsburg emperor ruling over the Low Countries in the sixteenth century from which, eventually, the mostly Protestant northern provinces separated from the mostly Catholic southern provinces.[34] During the 1570s and the 1580s, in the first phase of the war, the northern provinces were confronted with serious hardship while the southern provinces, and especially Antwerp, prospered. By 1585, the position had begun to reverse, and the northern provinces of the Netherlands (the Dutch Republic) had improved their defensive positions significantly and started to book important victories. The commercial expansion of Amsterdam at the expense of Antwerp became evident after 1585 when the blockade of the Scheldt River by Dutch forces (after the reconquest of Antwerp by Spanish forces) triggered

---

32 Jonathan I. Israel, "Sephardic Immigration into the Dutch Republic, 1595–1672," in *Studia Rosenthaliana*, vol. 23, Fall 1989, pp. 45–53.

33 Lesger, *The Rise of the Amsterdam Market* (2006). For a detailed discussion about the official Spanish trading regime, see the classical work by Clarence Henry Haring, *Trade and Navigation between Spain and the Indies in the Time of the Habsburgs* (Yale University Press, New Haven, 1917). The start of the Eighty Years' War was a revolt of the Seventeen Provinces of what are today the Netherlands, Belgium, and Luxembourg against Philip II of Spain, the sovereign of the Habsburg Netherlands.

34 The Eighty Years' War is generally considered the war of Dutch independence that started as a revolt against the overbearing rule of Philip II which was a mix of economic frustration about high taxes imposed on the cities and a deep disappointment with the political authorities in Madrid about the treatment of the Protestants living in Northern provinces which later united into the Dutch Republic.

the accelerated pace at which Amsterdam developed into Europe's major staple market. Meanwhile, the southern provinces remained aligned with the Habsburg Empire after being reconquered by Spanish forces. The siege of Antwerp by the Spanish troops as part of the reconquest efforts directed against the Dutch Republic and the spread of Protestantism drove merchants and investment out of Antwerp in the Southern (Spanish) Netherlands and toward northern European cities like Amsterdam, Hamburg, and Lübeck, which realigned their relationships with the German States through rerouting their trade via the Rhine River and other inland waterways.[35] As Portuguese merchants were key participants in the Iberian trade with Northern Europe and had settled in significant numbers in Antwerp in the course of the sixteenth century, their relocation to Amsterdam along with other Antwerp merchants toward the end of the sixteenth century meant that merchant networks transplanted to Amsterdam and that Portuguese *Converso* and Jewish merchants as part of the Portuguese Nation became part of the mix in Amsterdam's mercantile establishment.[36] Meanwhile, Amsterdam's trade prospects and merchants' wealth were to a large extent dictated by strategies of the warring parties which, in part, explain why illegal trade became an important component of mercantile enterprise among Amsterdam's Sephardic merchants.

The combination of forces due to war time conditions had an immediate impact on the sugar and tobacco trade with Brazil, *Tierra Firme*, and the Spanish Caribbean islands.[37] The Sephardic and *Converso* merchants shared in the ups and downs of the Atlantic and Caribbean staple trade as evidence from Amsterdam's freight and trade records show.[38] Trade among Portuguese New Christian merchants active in Spanish America and Portuguese Brazil and Portuguese Sephardic merchants resident in Amsterdam occurred

---

35 Lesger, *The Rise of the Amsterdam Market* (2006).
36 Israel, "The Economic Contribution of Dutch Sephardic Jewry," in *Empires and Entrepots* (1990), pp. 417–447. Israel marks 1595 as the year the "rich" trades were cut off from reaching Antwerp when a general and extended maritime blockade of the South Netherlands was imposed by the States General of the Dutch Republic.
37 Evidence from Bloom, *The Economic Activity of the Jews of Amsterdam* (1937), pp. 60–64; Israel, *Dutch Primacy in World Trade* (1989); Studnicki-Gizbert, *A Nation Upon the Ocean Sea* (2007). Swetschinski, *Reluctant Cosmopolitans* (2000), notes that by the late 1610s, Portuguese merchants residing in Amsterdam had begun to trade directly between Amsterdam and Brazil.
38 E. M. Koen (ed.), "Notarial Records Relating to the Portuguese Jews in Amsterdam up to 1639," *Studia Rosenthaliana*, volume 1, no. 2, 1967.

as early as the mid-1590s, and at the beginning of the seventeenth century, the members of the Portuguese Nation formed a thriving trade network provisioning *Tierra Firme*, the Spanish Caribbean islands, and Brazil with much needed supply goods and carrying colonial staple goods to the Iberian Peninsula and to market in Amsterdam.[39]

We have some evidence from freight records on how Amsterdam's resident Portuguese and Sephardic merchants insured and shipped cargo to and from Portuguese Brazil and carried sugar, indigo, tobacco, and brazil wood to market in Amsterdam via Portugal.[40] Freight contracts registered in Amsterdam offer some insight into commercial partnerships and show that skippers and merchants were often of different cultural or religious backgrounds. Skippers were almost always Christians and usually residents of the Dutch Republic. Merchants or freighters could be members of particular commercial communities resident in Dutch cities, and it was not unusual that members of the Portuguese Nation were *Converso* or Jewish (Sephardic) residents in Amsterdam or other Dutch cities. Some freight contracts were signed by multiple merchants or freighters some of whom may have had previous commercial partnerships abroad. Skippers usually knew the routes of transportation while the merchants had knowledge about specific production areas through the connections established during previous voyages and distribution markets in locations where skippers may not have been previously. This was particularly the case in the Atlantic

---

39 Ebert, "Dutch Trade with Brazil," (2003).
40 Swetschinski, *Reluctant Cosmopolitans* (2000), Chapter 3, pp. 102–164; Roitman, *The Same but Different* (2011). Swetschinski (2000), pp. 105–112, notes that, by and large, Portuguese Jewish merchants traded in a network of contacts comprised of Portugal and its colonies and trading partners in the Mediterranean region (including North Africa and the Barbary Coast) and the larger northern European market encompassing Rouen, London, Antwerp, Amsterdam, and Hamburg in the early to mid-seventeenth century. The sugar trade and trans-Atlantic trade were an important component of the circuit. He also notes that a collaborative effort between Spanish *Morisco* merchants and Portuguese *Converso* merchants led to successful preying on the Spanish fleets returning from Spanish America and that they became major interlopers interfering in the Seville import and export trade. Some of the illegal trade were transshipments via the Azores and Canary Islands and some concerned contraband trade via Cuba and Hispaniola. For transit via the Azores, see Gabriel de Avilez Rocha, "The Azorean Connection: Trajectories of Slaving, Piracy, and Trade in the Early Atlantic," in Ida Altman and David Wheat (eds.), *The Spanish Caribbean and the Atlantic World in the Long Sixteenth Century* (University of Nebraska Press, Lincoln, 2019), pp. 257–278. The importance of the Canary Islands in illegal trade is discussed in detail in Cromwell, *The Smuggler's World* (2018).

trading circuits. Sephardic merchants also often had specific knowledge and information about consumption markets and distribution outlets in particular in the Mediterranean areas.[41]

In Amsterdam, Sephardic merchants emerged as specialized intermediaries and became one of the main merchant groups in the trans-Atlantic colonial staple trade in the seventeenth century as evidence from freight records at the City Archives of Amsterdam illustrates.[42] In the tobacco trade, leaf was sold and processed in Amsterdam at the approximate same time as sugar was traded and refined as documented in histories of the city and in the literature on the seventeenth-century tobacco trade. But, were they of the same origin and engaged the same merchants in the same or similar trade networks? Records document that tobacco mixing and spinning became a most prominent industry in Amsterdam in the seventeenth century, and Portuguese New Christian and Sephardic merchants played a role of some sort in establishing the industry, but the tobacco freight records are obscure and hide rather than reveal the significance of the industry.[43] The question raised earlier, were sugar and tobacco merchants engaged in both the sugar and the tobacco trade at the same time, contracting with the same skippers, and loading both sugar and tobacco from the same source areas in the Caribbean region? Or, did sugar and tobacco trade constitute separate trade networks and engage different merchant groups? The question can only be answered if we compare freight records for both the sugar and the tobacco trade for the same decades in the early seventeenth century, but here the trade patterns diverge. Whereas Amsterdam's freight contracts documenting the sugar trade in the early seventeenth century show a clear pattern of trade in which Sephardic merchants took part, archives documenting the tobacco trade are essentially absent for *Tierra Firme*, Hispaniola, or Brazil which were the first and most important source areas for tobacco on the market in Europe at that time.[44]

---

41 Catia Antunes, "Cross-Cultural Business Cooperation in the Dutch Trading World, 1580–1776," in Catia Antunes, Franceso Trivellato and Leor Halevi (eds.), *Religion and Trade: Cross-Cultural Exchanges in World History, 1000–1900* (Oxford University Press, Oxford, 2014).

42 Swetchinski, *Reluctant Cosmopolitans* (2000), Table 3.1: "Occupations of Portuguese Jewish Males, 1655–1699," p. 103. Schreuder, *Amsterdam's Sephardic Merchants* (2019). See E. M. Koen (ed.), "Notarial Records Relating to the Portuguese Jews in Amsterdam up to 1639," *Studia Rosenthaliana*, volume 1, no. 2, 1967.

43 Bloom, *The Economic Activities of the Jews of Amsterdam* (1937), pp. 60–64. See also reference above; Swetchinski, *Reluctant Cosmopolitans* (2000), Table 3.1, p. 103.

44 Freight records available in the Notary Public records in the City Archives of Amsterdam, see pp. 119–158 (Chapter 4), in my book: *Amsterdam's Sephardic Merchants and the Atlantic Sugar Trade* (2019).

Furthermore, whereas sugar production moved westward from the Atlantic islands of Madeira and São Tomé to Brazil controlled by Portuguese merchants, and Cuba and Hispaniola in the sixteenth century under Spanish rule, tobacco cultivation originated in the Americas and was exchanged through illicit trade conducted by Portuguese, Dutch, English, and French mariners and merchants who explored the coastal areas and smuggled goods for and from the Spanish and Portuguese possessions along the Caribbean coast of South America (*Tierra Firme*), Brazil, and throughout the Caribbean region.[45] The supply goods were varied but usually included cloth, woolens, silks, and various tools and implements or arms, and the return cargo usually consisted of hides, tobacco, and pearls which were smuggled but were among the most valued staple goods for sale on the Amsterdam market.[46]

1.4 The Portuguese Nation and the Illegal Tobacco Trade

Although it is generally thought that by the late sixteenth century tobacco exchange at small scale took place among Dutch mariners, indigenous people, and Portuguese *Converso* merchants in *Tierra Firme* and Portuguese Brazil, Dutch freight records among Notary Public records in Amsterdam's Archives show at most only sketchy evidence of that. On the other hand, the fact that the Spanish Crown enforced a ten-year ban on growing tobacco in *Tierra Firme* and ordered the removal of coastal populations from Hispaniola in 1606 in order to undermine the trading or rather smuggling of tobacco by English, French, and Dutch mariners and Portuguese merchants suggests that tobacco had become an important trade good along the South American coast (*Tierra Firme*) and on the Spanish Caribbean island of Hispaniola. As noted, we also know from the records that Sephardic merchants in Amsterdam engaged in mixing and spinning of tobacco and in the tobacco wholesale, distribution, and retail trade in the seventeenth century, but we know little about when and how the tobacco trade in Amsterdam began.[47] Although Swetschinski (2000) and Roitman (2011) give us significant insight into the dynamics of trade among Amsterdam Sephardic merchants in the Atlantic circuits of the Portuguese Nation in the later part of the seventeenth century and the eighteenth century, we

---

45 Swetschinski, *Reluctant Cosmopolitans* (2000); Klooster, *Illicit Riches* (1998); Rupert, *Creolization and Contraband* (2012); Cromwell, *The Smugglers' World* (2018).
46 Goslinga, *The Dutch in the Caribbean* (1971), p. 55.
47 Bloom, *The Economic Activities of the Jews of Amsterdam* (1937), pp. 60–64.

are left with significant gaps in understanding the onset of the tobacco trade in particular as far as illicit trade in the first few decades of the seventeenth century is concerned.[48]

In *Reluctant Cosmopolitans*, Swetschinski (2000) hints at illegal trade networks among Portuguese merchants in Spain and Spanish America engaging Portuguese and Sephardic merchants from Amsterdam, but systematic records thereof do not exist.[49] Swetschinski (1982) does acknowledge that some Notary Publics in Amsterdam wrote contracts for merchants engaged in trade with Spain and the Spanish or Portuguese possessions but suggests that these documents were often forged and that Sephardic merchants used aliases.[50] Thus, as contraband trade was hidden from view, the public records are of little use to uncover the origin and the extent of the trans-Atlantic trade in tobacco. Although a handful of tobacco freight records were found in the Notary Public records at the City Archives of Amsterdam, they cannot be considered reliable or of much use for systematic research on the tobacco trade.[51] The Archives of the Amsterdam Exchange Bank provide a little more

---

48 Swetschinski, *Reluctant Cosmopolitans* (2000), Chapter 3, pp. 102–164 and Roitman, *The Same but Different* (2011). Cromwell, *The Smugglers' World* (2018), pp. 131–132; 138–146, details on the identities of smugglers along the Venezuela coast in the eighteenth century which reveals that crews of smuggling vessels were very often multinational (English, French, or Dutch) and that crew were of different religious and cultural backgrounds, including Protestants and Jews. Multilingual background and cultural fluidity was an advantage in the Hispanic world when engaged in smuggling activities. An important role was assigned to the *Practico* or pilot who was often an experienced coastal trader and very often, as in the case of Dutch privateers, of Portuguese *Converso* descent. Portuguese pilots often had trade links and family connections to the Canary Islands or the Azores which were in the sixteenth and early seventeenth centuries often the jumping-off point for Portuguese *Converso* merchants as related by Studnicki-Gizbert, *A Nation Upon the Ocean Sea* (2007). Portuguese *Converso* merchants had been permitted to trade with Portugal, Angola, and Brazil via the Canary Islands during the Habsburg reign of Philip II (1556–1598), and they often extended their activities to include the private trade with *Tierra Firme* and Hispaniola where they had established themselves in coastal areas earlier in the sixteenth century as suggested by Marcy Norton and Studnicki-Gizbert in "The Multinational Commodification of Tobacco, 1492–1650: An Iberian Perspective," in Peter C. Mancall (ed.), *The Atlantic World and Virginia, 1550–1624* (University of North Carolina Press, Chapel Hill, 2007), pp. 251–273.
49 Swetschinski, *Reluctant Cosmopolitans* (2000), pp. 119–123; see also Appendix, Table A.2.
50 Daniel M. Swetschinski, "Conflict and Opportunity in 'Europe's Other Sea': The Adventures of Caribbean Jewish Settlement," *American Jewish History*, vol. 72, no. 2, 1982, pp. 212–240.
51 E. M. Koen, "The Earliest Sources Relating to the Portuguese Jews in the Municipal Archives of Amsterdam up to 1620," in *Studia Rosenthaliana*, vol. 4, no. 1 (January 1970), pp. 25–42.

information as they contain the records of Portuguese brokers as go-between but records only start in 1612. An interesting register in the records of the Exchange Bank contains a list of "interlopers" with complaints about unlicensed brokers which show Portuguese names. Apparently, unlicensed brokers did buy and sell their merchandise in Amsterdam on the Exchange from time to time but no mention is made of tobacco traded by Portuguese merchants. Sugar was traded by both Portuguese and Amsterdam Sephardic merchants as the official records illustrate, but in order to conduct legitimate trade on the Exchange, merchants had to be sworn brokers.[52] An investigation requested by the Guildmasters to the Burgomasters in 1617 revealed that of the 365 sworn brokers listed, only eight were Jewish. Thirty-two Jewish and eighteen Christian merchants were listed as "interlopers."[53] Some of the Jewish merchants later became sworn brokers but illegitimate trade seems to have prevailed among Portuguese or Sephardic merchants at the Amsterdam market during the first two decades of the seventeenth century.[54]

During the Twelve Years' Truce (1609–1621), peace restored Dutch trade with the Iberian Peninsula, but after 1621, new hostilities marked another serious disruption of trade with merchants in the Spanish world.[55] At the same time, Portugal remained the primary center of the colonial

---

52 The Notarial Archives at the City Archives of Amsterdam contain at least 470 entries with Portuguese names for the period before 1620. About half of them were merchants and many of them were engaged in the sugar trade. See, E. M. Koen, "The Earliest Sources Relating to the Portuguese Jews in the Municipal Archives of Amsterdam up to 1620," in *Studia Rosenthaliana*, vol. 4, no. 1 (January 1970), pp. 25–42. The number of Portuguese residents in Amsterdam grew rapidly during the first two decades of the seventeenth century and particularly after 1609 which year marked the start of the Twelve Years' Truce of the Eighty Years' War during which time trade with the Iberian Peninsula resumed. During that time, many Portuguese residents began to openly practice Judaism and created their institutional base, including a synagogue and a cemetery. Portuguese immigrants arrived either directly from Portugal or from Antwerp and some seem to have come from southern France. The majority of them were merchants.
53 E. M. Koen, "The Earliest Sources Relating to the Portuguese Jews in the Municipal Archives of Amsterdam up to 1620," in *Studia Rosenthaliana*, vol. 4, no. 1 (January 1970), pp. 25–42.
54 According to a Notarial Deed of 1629, a Deputy Sheriff did notify the Jews at the request of Christian tobacconists that they were not allowed to keep tobacco shops. See Koen, "The Earliest Sources," (1970), p. 30, referred to in the previous footnotes. Jewish merchants were permitted to continue in the wholesale tobacco trade.
55 During the peacetime of the Twelve Years' Truce (1609–1621), Amsterdam was the major staple market in the Dutch Republic. After 1618 when renewed embargoes occurred, and after 1621 when war with Spain resumed, Hamburg regained its status as a staple market in the Baltic–Iberian trade circuit.

staple trade for Portuguese merchants in trade with East Asia, Brazil, and the Americas. As war time trade was illegal and trade goods became subject to confiscation, slowly but certainly, more and more of the colonial trade from both the East and the West was reoriented toward Northwestern Europe in the form of direct trade with Hamburg, London, and Amsterdam or the French port of Bayonne.[56] At the same time, in the 1620s, we see a steadily increasing immigration of wealthy New Christian merchants from Portugal to Spain where reform-minded officials—including the Count-Duke de Olivares during the reign of Philip IV—encouraged Portuguese New Christian merchants to engage in trade with Spanish America.[57] Under these circumstances, for as long as the Dutch Republic was still at war with Spain (until 1648), the situation was rife for an intensification of commerce (albeit illegal) between Spanish America and Amsterdam via Hamburg in Northern Germany, or Bayonne and other ports in Southwestern France, or London where Portuguese *Converso* and crypto-Jewish communities had emerged and where complex and intricate merchant networks had developed.

During this time, the Spanish King tried to coordinate and maintain trade relationships with the Southern Netherlands via Antwerp. As Count-Duke Olivares' influence unfolded from 1621 to 1643, Portuguese New Christian merchant-bankers were given a lead in government contracting and became engaged in the *Asiento* and tax-farming schemes as well as the Spanish tobacco

---

56 Swetschinski, "Conflict and Opportunity," (1982), pp. 223 ff. The town of Bayonne in Southwestern France was a hotbed for smugglers in which Sephardic merchants and *Converso* merchants actively participated. See, for instance, Carsten L. Wilke, "Contraband for the Catholic King: Jews of the French Pyrenees in the Tobacco Trade and Spanish State Finance," in Rebecca Kobrin and Adam Teller (eds.), *Purchasing Power: The Economics of Modern Jewish History* (University of Pennsylvania Press, Philadelphia, 2015), pp. 46–70.

57 Swetschinski, "Conflict and Opportunity," (1982), pp. 224–226. The Count-Duke's real name was Gaspar de Guzmán y Pimentel, 1st Duke of Sanlúcar. As prime minister and advisor to the Crown, from 1621 to 1643, Olivares proposed major commercial reforms and enhanced thereby the position of Portuguese New Christian merchants at the Court. Portuguese merchants subsequently received many concessions from the King and gained influential positions in commerce and finance as "merchant-bankers." At the same time, Olivares committed Spain to recapture Holland which led to a renewal of the Eighty Years' War while Spain was also embroiled in the Thirty Years' War (1618–1648) with the German States. Part of the reason, or perhaps the main reason, for more relaxed relationships between the Spanish Crown and New Christian merchants was the increasingly dire fiscal conditions the King found himself in. See also Studnicki-Gizbert, *A Nation Upon the Ocean Sea* (2007), Chapter 5, pp. 123–150, pp. 170–174.

monopoly which expanded their role in the slave trade and in colonial trade with Spanish America.[58] In Portuguese Brazil, meanwhile, the Dutch tried to take control of the sugar trade and founded the WIC (1621). At this time, some Portuguese New Christian merchants began to openly practice Judaism in Brazil and began to trade directly with Amsterdam.[59] From 1630 until 1654, Pernambuco resided under Dutch rule during which time New Christian immigration to Brazil and (re-)conversion to Judaism occurred and the sugar and tobacco trade with Amsterdam prospered.

Reportedly, more than 50 million pounds of tobacco were brought to Amsterdam for processing and distribution by the mid-seventeenth century mostly from South America and the Caribbean region.[60] Unlike Vlissingen or Rotterdam—two Dutch ports south of Amsterdam which received most of their shipments from Virginia or from London—the Amsterdam tobacco market was supplied mostly by Portuguese New Christian and Sephardic merchants via trade networks that dated back to the late sixteenth century.[61] Since the first half of the sixteenth century, New Christian merchants from Portugal had traded along the shores of Africa and in the sugar

---

58 As a consequence, Portuguese Jewish merchants of Amsterdam did not welcome the Dutch invasion of Bahia in 1624 as it weakened their connections with their brethren in Portugal. The Dutch occupation of Pernambuco (1630–1654) further weakened the position of the New Christian merchants in Portugal engaged in the sugar trade with Brazil. These circumstances would help explain why Portuguese New Christians shifted their business to Spain. The Portuguese rebellion in 1640 worsened the position of the *New Christian* merchants even further and when Olivares died and the Portuguese merchants lost their protector, large-scale relocation/migration occurred among *New Christians* from Seville, Madrid, and Antwerp to Amsterdam and within a decade (1646–1655), Amsterdam became the center of the Portuguese New Christian and Jewish world. See Jonathan I. Israel, "Spain and the Dutch Sephardic, 1609–1660," *Studia Rosenthaliana*, 12, 1978, pp. 1–61.

59 In 1621, after the resumption of hostilities with Spain, the WIC was founded. The Dutch WIC first attacked Bahia, Brazil, in an attempt to establish control over the sugar trade. Then, in 1630, Pernambuco was occupied which remained a Dutch colony until 1654. To assure that commerce in Dutch Brazil would thrive the Dutch colonial administration under WIC supervision assured the resident population that religious freedom and private trade were guaranteed. The WIC retained a monopoly in the slave trade and trade in arms, ammunition, and dye wood.

60 Wim Klooster, "The Tobacco Nation: English Traders and Pipe-Makers in Rotterdam, 1620–1650" in Laura Cruz and Joel Mokyr (eds.), *The Birth of Modern Europe: Culture and Economy, 1400–1800* (Brill, Leiden, Boston, 2010), pp. 17–34.

61 Studnicki-Gizbert, *A Nation Upon the Ocean Sea* (2007), Chapter 1, pp. 17–39. See also, Filipa Ribeiro da Silva, "The Portuguese Sephardi of Amsterdam and the Trade with Western Africa, 1580–1660," in *Le Verger V—Bouquet Histoire*, Janvier 2014, 1–22.

islands of Madeira and São Tomé extending their trade networks from the Mediterranean, including Livorno, Genoa, and Venice, via Antwerp where grain, lumber, and textiles were exchanged for olive oil, wine, spices, sugar, and gold. By the mid-sixteenth century, they were also trading in Brazil and sailed around the Cape of Good Hope to Asia.[62] Meanwhile, the Spanish had established colonial rule in South and Central America and in the Caribbean region and soon Portuguese New Christian merchants followed by way of the mid-Atlantic islands, the Azores and Canary islands, and began to engage in trade with Spanish America.[63] In the course of the sixteenth-century, trade with Portuguese New Christian merchants resident overseas in the Spanish colonies deepened but when Portugal became part of the Spanish Habsburg Empire in 1580, their position became more circumspect and New Christian merchants were persecuted for illegal activities with English, French, and Dutch privateers.[64]

At the same time, new opportunities opened up for Portuguese New Christian and Amsterdam's Sephardic merchants within the context of the Spanish Empire and Spanish possessions overseas including the Americas.[65] In fact, the well-connected Portuguese New Christian merchant networks proved to be indispensable for the expansion of Spanish control in the Americas in particular as it concerned the slave trade. As the colonies expanded and indigenous Amerindians succumbed to disease or proved unfit for hard labor, African slaves were imported from Portuguese colonies in West Africa under *Asiento* contracts. On the return voyage, colonial goods like sugar, tobacco, and later cacao were shipped to Portugal and Spain. Thus, Portuguese slave traders often gained legal access to Spanish America and were inevitably enticed to trade with local populations (including Amerindian, Mestizo, Mulatto, or Creole) to carry

---

62 Trivellato, *The Familiarity of Strangers* (2009).
63 Studnicki-Gizbert, *A Nation Upon the Ocean Sea* (2007), p. 129. During the Habsburg rule of Philip II (1556–1598), resident merchants of the Canary Islands, including New Christian merchants, had been permitted to trade openly and freely with foreign merchants.
64 Studnicki-Gizbert, *A Nation Upon the Ocean Sea* (2007), p. 39, pp. 154–174.
65 Swetschinski, "Conflict and Opportunity," (1982), pp. 218 describes how Old Christian merchants were inclined to join the landed aristocracy as fortune from commerce permitted whereas New Christians developed a niche in mercantile activities that stretched the whole geographic range of the Portuguese realm, including the Americas, West Africa, and Asia. Furthermore, New Christian merchants were engaged in commerce via their kin network and set up *Casas* (merchant houses) with correspondents or associates located in various port cities.

goods for the return voyage.⁶⁶ As a consequence, the coastal population in Spanish America and Portuguese Brazil included a growing number of Portuguese merchants, including crypto-Jews, with whom slave traders already had established contacts.⁶⁷ From the records we do know that the population of *Tierra Firme*, Cartagena, and New Granada increased substantially in the early seventeenth century when the tobacco trade first took hold along the Caribbean coast of South America and that a growing segment of the population of Hispaniola was Portuguese New Christian.⁶⁸ By then, Amsterdam had emerged as the main staple port and Portuguese merchants who had been engaged in the sugar and tobacco trade before were offered the opportunity to trade and reside in the Dutch Republic and to trade as they wished which included the Baltic region as well as the Mediterranean region and the Levant. Thus, in the early seventeenth century, the Atlantic commercial networks engaged besides Flemish, Dutch, German, English, and French merchants, also Portuguese New Christian and Sephardic merchants as evidenced in freight records of the Notary Public records at the City Archives of Amsterdam.⁶⁹ For most of the first half of the Eighty Years' War, Amsterdam's trade with Portugal continued despite official trade bans in effect. Apparently, merchant networks that had been established in the sixteenth and early seventeenth centuries were deemed too important for Spain and Portugal to abolish or render "illegal." As Amsterdam became the primary port in Western Europe in the grain trade with the Baltic, a trade both Portugal and Spain depended on, Portuguese New Christian and Sephardic merchants extended their trading networks to include the North Sea and

---

66 Morris, "Cultivating Colonies," (2017, p. 101, Figure 18) refers to tobacco cultivation in West Africa before 1620 and suggests that Africans were early adopters who consumed tobacco before Europeans did. Portuguese trade networks included West Africa well before the Americas became important in trade with Northern Europe and regular contacts among Portuguese merchants along the coasts of *Tierra Firme*, Guyana, and West Africa had led to a substantial mixing of New Christians, crypto-Jews, and Africans during the sixteenth century. In the mid-sixteenth century, they were recognized as Mestizos on La Margarita Island.
67 Jonathan I. Israel, *Diasporas within a Diaspora: Jews, Crypto-Jews and the World of Maritime Empires* (1540–1740) (Brill's Series in Jewish Studies, volume 30, 2002).
68 Swetschinski, "Conflict and Opportunity," 1982, p. 222. See also John V. Lombardi, *People and Places in Colonial Venezuela* (Indiana University Press, Bloomington, 1976) and Juan Jose Ponce Vazquez, *Islanders and Empire: Smuggling and Political Defiance in Hispaniola, 1580–1690* (Cambridge University Press, published online, October 2020).
69 Koen (ed.), "Notarial Records Relating to the Portuguese Jews in Amsterdam up to 1639," *Studia Rosenthaliana*, volume 1, no. 2, 1967.

Baltic Sea coastal areas. In addition, they extended their reach to include the trade in colonial staple products like sugar and tobacco. In doing so, they entered into the European sugar and tobacco distribution networks and established a significant foothold in Amsterdam's colonial economy of the seventeenth century.[70]

1.5 Evidence from the Amsterdam Notary Public Records

As noted, archival records about illegal trade are scant and intermittent, but some freight contract entries in the Notary Public records in the City Archives of Amsterdam illustrate that tobacco from the Spanish and/or Portuguese territories was on board several vessels that had sailed in convoy from the Caribbean region. The first reported case concerned a merchant from Middelburg in the province of Zeeland who on his return voyage had contracted with a skipper from Enkhuizen in the province of Holland. The insinuation was that the skipper had brought contraband tobacco on shore in Amsterdam which was to be exchanged with a relative to be sold in England. From the records it appears that the cargo was illegal. Witnesses denied the allegation, but the crew members were searched for possession of tobacco as they had been prohibited from taking tobacco on board for the return voyage. The vessel had sailed out with two other vessels, one of which had taken on 400 pounds of tobacco in the name of two merchants from London to be delivered and sold there.[71] The prohibition was likely in response to the efforts made by the Spanish to ban and root out contraband trade by Dutch and English merchants and mariners in the Spanish territories. Or, the prohibition may have been an effort on the part of Dutch officials to comply with official trade restrictions in order not to antagonize

---

70 Israel, *Dutch Primacy in World Trade* (1989) and Swetschinski, *Reluctant Cosmopolitans* (2000).
71 The merchant's name was Cornelis Quatghbuyr. See Notariele Akten (NA), Archief van S. Hart (inventaris nummer 30452: Toegang op de notariële archieven Tabak: nummer 479), Notary J. Fr. Bruyningh: September 28, 1606, NA 103/202, October 1, 1606, NA 57/255 v; October 11, 1606, NA 57/262; October 18, 1606, NA 195/v.54. NA 195/v. 55; October 19, NA 106/12; November 4, 1606, NA 195/64; December 1, 1606, NA 106/38 v. One of the Notary Public's acts states that the crew of the vessel had been prohibited to take tobacco on board and that the skipper had checked that the mariners complied with the order. As was the case, the skipper himself had brought tobacco on shore and was likely aware of the much larger tobacco shipment to London on one of the three vessels that had sailed in convoy to the Caribbean. The name of the merchant, Quatghbuyr, appears on a bill of exchange.

the Spanish authorities as the two parties were in negotiation with each other to end the war or to establish truce. In a separate case, in November 1607, several crew members declared and signed an affidavit for small amounts of tobacco delivered to an Amsterdam cloth merchant.[72] In March 1608, record is made of a voyage to the Orinoco River and *Tierra Firme* in which knives, axes, and corals were exchanged for tobacco with reference to a member of an indigenous tribe who had delivered the tobacco and who had come on board and sailed back with the vessel to Amsterdam.[73] Thirty miles up the Orinoco, the crew had exchanged three tons of wheat for vegetables, pineapple, bananas, chickens, and rabbits. The tobacco was valued at 195 pounds.[74]

During the Twelve Years' Truce from 1609 to 1621, several freight acts were drawn up with Notary Publics in Amsterdam. They concerned bills of sale and payments for tobacco delivered by various merchants. The time of truce between the warring parties partially restored trade relations between merchants in the Dutch Republic and Spain or Portugal but not with the Spanish or Portuguese American possessions. In 1611, a large shipment of tobacco was made via official Spanish channels (*Licendiado*).[75] All the merchants were Dutch, and a variety of supply sources, including Trinidad, were mentioned in the records. In January 1612, an entry in the Notary Public records of Amsterdam mentions that Francisco Nunes Homen, an Amsterdam Portuguese merchant, had granted power of attorney to some Zeeland merchants and to Francisco Lopes Pereira, an Amsterdam Sephardic merchant related to him. To manage his affairs in the province of Zeeland and to reclaim the pipes or casks of tobacco that had arrived from San Lucar (Spain), Francisco Nunes Homen had to defend his claims for the tobacco shipment before the Admiralty.[76] In March 1612, a deed of conveyance was made of a case of tobacco in which another Amsterdam Portuguese merchant appears in the records. The deed conveyed payment to an Amsterdam Dutch merchant for delivery of 324 pounds of tobacco

---

72 November 27, 1607, NA 20/K1-15.
73 Norton, *Sacred Gifts* (2008) suggests that it was not uncommon to take Indians back to Europe in order to improve communication between Indian, Portuguese, and Dutch or English mariners and to learn their languages. See also Morris, "Cultivating Colonies" (2017), p. 132.
74 March 15, 1608, NA 195/497, Notary J. Fr. Bruyningh.
75 August 26, 1611, NA 125/172.
76 Both the Nunes Homen and the Lopes Pereira families were among the first New Christian/Sephardic merchants settled in Amsterdam in the late sixteenth/early seventeenth century.

for a Portuguese merchant in London.[77] Until then, at least according to the Notary Public records, Portuguese merchants in Amsterdam were mostly engaged in the sugar trade with Brazil, shipped via Portugal. In the records, sugar is mentioned predominantly, while ginger or brazil wood is sometimes mentioned along with "other merchandise."[78] We can only guess what was included in "other merchandise," but if the records just reviewed are any guide, it is quite possible that illegal or contraband tobacco was shipped from Brazil by Portuguese or Sephardic merchants alongside regular sugar deliveries or that, by means of transfer in the Canary islands or Portugal, tobacco reached the Amsterdam market.[79]

Until 1621, only Brazil, Caribbean, and *Tierra Firme* tobacco source regions appear in the Amsterdam Notary Public records. In 1621, with the resumption of war with Spain, the first Virginia delivery was made to Amsterdam. By mid-century, tobacco shipments to the Dutch Republic were regular occurrences from both North America (Virginia and Maryland) and the Caribbean and *Tierra Firme* as well as Brazil in which both Dutch and Sephardic merchants participated and from non-Hispanic Caribbean islands.[80] As reported and as evidence from historical records shows, Amsterdam's Portuguese merchants, including Sephardic merchants, were engaged in tobacco processing, wholesale, and retail trade in Amsterdam and in the distribution trade with various markets in Europe. Indirect evidence suggests that the tobacco import trade among Portuguese merchants was substantial and that tobacco entered the Amsterdam market by means

---

77 January 9, 1612, nr. 510; March 27, 1612, nr. 535, in E. M. Koen, "Notarial Records Relating to the Portuguese Jews in Amsterdam up to 1639," in *Studia Rosenthaliana*, vol. 5, no. 2, July 1971, p. 245.
78 Brazil and Portugal had continued their sugar trade and Portuguese New Christian and Sephardic merchants from Amsterdam maintained regular trade connections via Portugal's Atlantic ports as evidenced from the Notarial records in the City Archives of Amsterdam. Whereas sugar was traded freely and legally, tobacco was not and any merchants who were found shipping tobacco via regular trade routes were engaged in illegal or contraband trade.
79 As referenced earlier, the Canary Islands had traditionally offered free transit in trade between the Iberian Peninsula and the Portuguese and Spanish-American possessions. Cromwell, *The Smugglers' World* (2017), p. 49.
80 The first freight records deposited with a Notary Public in Amsterdam in trade with Barbados and some other non-Spanish Caribbean islands was in 1635. It concerns a shipment of wine to Barbados in return for tobacco. In a second version of the same contract, reference is made to provisioning as well. The second record also makes reference to "other free islands" (Tortuga and St. Christopher), in case goods cannot be delivered to Barbados. See City Archives of Amsterdam (Gemeente Archief Amsterdam (GAA)), Notarial Archives (NA), December 11, 1635, 1143/117, and

of various contacts among *Converso* and Portuguese Jewish merchants resident in Portuguese Brazil, Spanish America, the Canary islands, London, Bayonne, and Hamburg, as well as several Portuguese Atlantic ports. In 1620, Amsterdam listed two registered or sworn Jewish tobacco brokers.[81] Research suggests that tobacco, per shipment as compared to sugar, was traded in much smaller quantities and that less wealthy merchants could thus participate in the tobacco trade.[82] It has also been suggested that mariners on board Dutch vessels traded small amounts of tobacco as opportunities occurred. In either scenario, it is unlikely that official tobacco trade contracts were submitted to the officials (i.e., Notary Publics). Furthermore, tobacco processing (spinning and mixing) required less capital investment than sugar refining and spinning, and mixing of tobacco was often conducted in small shops depending on manual labor supplied by the merchant's family suggesting that trade, processing, and distribution were often combined in the same family household. In 1629 and again in 1631, Dutch merchants and retailers complained that Jews were selling tobacco in retail shops which, by regulations imposed, was prohibited. In a formal statement of the "poortersneringen" (a trade or profession organized in a guild), introduced in 1632, Jews were banned from engaging in the retail tobacco trade in Amsterdam but were still permitted to engage in spinning and mixing of tobacco and in the wholesale trade in which they continued to thrive well into the eighteenth century.[83]

In conclusion, the tobacco trade remained mostly hidden and Amsterdam's Notary Public records are therefore of only limited use in research on the origin of the Amsterdam tobacco trade. To unearth the very beginnings

---

December 12, 1635, 1143/118. Most of the trading partners were Dutch, but in 1638, we find the first reference to Portuguese (New Christian or Sephardic) merchants trading from Amsterdam with Barbados. See Notarial Archives dated November 30, 1638, 867/401, and December 1, 1638, 867/403. The name of the merchants appears to be Hebrew (first names) and Dutch (last names). The entries suggest that there was some uncertainty about the return destination, Amsterdam or Hamburg. Many Amsterdam Sephardic merchants had trade connections with Hamburg at the time as the Dutch Republic was still at war with Spain (Eighty Years' War), and several merchants had agencies in Hamburg in order to divert trade. In December 1639, a tobacco planter from Barbados sailed to Amsterdam with a Dutch vessel contracted for by one of the Sephardic merchants in order to negotiate a shipment of tobacco in Amsterdam. See Notarial Archives, 599/587. See also Bloom about Hamburg and Amsterdam connection, pp. 107 ff.

81 Bloom, *The Economic Activity of the Jews of Amsterdam* (1937), p. 61.
82 Swetschinski, *Reluctant Cosmopolitans* (2000), p. 155.
83 "Poortnersneringen" refers to burgher trade or retail shops. To be able to buy or sell in small quantities in the seventeenth century in Amsterdam, one had to be a resident (a "poorter" or "burgher") of the city.

of Amsterdam's tobacco trade, I will discuss and analyze a collection of documents which until recently have been used only sparingly in historical research. These are the records in the Engel Sluiter Documents Collection described in the next chapter. The Collection concentrates on the trade rivalry between the Dutch Republic and the Spanish Habsburg regime during the Eighty Years' War and the concerns Spanish officials expressed with respect to illegitimate trade in which English, French, and Dutch privateers participated. Before the arrival of the Portuguese in Brazil and the Spanish in *Tierra Firme* and the Caribbean islands, indigenous Indians had collected and exchanged tobacco among each other and tobacco had served ritual and social functions in indigenous societies before the arrival of European settlers. With the advent of European trade goods arriving along the South and Central American coasts, tobacco exchange moved into the European colonial sphere as a commodity.[84] Initially, exchange occurred through occasional contacts with indigenous populations along the coasts but, in due time, as Portuguese merchants and English, French, and Dutch explorers and mariners passed through more frequently, points of contact were established and at set times of the year when ships arrived from Europe, supplies and provisions were unloaded and hides, log wood, pearls, salt, and tobacco were taken on board for the return voyage. It were the English, the French, and the Dutch in particular, who ventured out to trade in the Spanish and Portuguese territories in the late sixteenth century, and it were Portuguese *Converso* and Sephardic merchants who, in due time, formed a crucial link in ongoing trade with Northwestern Europe.[85] As all this took place during the Eighty Years' War, the trade conducted with the Spanish and Portuguese American colonies was illegal and contraband.

---

84 Norton, *Sacred Gifts* (2008), Chapters 2, 3, and 4; Cromwell, *The Smugglers' World* (2018), Chapters 1 and 2.
85 Studnicki-Gizbert, *A Nation Upon the Ocean Sea* (2007). See also, Morris, "Cultivating Colonies" (2017).

Chapter 2

THE CONTRABAND TOBACCO TRADE WITH SPANISH AMERICA: *TIERRA FIRME* AND HISPANIOLA

2.1 Trade and Navigation between Spain and Its Colonies

Trade rivalry between the Dutch Republic and the Spanish Habsburg regime during the Eighty Years' War was fierce and concerns expressed by Spanish officials with respect to illegitimate trade in which English, French and Dutch privateers participated and Portuguese merchants assisted in trade between Spain and its colonies were omnipresent in reports sent from *Tierra Firme* and Hispaniola. In the Preface to *The Dutch in the Caribbean and on the Wild Coast, 1580–1680*, Goslinga (1971) notes that the documentation on the role the Dutch played in the Caribbean region and along the coast of *Tierra Firme* during the seventeenth century derived mostly from accounts of their foes.[1] To explore the extent and nature of the tobacco contraband trade in the late sixteenth century and early seventeenth century we will therefore depend to a large extent on Spanish and Portuguese accounts and records most of which are found in the Archives of Seville and Lisbon. Besides a discussion of the Engel Sluiter Historical Documents Collection as a source of information for the study of the tobacco contraband trade in the early seventeenth century, this chapter will thus present a brief discussion about the early history of trade and navigation between Spain and its colonies which was subjected to a strict set of rules and for the most part excluded foreigners. The records of *the Casa de Contratacion* in Seville reveal the extent of illegitimate trade as documented by Spanish officials responsible for reporting on trade and navigation to and from the colonies. In addition, in the reports sent by the *Audiencias* to the Crown and Council, there is frequent mention of interlopers and foreigners interfering in Spanish maritime interests and about efforts made

---

1 Cornelis Ch. Goslinga, *The Dutch in the Caribbean and on the Wild Coast, 1580–1680* (University of Florida Press, Gainesville, 1971). See also Jonathan I. Israel, *The Dutch Republic and the Hispanic World 1606–1661* (Oxford University Press, Oxford, 1986).

by the officials to control colonial trade in particular as it involved Dutch merchants and mariners during the Eighty Years' War.

Trade and navigation between Spain and its colonial possessions was dominated by the Seville monopoly; the *Casa de Contratacion*.[2] The first Royal ordinances for the *Casa de Contratacion* were issued in 1503 and officials were appointed by the Crown to administer the possessions and issue licenses to trade but it was soon clear that strict schedules and regulations did not work. In 1504 the settlers on Hispaniola complained that they lacked provisions and supplies and requested a new order which permitted Castilian merchants to deliver needed supplies to the colony without special licenses. Excluded from the free trade provisions were slaves, arms, horses, or gold and silver. In name the *Casa de Contratacion* administered affairs but in practice it were the officials consisting of a treasurer, a factor, and a *contador* who collected customs fees and registered cargoes shipped to and from the colonies. In the colonies, similar functions were assigned to officials of the *Audiencias*.[3] It was assumed that under all circumstances trade would be conducted by merchants from Castile and that no foreigners would participate. This principle of exclusiveness formed the basis of most colonial trade conducted in the sixteenth and seventeenth century under Habsburg rule and included rights of residency which excluded foreigners. In 1614, Spain declared Seville the tobacco capital of the world. This meant that all the tobacco produced in the New World had to first be shipped to Seville before being distributed to the rest of Europe.

Here the interesting question arises, were the Portuguese and Dutch and Flemish merchants foreign merchants?[4] In the early sixteenth century, under the rule of Ferdinand and Isabelle only residents of Castile and Leon could emigrate to and trade with the Spanish possessions in the West Indies. This early on changed to be extended to Aragon and then to all of Spain. Under the reign of Charles V (1516–1556), the Low Countries and a good part of the German lands became part of the Habsburg Empire

---

2 Clarence Henry Haring, *Trade and Navigation between Spain and the Indies in the time of the Habsburgs* (Yale University Press, New Haven, 1917), Chapter 1, pp. 3–20; Chapter 2, pp. 21–45. In this section, I draw information almost exclusively from Haring, *Trade and Navigation* (1917) in order to present a brief introduction. For an overview of more recently published information on specific topics on trade and navigation between Spain and the Caribbean region see Ida Altman and David Wheat (eds.), *The Spanish Caribbean and the Atlantic World in the Long Sixteenth Century* (University of Nebraska Press, Lincoln, 2019).

3 Haring, *Trade and Navigation* (1917), Chapter 3, pp. 46–58; Chapter 4, pp. 47–95.

4 Haring, *Trade and Navigation* (1917), Chapter 5, pp. 96–122.

and in 1526 Charles issued the edict that commercial rights also be applied to subjects of the non-Spanish dominions.[5] With great ambition Charles V tried to keep his territories united under Catholic Habsburg rule as the Holy Roman Empire but failed when Protestant movements undermined his authority. In 1556 Charles V abdicated rule to his son Philip II who ruled the Habsburg Empire until 1598. It was during Philip's reign that the Eighty Years' War with the Netherlands (then known as the Dutch Republic) broke out. In 1580, Philip also became King of Portugal which meant his rule extended to include Portuguese subjects. At that time, he applied the rule of exclusivity of residency and trading rights to Spanish subjects only, while granting Portugal its traditional rights to conduct trade with Brazil and its other territories in West Africa and Asia where they had established colonial rule earlier.

During the sixteenth century, the Spanish confined the rights to trade and residence in the territories to subjects of "unquestionable orthodoxy".[6] This rule had been in existence since 1508 when Spanish colonists in Hispaniola requested the Crown to prohibit descendants of "infidels and heretics" to inhabit the island. The Crown subsequently issued the verdict that sons and grandsons of Jews, Moors, and *Conversos* and sons of those who had been charged by the Inquisition be barred from Hispaniola and other Spanish territories. The rule was difficult to enforce as it were Portuguese New Christians who proved to be effective in trade and possessed the financial resources to develop the colonies and help fund the Spanish Treasury. Thus, throughout the sixteenth century, Portuguese New Christians were given permission to emigrate to Spanish America. By the late sixteenth and in the early seventeenth century, Portuguese merchants were found almost everywhere in the Spanish overseas realm and were operating usually without licenses and frequently in the service of foreign merchants (privateers) from England, France

---

5 Charles V was Holy Roman Emperor and Archduke of Austria from 1519, King of Spain from 1516, and Lord of the Netherlands as titular Duke of Burgundy from 1506. He also became King of Naples and Sicily in 1554, and *jure uxoris* King of England and Ireland (during his marriage to Queen Mary I from 1554 to 1558). On trade and residency rights during his reign, see Haring, *Trade and Navigation* (1917) p. 98–101 who describes the intricacies in extending commercial and banking rights to the German bankers and merchants including the Welser and Fugger families in *Tierra Firme* and Hispaniola. See also, Spencer Tyce, "The Hispano-German Caribbean: South German Merchants and the Realities of European Consolidation, 1500–1540," in *The Spanish Caribbean and the Atlantic World* (2019), pp. 235–256. In 1549, the rights of "foreigners" to trade with the colonies was rescinded and the privilege to trade was again exclusively reserved for Spanish subjects.

6 Haring, *Trade and Navigation* (1917), pp. 104–105.

and the Dutch Republic.[7] During the sixteenth century many of the original Spanish settlers from *Tierra Firme* and Hispaniola had moved on to Mexico and Peru and Spanish immigration to *Tierra Firme* and Hispaniola was greatly reduced. This led the Spanish government to entice immigrants (including Portuguese immigrants) to settle in *Tierra Firme* and Hispaniola by paying for their crossing and furnishing land title, livestock, and tools to till the soil. Also, new immigrants were usually excluded from paying *alcabala* (the Royal sales tax imposed by the Habsburg rulers) for a number of years.[8]

During Philip's rule (1556–1598), by edict as noted, all trade from Seville to the colonies had to be conducted by native-born Spanish subjects. In practice, and as mentioned, this proved to be difficult to enforce and often exceptions were made, especially in those areas where foreign merchant-bankers were involved or, as in the case of Portuguese merchants, at service of the Crown or Treasury.[9] Another way to avoid the edict was to proclaim that the Canary Islands were the end destination while sailing on to the Americas without a license. The Canary Islands had traditionally been a staging or transfer point and had developed into a kind of staple market for products in demand in both the East and West Atlantic and had begun to form a part of the Portuguese merchant network. Another way to avoid official trade regulations was to claim status as Fleming or Italian merchant as Flanders and some Italian cities resided under official Spanish Habsburg rule and could thus declare residency in Seville. And finally, if necessary, one might pay a fine and bribe the officials. All these tactics and more were used and in effect for most of the sixteenth and early seventeenth centuries. The net result was that much trade was technically illegal. A common practice among Portuguese merchants was to sail from a Spanish port to the Canary Islands and then set course to Spanish America or Portuguese Brazil, and in return take cargo which they then carried directly to Portugal. Since most of the outbound trade of provisions from the Iberian Peninsula to the American territories was compromised trade to begin with because Spain did not manufacture enough goods and had to purchase goods in their vassal states in Northern Europe, a system of fines and fees (*indultos*) was introduced to compensate for lost revenue. Another way to supply the colonies was by contraband derived from Northwestern Europe involving French, English, and Dutch merchants

---

7 Haring, *Trade and Navigation* (1917), pp. 104–105. By 1630, measures were taken by the Spanish Crown to curtail the activities of Portuguese merchants on the Iberian Peninsula and in Spanish overseas territories including Mexico and Peru where the Inquisition was installed to persecute *Conversos* suspected of adhering to Jewish practices.
8 Haring, *Trade and Navigation* (1917), pp. 106–107.
9 Haring, *Trade and Navigation* (1917), pp. 107–109.

alongside Portuguese merchants. The *Asiento* slave trade also contributed to the contraband trade as *asentistas* were usually Portuguese merchants who were familiar with the slaving source areas in West Africa and maintained extensive trade networks.[10]

By the end of the sixteenth century, Spanish officials in the territories began to sound the alarm bell as Portuguese merchants and immigrant residents began to outnumber Spanish subjects in the colonies. After 1580, loyalty of the Portuguese immigrant population was in question and the Portuguese merchants resident in Castile where they could obtain *vecindad* (residency), were often suspected of illegal activities. In the Spanish colonies Portuguese residents were often serving foreign merchants and mariners as pilots, hired to explore the coast for trade or barter.[11] The Dutch were prominent participants in the coastal trade and barter in the late sixteenth and early seventeenth century as they frequented the Punta de Araya salt pans and sold cloth, axes, and other implements to the local population in exchange for silver, pearls, emeralds, and tobacco. The takeoff of tobacco exchange occurred during the expansionary phase of the development of Spanish America and Portuguese Brazil in the late sixteenth and early seventeenth century when new colonists began to arrive and settled the Caribbean Islands and *Tierra Firme* between the Orinoco and Amazon river deltas.[12] As pearl fishing, silver mining, and sugar plantations expanded, more merchants from Europe came up along the shores of *Tierra Firme*, and the Caribbean islands. At the same time, and in order to secure their territorial claims, the Spanish Crown encouraged the settlement of planters and merchant colonists along the coast and deltas of the major river systems like the Orinoco and Amazon River basins and stimulated the tobacco cultivation.[13] In due time, Trinidad became the major center of tobacco plantations and trade but Hispaniola was also targeted for

---

10 Haring, *Trade and Navigation* (1917), pp. 110–119.
11 Brian Hamm, "Between Acceptance and Exclusion: Spanish Responses to Portuguese Immigrants in the Sixteenth-Century Spanish Caribbean," in *The Spanish Caribbean and the Atlantic World* (2019), pp. 113–135.
12 See also Marcy Norton and Studnicki-Gizbert in "The Multinational Commodification of Tobacco, 1492–1650: An Iberian Perspective," in Peter C. Mancall (ed.), *The Atlantic World and Virginia, 1550–1624* (University of North Carolina Press, Chapel Hill, 2007), pp. 251–273, p. 260.
13 Trinidad was the first recognized Spanish Caribbean colony specifically targeted for tobacco cultivation at around 1590. Before then, most of the tobacco exchange that occurred was between English, Dutch, and French mariners and Amerindians or Creoles. See, Marcy Norton, *Sacred Gifts, Profane Pleasures: A History of Tobacco and Chocolate in the Atlantic World* (Cornell University Press, Ithaca and London, 2008), pp. 150–151, and Melissa N. Morris, "Cultivating Colonies: Tobacco and the Upstart Empires, 1580–1640," (PhD dissertation, Columbia University, 2017), pp. 160–161.

tobacco production and trade.[14] Gradually, settlements of French, English and Dutch merchants sprung up along the coast of South America and on the Caribbean islands.[15] In addition, several islands were settled by the French and the English and became tobacco colonies including Barbados which was founded by the English in 1627. With the help of Dutch merchants Barbados became one of the main tobacco export colonies in the 1630s to change over to sugar cultivation in the 1650s.[16]

Meanwhile, Dutch merchants focused their attention still primarily on the Amazon and Orinoco delta regions and in rivalry with Spain began to exchange their trade goods including linen and hardware to access coastal areas where tobacco was exchanged or cultivated while establishing short-lived colonies between the Amazon and Orinoco rivers.[17] In 1634, the Amsterdam

---

14 A. G. Escudero, "Hispaniola's Turn to Tobacco," in B. Aram and B. Yun-Casalilla (eds.), *Global Goods and the Spanish Empire, 1492–1824* (Palgrave Macmillan, London, 2014), pp. 216–229.
15 The first Dutch voyage to Trinidad was undertaken to deliver slaves in 1606. See Vincent T. Harlow, *Colonizing Expeditions to the West Indies and Guiana, 1623–1667* (London, 1925), p. 125. See also, Goslinga, *The Dutch in the Caribbean and on the Wild Coast* (1971), pp. 340–341.
16 Robert C. Batie, "Why Sugar? Economic Cycles and the Changing of Staples on the English and French Antilles, 1624–1654," 1–41; 4–13. Besides Barbados (1627), St. Christopher (1624), Nevis (1628), Antigua (1632), Montserrat (1632), Guadeloupe (1635), and Martinique (1635) were settled by the French and the English. For a historical documentation of the early settlement of Barbados and the relationship to Dutch trade interests and tobacco, see George Edmundson, "The Dutch in Western Guiana," *The English Historical Review*, vol. 16, no. 64, October 1901, pp. 640–675. The settlement and colonization of Barbados was in the realm of Dutch-Anglo trade interests and involved Anglo-Dutch merchants from *Tierra Firme* who brought the plants and financial resources to develop a plantation economy focused on tobacco. The tobacco grown in Barbados turned out to be of inferior quality compared to Venezuelan or Virginia tobacco and was sold at lower prices in the European market. During the 1620s, 1630s, and 1640s, Dutch merchants shipped tobacco from Barbados and Virginia to the Amsterdam market. Christian J. Koot, *Empire at the Periphery: British Colonists, Anglo-Dutch Trade, and the Development of the British Atlantic, 1621–1713* (New York University Press, New York and London, 2011), pp. 17–46. For an overall view Dutch merchants played in the colonization of the *Tierra Firme* and the Caribbean islands see Wim Klooster, *The Dutch Moment: War, Trade, and Settlement in the Seventeenth-Century Atlantic World* (Cornell University Press, Ithaca, 2016).
17 George Edmundson, "The Dutch on the Amazon and Negro in the Seventeenth Century. Part I.- Dutch Trade on the Amazon," *The English Historical Review*, Vol. 18, No. 72, October 1903), pp. 642–663, and Engel Sluiter, "Dutch-Spanish Rivalry in the Caribbean Area, 1594–1609," *The Hispanic American Historical Review*, vol. 28, no.2, May, 1948, pp. 165–196; pp. 182–183. See also, Jessica Vance Roitman, "Second Is Best: Dutch Colonization on the 'Wild Coast'", in L. H. Roper (ed.), *The Torrid Zone: Caribbean Colonization and Cultural Interaction in the Long Seventeenth Century* (University of South Carolina Press, 2018).

Chamber of the West India Company (WIC) unanimously agreed to seize Curacao from the Spanish and in due time established a thriving colony and transshipment center under the directorship of the WIC.[18] Soon after the Amsterdam Chamber of the WIC declared Curacao a Dutch colony, the first Amsterdam Sephardic merchants established themselves as resident merchants and became engaged in delivering cloth and hardware and sometimes slaves to planters and settlers in *Tierra Firme* in return for tobacco and cacao for the Amsterdam and European market.[19] In the late seventeenth and early eighteenth century, these contacts concentrated on Coro in the central coastal region of Venezuela close to Curacao from where cacao was shipped and where for a period of time a Jewish settlement developed in Tucacas. However, these developments occurred almost a century after the Dutch and Portuguese merchants had first begun to trade along the Orinoco section of the coast of *Tierra Firme*, further east.

2.2 The Engel Sluiter Historical Documents Collection[20]

The Engel Sluiter Historical Documents Collection is kept at Bancroft Library at the University of California - Berkeley. The records in the collection are copies of documents dating back to the 1590s and include records for

---

18 Linda M. Rupert, *Creolization and Contraband: Curacao in the Early Modern* Atlantic World (University of Georgia Press, Athens, Georgia, 2012) Chapter 1, pp. 17–42. Curacao resided under a Spanish governor prior to 1634. English and Dutch privateers had visited and traded with the local population going back to 1565 when the Hawkins traded cloth and some slaves for hides. Contact between Curacao's Caquetios Indians and tribes of *Tierra Firme* was common before Spanish settlement of the island. In the sixteenth century, Curacao's indigenous population served as slaves on Hispaniola and *Tierra Firme*. Mostly ignored and neglected by the Spanish, Dutch merchants began to explore the salt pans of the Lesser Antilles (Aruba, Bonaire and Curacao) in the 1620s. When the Dutch lost control of St. Martin (where they had mined salt) in 1633, the Amsterdam Chamber of the WIC set its eye on Curacao.

19 Rupert, *Creolization and Contraband* (2012), p. 48, 59, 78–79. See also, Wim Klooster, "Contraband Trade by Curacao's Jews with Countries of Idolatry, 1660–1800," in *Studia Rosenthaliana*, Vol. 31, no. 1–2, 1997, pp. 58–73, and Jonathan I. Israel, "The Jews of Curacao, New Amsterdam and the Guyanas: A Caribbean and Trans-Atlantic Network, 1648–1740," in *Diasporas within a Diaspora: Jews, Crypto-Jews, and the World Maritime Empires: 1540–1740* (Brill, Leiden, 2002), pp. 511–532.

20 The collection of the documents took place during a 70-year period from approximately 1930–2001. The collection is approximately 116 linear feet, 92 cartons and a few oversized folders. The Engel Sluiter Historical Documents Collection was donated to the Bancroft Library, University of California, Berkeley in 1996. The collection is open for research but advance notice is required for use. For a more detailed description of the collection see Julie van den Hout, *Listing of the Engel Sluiter Historical Documents Collection*, Collection number BANC MSS 98/79 z.

specific regions of Spanish America and Portuguese Brazil where tobacco smuggling occurred and where Portuguese merchants were active in trade. The collection consists of records in which Spanish officials express concern and develop plans to combat illegal trade in efforts to regain control over their territory. The records also illustrate the extent to which Spanish officials were prepared to go to combat smugglers or engage in bribery and in manipulating the circumstances that enticed the local populations to participate in illegal exchange. In my research I focus on merchants active in illicit trade with *Tierra Firme* and Hispaniola; coastal areas of Spanish America abutting the Caribbean Sea. The areas were relatively scantily populated and relatively poorly defended by the Spanish authorities and over time became a smugglers paradise.[21] The story told by Sluiter in his own words derived from documents he collected, transcribed, and then provided with annotations in English revealed a close-knit relationship between smugglers and their go-betweens, the Portuguese merchants resident along the coast and on the islands on whom the Spanish officials depended for needed supplies and income.[22]

The Collection was cataloged and provided with an inventory and description in 2016 by Julie van den Hout under the auspices of the New Netherland Institute.[23] The collection contains historical documents from archives throughout Europe and Latin America. The documents collected include government records, fiscal and business accounts, and reports on military matters. The main theme of Sluiter's Historical Documents Collection is Dutch-Iberian rivalry at the time of the Eighty Years' War from 1568 to 1648. The documents also include Dutch, English, French, Spanish, and Portuguese voyages to the New World in rivalry

---

21 Most of what has been written about smuggling along the coast of Hispaniola or *Tierra Firme* concerns illicit trade in the eighteenth century. My study, I hope, will illustrate that the contraband trade had deep roots in the Eastern Caribbean coastal areas and laid the basis for illicit trade conducted in the eighteenth century. See for instance, Jesse Cromwell, *The Smugglers' World: Illicit Trade and Atlantic Communities in Eighteenth-Century Venezuela* (University of North Carolina Press, Chapel Hill, 2018), and Rupert, *Creolization and Contraband* (2012).

22 In this chapter, I will refer to Portuguese merchants without suggesting that they were New Christian merchants. Old Christian and New Christians are not distinguished by name. In those instances in which it seems obvious or likely that they are Portuguese New Christian merchants, I will specify.

23 For a description of the documents included in the collection, see Julie van den Hout, *Listing to the Engel Sluiter Historical Documents Collection* available at Bancroft Library and on-line (Collection number BANC MSS 98/79 z) completed 2016.

with each other in search of gold, silver, and goods to trade. Copies of unpublished manuscripts are included in the collection and are provided with transcriptions. Economic and fiscal records predominate which document the rise to commercial prominence of the Dutch Republic, the intricacies of Spanish and Portuguese trade and navigation, and the *Contaduria* which report revenue and expenditures of the Crown along with import and export duties. Many of the records were filed with the Archives of the Indies in Seville. The documents in the collection relate mainly to Dutch, Spanish, and Portuguese affairs in Europe and in the overseas Spanish and Portuguese possessions but include references to English and French accounts of affairs with Spain as well.

Besides the collection documenting Spanish America, Sluiter also collected documents on Portuguese Brazil. The Brazil collection starts in 1500 but primarily documents events after 1580 when Portugal was united with Spain and when Dutch trade and navigation with Portuguese Brazil became more compromised although Portugal maintained some order of independence from Habsburg rule concerning its mercantile and colonial affairs. The collection includes the period of Dutch conquest and occupation of North-East Brazil (Pernambuco) during the period from 1630 until 1654. The documents uncover Portuguese resistance to encroachment by foreigners (i.e., the Dutch) and information on sugar, brazil wood and the slave trade, and illustrates merchant networks between West Africa, Brazil and Portugal. References to the tobacco trade seem incidental but the collection includes references to Portuguese and Sephardic merchants in contact with Portugal, Brazil and the Dutch Republic. The collection on Brazil contains two parts: Portuguese Brazil before 1630, and the Dutch occupation of Pernambuco from 1630 until 1654.

The Caribbean collection (including *Tierra Firme* and the Spanish Caribbean islands) covers English, French, Spanish and Dutch merchant trade and documents aspects of Spanish colonial administration, defense policy, fortification, along with mining and trade regulation. Throughout the collection, smugglers, buccaneers, corsairs, privateers and foreigners involved in illegal trade are referred to, often in the context of capture, corruption, and bribery. Remarkable are the detailed considerations to depopulate areas where smuggling occurred and tobacco was cultivated and exchanged. The collection on *Tierra Firme* and the Spanish islands also describes involvement of or with indigenous Amerindian tribes, Creoles, run-away African slaves, as well as Portuguese and Mestizo merchants in coastal areas where they had settled to conduct trade or engage with smugglers in the tobacco contraband trade. From the documents presented it is clear that Dutch merchants were interlopers and were not welcome and

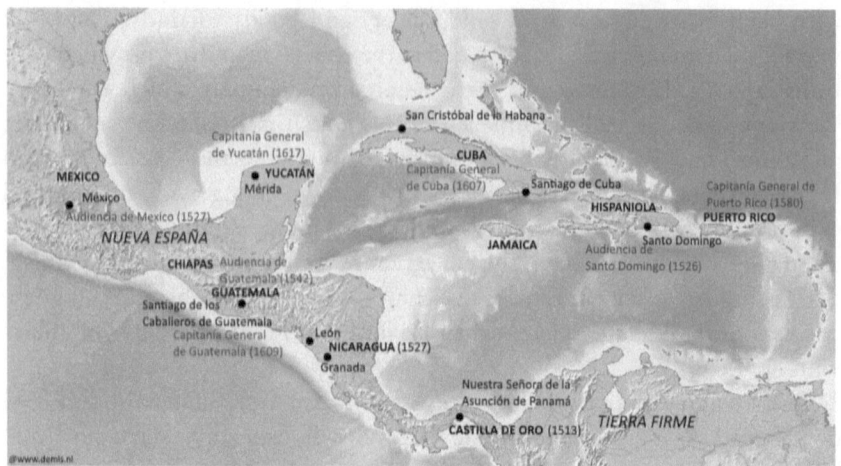

Figure 2.1 Spanish provinces, audiencias, and captaincies general in the Caribbean and Gulf of Mexico in the sixteenth to seventeenth centuries.

Source: See Wikimedia Commons, Author Simon Burchell: www2.demis.nl/worldmap.

that contacts with Portuguese merchants in the colonial Iberian world of the late sixteenth and early seventeenth century were suspect (Figure 2.1).[24]

The focus of the Engel Sluiter Caribbean collection is on Hispaniola (Santo Domingo), Margarita Island, Punta de Araya, Cumana, Santa Marta and Cartagena, Guyana, and Trinidad.

Most of the evidence presented is from Spanish colonial administrators (the *Audiencia*), who reported to the King and Council from territories administered about threats of smugglers and buccaneers with specific mention of Dutch mariners and merchants in contact with local indigenous or coastal populations. Quite often exchange contacts took place in rather remote locations away from the main ports where the Spanish galleons (or *Flotas*) frequented during their annual voyages. The smuggling trade with Portuguese (i.e., New Christian) merchants included the slave trade. Frequent reports were made of Dutch (or French and English) vessels lying at anchor delivering goods and receiving pearls, ginger, hides, or tobacco in return. Sometimes, when ships were captured and hauled into port, mariners or merchant smugglers were reported by name and their port of origin and voyage details were recorded and we thus gain some insight

---

24 For scope and content of the cartons and file folders see Listing Julie van den Hout, *Engel Sluiter Historical Documents Collection*.

into the specifics of the merchants and their trading networks as well as the goods being smuggled.²⁵ Concern about the frequency of tobacco smuggling is referred to in several of the reports and resulted in plans to prohibit tobacco cultivation or allow cultivation with royal permission only. In several instances, recommendations were made to undermine smuggling activities in specific coastal regions and depopulate specific areas. So, for instance, along the coast of Hispaniola, Cumana, Guyana, Trinidad, and Punta de Araya. The same areas were also mentioned as being populated by Portuguese referring to New Christian merchants who had settled in coastal regions in earlier decades.²⁶ In the Spanish documents we sense disdain for Portuguese merchants as they were associated with contraband trade and were thought to be in cahoots with the French, Dutch and English smugglers. The records suggest that Portuguese merchant networks extended to include contacts in Bayonne in Southwest France, London, and Amsterdam which were implicated in tobacco smuggling activities. Furthermore, the salt pans of Punta de Araya, frequented by Dutch vessels to transport salt to the Dutch Republic were of particular concern as the Spanish administrators were well aware that besides salt, tobacco and pearls were also smuggled to Amsterdam and to other ports in the Dutch Republic.²⁷

---

25 A particularly interesting case is Simon de Herrera, a Jewish merchant, who is persecuted by the Inquisition, whose goods are confiscated after he tried to sell his ship to the enemies, and who sent for safe conduit in order to escape to Holland or Zeeland in the Dutch Republic. He was eventually put to death when he was convicted. Or the case of Don Fernando de Berrio who pursued the search for El Dorado which caused him great economic losses which he compensated by trading tobacco illegally with the English and the Dutch. He was denounced by the Council of the Indies in the province of Venezuela. Both cases will be discussed in more detail in the main text.
26 Daviken Studnicki-Gizbert, *A Nation Upon the Ocean Sea: Portugal's Atlantic Diaspora and the Crisis of the Spanish Empire, 1492–1640* (Oxford University Press, Oxford, New York, 2007).
27 Salt was an important commodity for the North Sea fisheries and had been obtained in Portugal prior to 1580 after which date salt shipments were boycotted when Portugal united with Spain in the Eighty Years' War against the Dutch Republic. See Jonathan I. Israel, "Spain and the Dutch Sephardic, 1609–1660)" *Studia Rosenthaliana*, vol. 12, no. 1/2 (July 1978), pp. 1–61; pp. 5, 19, who refers to Setubal as the main salt shipment port and Sephardic merchants as the predominant merchant group engaged in the salt trade during the Twelve Years' Truce from 1609–1621. Earlier, salt was mined and shipped from the Spanish territories in the Americas, particularly Punta de Araya. See also, Catia Antunes, "The Commercial Relationship between Amsterdam and the Portuguese Salt-Exporting Ports: Aveiro and Setubal, 1580–1715," in *The Articulation of Portuguese Salt with Worldwide Routes: Past and New Consumption Trends* (University of Porto, Porto, 2008) pp. 161–181.

2.3 Engel Sluiter's Analysis of the Documents Collection

Whereas the Engel Sluiter Collection is rich in evidence about smuggling, including the smuggling of tobacco and the role of Portuguese merchants in smuggling activities, Engel Sluiter published relatively little over his lifetime compared to the extensive collection of documents he assembled. Two articles on Dutch maritime activities and Dutch-Spanish rivalry during the Eighty Years' War appeared in the 1940s in which he detailed primarily on the expansion of the emerging maritime power of the Dutch Republic and smuggling in the Caribbean region. In the first paper, published in 1942, he describes the unique character of Dutch maritime power and the superiority of resources, technology, seafaring and navigation skills of the Dutch in their push to undermine the Spanish at sea during the Eighty Years' War.[28] He describes the period from roughly 1585 until 1597 as exploratory during which Dutch merchants venture out across the Atlantic to the Caribbean region to secure commodities which they previously obtained in the Iberian Peninsula including salt needed for the fisheries to preserve the North Sea herring catch. The first voyages to Brazil occurred in 1587 when Dutch vessels and crews in the employ of Portuguese merchants were first banned from trade with Portugal at the time when the first embargoes were imposed.[29] Soon thereafter in 1592 or 1593, Dutch ships were exploring the coast of Guyana and in 1595 Dutch ships appeared at Cumana along the coast of *Tierra Firme*, and at Santo Domingo, Hispaniola. In 1598 several Dutch vessels were exploring and trading along the Amazon and the Orinoco rivers.[30] From the records collected for the years 1598 to 1605, Sluiter counted twenty to twenty-five vessels annually sailing between the Dutch Republic and *Tierra Firme*, Cuba, and Hispaniola engaged in barter trade with Spanish colonists, Portuguese merchants, and Amerindians and Creoles in exchange for hides, sugar, ginger, and pearls. Somewhat surprising, Sluiter does not mention tobacco in his 1942 journal article although records in his Historical Documents Collection frequently mentioned tobacco as a trade good and we do know that in 1606 Spanish colonial administrators contemplated depopulating coastal areas where tobacco cultivation and smuggling occurred. Salt hauling as referred to above is reported frequently

---

28 Engel Sluiter, "Dutch Maritime Power and the Colonial Status Quo, 1585–1641," *Pacific Historical Review*, vol. 11, no. 1 (March 1942), pp. 29–41.
29 See also, Daniel M. Swetschinski, "Conflict and Opportunity in 'Europe's Other Sea': The Adventure of Caribbean Jewish Settlement," *American Jewish History*, vol. 72, no. 2 (December 1982), pp. 212–240.
30 Engel Sluiter (1942), pp. 30–31.

and it is likely that tobacco was exchanged at Punta de Araya in barter for goods the Dutch delivered to coastal populations nearby which was usually not recorded.[31]

The Sluiter Collection contains a great deal of detail on the number of vessels engaged in salt shipments and smuggling for the period 1600–1605. From letters sent by the Governor of Cumana (Don Diego Suarez de Amaya) to the King, Sluiter calculates that almost six hundred Dutch salt ships besides more than fifty smuggling vessels arrived at or passed by Cumana during that time.[32] In response, the Spanish mounted a concerted effort to attack the Dutch salt fleet and General Don Luis Fajardo of the Spanish Armada sent fourteen galleons and four auxiliary vessels to fend off the Dutch in 1606. A year later Fajardo's fleet dispersed a smuggling fleet of twenty-four Dutch vessels, six French ships and one English vessel off the coast of Cuba.[33] In response, the Dutch outfit a fleet of 130 privateers to harass the Spanish and Portuguese at sea and off the coasts of Spain and Portugal. In 1607 and 1608, negotiations began between the Dutch Republic and Spain to end the war and in 1609 a truce was signed which honored unobstructed shipping between Amsterdam and the Atlantic coasts of Spain and Portugal. The truce agreed to in 1609 held until 1621 (known as the Twelve Years' Truce in the Eighty Years' War) during which time Dutch merchants resumed direct trade with the Iberian Peninsula to obtain commodities (including salt from Setubal in Portugal) which were now safely carried to Amsterdam while the smuggling trade with *Tierra Firme* diminished some but did not cease.[34] In fact, tobacco smuggling expanded during the Twelve Years' Truce from 1609–1621 as embargoes on trade with Spanish America and Portuguese Brazil remained in effect during that time. From the documents collected, Sluiter (1942) demonstrates that tobacco smuggling with *Tierra Firme* coastal communities intensified and that trade with Brazil grew substantially

---

31 Engel Sluiter (1942), pp. 30–31. See also, Cromwell, *The Smuggler's World* (2018), pp. 54–55.
32 Engel Sluiter (1942), p. 32.
33 Engel Sluiter (1942), p. 33.
34 The Twelve Years Truce (1609–1621) was a prosperous period in the Dutch-Iberian relationships. The end of the Spanish and Portuguese embargos on Dutch trade had ended and bilateral contacts were re-established. In the Atlantic, especially in the Caribbean, Dutch expansion as it had occurred during the first phase of the War was temporarily halted but smuggling did not cease. See also Jonathan I. Israel, *Dutch Primacy in the World Trade, 1585–1740* (Oxford: Clarendon, 1989), 38–79 and Jonathan I. Israel, *Empires and Entrepots: The Dutch, the Spanish monarchy and the Jews, 1585–1713* (The Hambledon Press, London, 1990), 135–141.

more pronounced during the Twelve Years' Truce. As the Spanish Crown restricted legal trade engaging foreign merchants and prohibited tobacco cultivation and exchange in coastal areas of *Tierra Firme* and the Caribbean islands, the contraband trade or smuggling, apparently, more than doubled.

Dutch trade with Brazil during the Twelve Years' Truce developed very differently. According to Sluiter (1942), based on his document collection, Portuguese merchants and New Christian or Sephardic merchants from Amsterdam with family and commercial connections in Lisbon, Viana, Oporto, and Brazil, continued to trade with Brazil unabatedly. In 1621, at the end of the truce, reports revealed that ten to fifteen ships were built annually in the Dutch Republic used exclusively for the Brazil trade, and forty to fifty thousand chests of Brazil sugar were imported every year while twenty-five sugar refineries were operating in the Dutch Republic, most of them in Amsterdam. The sugar traded and processed in Amsterdam, in fact, accounted for one-half or two-thirds of the carrying trade between Brazil and the European market.[35] As sugar was the primary colonial trade good, tobacco was likely exchanged or traded alongside and taken on board for the return voyage, as seaman's ration or as contraband.[36] In Guyana, in the meantime, from the Essequibo to the Amazon rivers, Dutch attempts at establishing control over territory occurred but attacks by Spanish forces ended the early attempts at establishing permanent colonies. In 1616, the first semi-permanent colony emerged on the Essequibo River.[37] Only later in the seventeenth century did the Dutch render some success in colonizing territory. The Twelve Years' Truce expired in 1621 and the Dutch-Iberian conflict resumed. The WIC, chartered in 1621, was founded in response to the renewed war threats and trade embargoes and became the driving force behind Dutch trade and colonization schemes in the Caribbean region for the next few decades. Meanwhile hundreds of Dutch salt ships and scores of privateers reappeared at Punta de Araya and along the coasts of South America and islands of the Caribbean. In response to the obvious re-emergence of Dutch naval power and commercial intrusions, the Spanish built a fort at Punta de Araya in 1622 and closed off the salt pans to Dutch salt mining and the Portuguese expelled Dutch colonists from the Amazon delta region. In May 1624, the WIC naval force moved against Salvador, the capital of the province of Bahia in Brazil, which

---

35 See Engel Sluiter (1942), p. 35.
36 See Engel Sluiter (1942), p. 36.
37 Roitman, "Second Is Best" in Roper (ed.), *The Torrid Zone* (2018) describes the colonizing efforts during the first few decades of the seventeenth century as an unending, unmitigated disaster.

was recaptured by the Portuguese a year later. In 1630 a second WIC attempt at establishing control over the Brazil sugar trade by invading Pernambuco succeeded and the province became a Dutch colony from 1630 until 1654. Curacao was seized by the Dutch from the Spanish in 1634 and became the main transfer point in trade between Spanish America and the Dutch Republic.[38] This turbulent history between Spain, Portugal, and the Dutch Republic ended with the Peace Treaty of Munster in 1648 at which time more or less regular trade relations between Spain and the Dutch Republic were re-established.[39]

In an article published in 1948, Sluiter deals more specifically with the Spanish response to Dutch trade emerging in the Atlantic world addressing the question as to what extent the Dutch jeopardized Spain's position in the region.[40] More precisely, Sluiter (1948) asks to what extent the Dutch drained the Spanish and Portuguese of their wealth and corrupted its officials and forced them to increase defense spending. To understand and explain the impact of the Dutch revolt against Spanish Habsburg rule at home and commercial expansion in the Atlantic region, Sluiter describes the history of the Eighty Years' War (1568–1648) and the impact it had on Dutch trade in some detail. By 1595 the defensive phase of the Dutch resistance to Habsburg rule had ended and the Dutch offensive to Spanish hegemony in Europe and its imperial rule in the rest of the world had begun.[41] Inter-European trade at the time reached from the Baltic to the Iberian Peninsula and concerned commodities like timber, naval stores, hemp, flax, metals and grain to supply the Iberian Peninsula and the Mediterranean region while shipments of wine, wool, salt, fruits, sugar, spices, dyestuffs, and bullion were made to the Northern European market. The main share of this trade passed through the Dutch Republic and Flanders. During the decade and a half of the Eighty Years' War when Portugal was not yet officially unified with Spain, most of the trade from the Mediterranean and the Iberian Peninsula continued to be transferred through Lisbon and other ports in Portugal, and via Antwerp where Portuguese merchants were resident. As discussed

---

38 See Engel Sluiter (1942), p. 38–39.
39 The Dutch remained at war with Portugal until 1660.
40 Engel Sluiter, "Dutch-Spanish Rivalry in the Caribbean Area, 1594–1609," *The Hispanic American Historical Review*, vol. 28, no. 2, May 1948, pp. 165–196.
41 Conveniently, France and England had also declared war on Spain and thus the Spanish aggressive stand against the Dutch Republic diminished because of divided attention paid to all its enemies.

in Chapter 1, after 1580 this changed and in 1585 the first of several Dutch offensives and Spanish counter-offensives in the form of embargoes and blockades of the Scheldt river and the Flemish coast occurred and by the end of the sixteenth century, Antwerp's colonial transfer trade had been greatly diminished while Amsterdam's trade had increased.[42] Amsterdam profited from this situation as Portuguese merchants transferred their business to the Dutch Republic. Subsequently, many Antwerp merchants, including Portuguese New Christian merchants, moved to Amsterdam as well and as a result many New Christian and Sephardic merchants with ties to the Mediterranean, the Iberian Peninsula, and Southwestern France began to settle in Amsterdam and engage in the Iberia-Baltic and Mediterranean trade and in the sugar trade with Madeira, São Tomé and Brazil, bypassing Antwerp. But trade with the Dutch Republic was illegal as seen from the Spanish perspective and Dutch and Portuguese merchants in Amsterdam or merchants resident in other cities of the Dutch Republic sailing under the Dutch flag were suspected and frequently under attack. Several attacks at sea and confiscations of vessels in Portuguese ports occurred and as a consequence, trade with the Iberian Peninsula was severely affected. The most affected were Dutch salt merchants, including Sephardic merchants, who had traded with Setubal and Aveiro in Portugal. As vessels were confiscated, salt merchants transferred their trade to the Cape Verde Islands in the late sixteenth century and thus the first step towards establishing a trans-Atlantic trade network had occurred.[43]

The main supply sources for colonial staple commodities in which the Portuguese had traded, first via Antwerp and then via Amsterdam, in the North-South Baltic-Iberia circuit were the islands of the Caribbean (Cuba, Hispaniola, Jamaica, Puerto Rico and Trinidad), the coast of *Tierra Firma* (Cartagena, Santa Marta, Margarita Island and Cumana) and Central America (Vera Cruz) as well as Brazil (Salvador in Bahia, and Recife in Pernambuco). In order to continue the profitable trade it became ever

---

42 See C. Lesger, *The Rise of the Amsterdam Market and Information Exchange* (Ashgate, Aldershot, UK and Burlington, VT, 2006), pp. 100–138. As Portugal became part of the Spanish Habsburg Empire in 1580 and Antwerp remained under Spanish rule, Antwerp became more vulnerable as a target in the Eighty Years' War between the Dutch Republic and Spain. Many of the merchants were New Christian or *Conversos* who later reconverted to Judaism as the Dutch granted Jews special privileges to trade and allowed them to found and establish their own Jewish congregations.

43 Engel Sluiter (1948), pp. 165–170, describes and documents that 400–500 vessels in Spanish and Portuguese ports were confiscated during the period 1585–1598.

more important to establish more direct trade relationships with *Tierra Firme*, Hispaniola, Cuba, and Brazil.⁴⁴ In the case of *Tierra Firme*, these commodities included salt, pearls, sarsaparilla, silver and gold, as well as cacao and tobacco. Hispaniola and Cuba, provided hides, ginger, sugar and tobacco. In general, along the coast of *Tierra Firme*, the Spanish held only intermittent or limited control over the areas where these products were mined or grown and from the records it is obvious that indigenous Amerindians, run-away slaves and Creoles, as well as itinerant foreigners including Portuguese merchants who made up part of the coastal populations all participated in trade or smuggling. The territories were nominally governed by administrators assigned by the Spanish King and his Council but the centers of control were wide and far between and the territories were rather scantily populated. It is from reports made by the governors of the province of Cumana, in New Andalusia, and assigned to the territories covered in the Engel Sluiter Historical Documents Collection that we learn about smugglers and tobacco planters and Spanish officials who ordered removal of coastal populations and resettlement. From these documents we gain the first impression of how the colonial or smuggling trade was conducted, who participated in illegal trade, how officials interfered, and how the Spanish administrators (governors included) colluded with the merchant-smugglers, including New Christian and Sephardic merchants engaged in the contraband trade.⁴⁵

The first Portuguese Jewish or Sephardic merchants mentioned in Sluiter's collection of documents are Simon de Herrera, Manual Cardozo, and Juan de Riberos who had been apprehended for possession of multiple passports and had associations with both English and Dutch merchants and smugglers. They were captured in Hispaniola in 1596.⁴⁶ Among Simon de Herrera's confiscated documents were account books, bills of lading, and letters which implicated him with foreign commercial interest. He was taken to the Inquisition and put on trial in Mexico and executed in 1604 after it became known that he had tried to sell his vessel which had routinely sailed from Santo Domingo on Hispaniola to

---

44 In March 1595, Balthasar de Moucheron, an Antwerp merchant of French extraction who had transferred his business to the Dutch Republic, applied to the States of Zeeland for an exemption of payment of export duties on goods he planned to send to the Spanish Indies. That year he was found trading in Cumana. In November 1595, the States of Zeeland waived payment of export duties on cloth, silks, linen, velvet, and other small wares to be traded on the north coast of the Indies (Cumana?). See Engel Sluiter (1948), p. 171–173.
45 Engel Sluiter, 1948. See also Cromwell, *The Smugglers' World* (2018) for the eighteenth century.
46 Engel Sluiter, 1948, p. 174.

Seville in Castile to the enemy and then applied for a safeguard to take him to Holland or Zeeland in the Dutch Republic.[47] Dutch and English merchants arriving along the coast of South America in the 1590s welcomed the opportunity to trade or smuggle with Portuguese merchants and in the course of the first few decades of the seventeenth century trade exchange took place regularly among Amsterdam's Portuguese merchants, including Sephardic merchants, and New Christian or crypto-Jewish merchants in the Caribbean.[48] When the first Dutch voyages to *Tierra Firme* and the Caribbean islands occurred, Dutch ship captains preferred to take Portuguese pilots on board as they were acquainted with the territory and the merchant communities on shore.[49] The mutually beneficial relationship between Dutch, Sephardic and Portuguese merchants as analyzed and discussed by Sluiter (1948) based on his collection of documents, however, made the Portuguese merchants suspect in the eyes of the Spanish officials as smuggling activities increased.

Due to embargoes imposed on Dutch salt carriers embarking at Portuguese ports as discussed earlier, Dutch merchants began to sail to the Caribbean region on a regular basis starting in 1594 and in 1598 they explored opportunities to access the salt pans off the coast of *Tierra Firme*. They soon began to transport salt in substantial quantities from Punta de Araya, situated halfway between the island of La Margarita and Cumana. According to Sluiter (1948) based on calculations derived from accounts sent by the Governors of Cumana and Caracas in 1600, between thirty and forty salt carriers sailed back from Araya to the Dutch Republic that year. Reports also implicated Dutch mariners and merchants for smuggling as they were lying at anchor off the coast to load salt. According to the Governor of La Margarita, smuggling also disrupted the pearl fisheries and he recommended to inundate the salt pans at Punta de Araya and fortify the location in order to retake control over the situation.

---

47 In both Spain and Portugal, New Christians were regularly persecuted and executed under suspicion of practicing Judaism and in 1499, Manuel I the King of Portugal had issued a decree that New Christians could not leave the country without special permission. Interestingly, the ban did not apply to the Portuguese colonies and many New Christian families decided for commercial opportunities and under safeguards from the Inquisition to move overseas. Later, in 1571 the Spanish King Philip II who also became king of Portugal after 1580, instituted an Inquisitorial tribunal in Mexico.

48 Daniel M. Swetschinski, "Conflict and Opportunity in 'Europe's Other Sea': The Adventures of Caribbean Jewish Settlement," *American Jewish History*, vol. 72, no. 2, 1982, pp. 212–240.

49 See Engel Sluiter (1948), p. 175. About "Portuguese" pilots or *Practicos*, see Cromwell, *A Smugglers' World* (2018), pp. 131–132.

Nonetheless, regular voyages were made by Dutch salt carriers and smuggling vessels in the following years, as reported by Sluiter (1948).[50]

Evidently, the salt trade and tobacco smuggling took place side by side. The ships usually sailed from the Dutch Republic in squadrons of six vessels, escorted by naval ships to protect them. Outbound, they sailed via the Canary Islands, the Lesser Antilles, the Los Testigos Islands, La Margarita Island, to anchor at Punta de Araya. On the return voyage, following the prevailing winds and currents, they sailed via the Mona Passage between Puerto Rico and Hispaniola to Bermuda. Sailing round trip between Amsterdam and the Caribbean took twelve weeks, thereabouts. An average crew numbered twenty to fifty men depending on the tonnage of the vessel ranging in size from two hundred to six hundred tons for salt carriers and one to two hundred tons for smuggling vessels. Most vessels carried some armaments in the form of cannons and muskets. At the salt pans or at anchor in the lagoons, small jetties were built and salt was broken into pieces and then loaded on board. Apparently, labor was provided by the crew and no slave labor was used. The area lacked fresh water and crew were sent weekly to mainland rivers where the Spaniards occasionally waited in ambush. However, due to undermanned Spanish command posts and townspeople willing to exchange goods, the fresh water stations subsequently became smuggling centers. Clearly, these activities undermined Spanish control and fiscal prudence and soon this became the core of concerns expressed by Spanish administrators.[51]

In addition to coastal smuggling, Dutch naval vessels also formed a serious threat to the Spanish supply and carrying trade consisting of provisions and merchandise from Puerto Rico, Santo Domingo, and Cartagena bound for La Margarita Island, Cumana, and Caracas. On a more or less regular basis, Spanish *pinnaces* sailed the Caribbean coastal routes to supply the coastal areas following the prevailing winds and currents. As reports were made about the unrelenting Dutch attacks along the coast of *Tierra Firme*, repeated requests from the Governors to the Spanish King followed for more frequent and direct service and protection to re-supply the forts and towns along the coast and to handle and improve trade and exchange for the benefit of local residents. As the situation worsened, coastal communities resorted to

---

50 See Engel Sluiter (1948), p. 176–179.
51 See Engel Sluiter (1948), pp. 180–181. Goods smuggled included pearls from pearl beds of La Margarita, Cubagua, and Araya Bay. The estimated value based on calculations done by Sluiter from reports filed by the Spanish governors and administrators was in the amount of thirty thousand pesos. In 1603, the royal *quinto* at Cumana was down to three thousand pesos and lower still in the following year suggesting smuggling pearls prevailed over regular trade.

smuggling with Dutch merchants and mariners who brought badly needed supplies of cloth and hardware at prices well below what the Spanish were charging. In return, residential coastal communities, including Portuguese resident merchants specifically referred to, offered a variety of trade goods including tobacco. As Sluiter (1948) points out and as will be documented in more detail in the next two chapters, the Dutch demand for tobacco subsequently stimulated tobacco cultivation and led to prohibition of tobacco growing, depopulation, and resettlement of coastal populations in Hispaniola, Cumana and La Margarita as ordered by Spanish officials.[52] The case studies presented in Chapters 3 and 4 illustrate how the economic, military, and political or administrative decisions made by the Dutch and the Spanish conditioned by mercantile and military circumstances in the context of the Eighty Years' War in the early seventeenth century, engaged Portuguese New Christian merchants in *Tierra Firme* and Hispaniola and Sephardic merchants in Amsterdam and contributed to Amsterdam's colonial staple trade and wealth creation. As the Spanish and Dutch became more and more entangled in affairs of state and war, Amsterdam merchants including Sephardic merchants and coastal populations in *Tierra Firme* including Portuguese and crypto-Jewish or Jewish merchants saw opportunities to trade or smuggle and became more engaged with each other and with Dutch merchants.

In summary, the Dutch had first become acquainted with *Tierra Firme* through contacts with Portuguese mariners in the 1580s and by the mid-1590s Amsterdam merchants had become engaged in the contraband trade by means of contacts with Portuguese merchants as noted by Sluiter (1948) here and discussed earlier. War with Spain (from 1568 onwards) and Portugal (starting in 1580 with the Portugal-Spain unification) had interrupted the flow of staple goods to the Amsterdam market as frequent attacks at sea meant loss of cargo. Toward the end of the sixteenth century a growing number of vessels from Holland and Zeeland made their way westward to trade or barter directly with Amerindians along the Orinoco and Amazon river estuaries. In Punta de Araya, just west of the mouth of the Orinoco River, Dutch merchants had begun to explore opportunities to mine salt after the salt pans in Portugal became off-limits. Gradually, Dutch merchants established themselves in the area by assigning factors, including Portuguese merchants, with supply goods to barter in exchange for access to fresh water and food, and for tobacco and other commodities, including dye woods, for the return voyage. Thus, the early Dutch voyages to *Tierra Firme* were in part to serve the salt trade

---

52 See Engel Sluiter (1948), pp. 181–183.

which previously had been conducted from the Iberian Peninsula (Setubal) and the Cape Verde Islands.[53] As a consequence of embargoes imposed by Spain on Dutch trade with the Iberian Peninsula during the Eighty Years' War especially after 1594, shipping was re-routed and frequently illegal passages were made to the Spanish West Indies in search of salt. The presence of the Dutch mariners also affected the pearl fisheries at Cumana, La Margarita Island, and Cubagua as they readily exchanged cloth and hardware for pearls for the return voyage.[54]

As the Dutch delivered needed supplies and provided demand for colonial staple goods traded along the coast, including tobacco, cultivation of the crop carried out by local Amerindians and Creole populations expanded and interest in investment in tobacco plantations by Spanish settlers increased. In not too long, the contraband trade began to flourish and became of great concern to the Spanish officials in charge.[55] In 1603, the town of Nueva Ecija de los Cumangotos, an Amerindian village near Cumana, harvested 30 thousand pounds of tobacco and Suarez de Amaya, nearby, became the most notorious port from where tobacco was smuggled. To eradicate the contraband trade, the *Consejo de Indias* recommended depopulation of the area.[56] Thus, in effect, the great volume of Dutch salt shipping at Punta de Araya, made *Tierra Firme* the center of Dutch penetration in the Caribbean region but merchants also operated in the Spanish Antilles, Cuba and Hispaniola in particular, where Dutch mariners along with English and French privateers or buccaneers smuggled tobacco along with hides which was the main staple good exchanged on the islands. Here too depopulation was ordered and pursuits of Dutch merchants by the Spanish navy was conducted.[57]

By the second decade of the seventeenth century Dutch ships sailed to the West Indies on a regular basis to resupply stores and collect the staple goods and, it appears, that among the first agents from Amsterdam were Portuguese merchants and former merchants from the Southern Netherlands

---

53 In the Portugal salt trade via Setubal, Portuguese merchants from Amsterdam were engaged in the period before 1580 and it would seem reasonable to suggest that the same merchants became engaged in the salt trade conducted via Porto de Araya. See Catia Antunes, "The Commercial Relationships between Amsterdam and the Portuguese Salt-Exporting Ports Aveiro and Setubal, 1580–1715," in *Journal of Early Modern History*, vol. 12, no. 1, 2008, pp. 25–53.
54 Goslinga, *The Dutch in the Caribbean* (1971), p. 54.
55 See also, Wim Klooster, *Illicit Riches: Dutch Trade in the Caribbean, 1648–1795* (KITLV Press, Leiden, 1998), pp. 31–33.
56 See Engel Sluiter (1948), pp. 182–183.
57 Engel Sluiter, (1948) pp. 183–184, pp. 187–189, pp. 193–194.

who journeyed up the various tributaries of the Amazon and Orinoco rivers in pursuit of goods of value and booty.[58] Accounts of explorers illustrate that there were close associations between Dutch and the English merchants and mariners in which Portuguese merchants often engaged as go-between.[59] Engel Sluiter's analysis and interpretation of the documents collected during a lifetime confirms that in this network of contacts, war and rivalry played an important role which strengthened the bonds between allies and enhanced rivalries among the warring parties. War with Spain and divided interests for territorial control in the Caribbean set the stage for private parties to engage in smuggling in which Portuguese and Sephardic merchants were more often than not willing to side with the interest of the enemy, the rebels, and heretics. In their efforts to engage in trade with the Dutch and English merchants they operated through their kin and merchant networks connected along the coast of South America (*Tierra Firme*), Brazil, the Caribbean islands, the Azores and the Canary Islands, and the Iberian Peninsula as well as Antwerp, Amsterdam and London.[60] Thus, in the early seventeenth century, connections between earlier generations of Portuguese merchants and Spanish-America and Portuguese Brazil extended to include Sephardic merchants in Amsterdam and most of the trade continued to be conducted via these merchant networks which remained the case until at least two decades into the seventeenth century.[61]

2.4 Tobacco Monopolies and Tariff Systems

After the turn of the seventeenth century, tobacco consumption was expanding rapidly in Europe and much of the market supply was provided by Dutch and English merchants who together with Portuguese merchants shipped tobacco

---

58 Goslinga, *The Dutch in the Caribbean* (1971), pp. 80–84.
59 Norton and Studnicki-Gizbert, "The Multinational Commodification of Tobacco," (2007), pp. 251–273. Anglo-Dutch trade was enhanced by the Treaty of Nonesuch, in effect between 1585 and 1616, in which the English helped finance the Dutch in their war effort against the Spanish. As compensation, the English obtained extraterritorial rights to trade and settle in the province of Zeeland at which time the Merchant Adventurers gained a significant foothold in the Dutch Republic.
60 The Dutch and the English had begun to engage in regular trade across the Atlantic in the last decade of the sixteenth century when Dutch cloth textiles were traded for tobacco. In the trade triangle that developed between Northern Europe, West Africa, and the West Indies, English and Dutch merchants transported tobacco and other American products across the Atlantic in order to enhance the prospects of acquiring slaves in West Africa and to fulfill the consumer demands for tobacco in the Northern European market. See Norton and Studnicki-Gizbert, "The Multinational Commodification of Tobacco" (2007), pp. 251–273; p. 259, ftn. 16.
61 Swetschinski, "Conflict and Opportunity," 1982, p. 238.

directly from the Caribbean islands or *Tierra Firme* to various East Atlantic ports for delivery to both the Northern European and the Iberian-Mediterranean markets. As the ports of the Iberian Peninsula had reopened for legal trade with the Dutch merchants during the Twelve Years' Truce in the Eighty Years' War (1609–1621) and incentives to trade directly in Spanish America and the Caribbean were diminished, some of the merchants engaged in the salt and tobacco trade in *Tierra Firme* and the Spanish Caribbean islands returned to their traditional Baltic-Iberia trade in which Portuguese merchants from ports up and down the Eastern Atlantic in France, Spain, and Portugal and Sephardic merchants from Amsterdam participated. During the truce, some Amsterdam merchants sent agents to Spain and Portugal. These agents settled in Lisbon and Seville connecting the Atlantic trade circuits with the Northern European trade routes and the tobacco trade was a natural extension of these circuits.[62] Thus, trade with the Iberian Peninsula was conducted by both legal and illegal means during the years of truce but was almost always tied to the established interlocking trade networks which had formed in the course of the late sixteenth and early seventeenth century and had expanded with the accession of Philip IV to the throne in 1621 when Olivares was installed as his advisor.[63]

---

62 Catia Antunes and Amerila Polonia (eds.), *Beyond Empires: Global, self-organizing, cross-imperial networks, 1500–1800* (Brill, Leiden, 2016). Merchants in long-distance trade operated both inside and outside imperial boundaries which often transcended official or institutional controls and which proved to be remarkably resilient over time. See also, Catia Antunes, "International Positioning of Portuguese Seaports, 1580–1640: The Economic Link to Northwest Europe," in Antunes and Polonia (eds.), *Seaports in the First Global Age: Portuguese Agents, Networks and Interactions (1500–1800)* (UPorto Edicoes, Porto, 2016), pp. 95–114. Note also that many Portuguese New Christian merchants had connections with Sephardic merchants in Amsterdam engaged in the sugar trade, see Jessica Roitman, *The Same but Different: Inter-Cultural Trade and the Sephardic, 1595–1640* (Brill, Leiden, 2011).
63 Swetschinski, "Conflict and Opportunity," 1982, pp. 225. See also, Jonathan I. Israel, "Spain and the Dutch Sephardic, 1609–1660," *Studia Rosenthaliana*, 12, 1978, pp. 41–42. Swetschinski, "Conflict and Opportunity," 1982, pp. 226–228 suggests that, as a consequence, the Portuguese Jewish merchants of Amsterdam did not welcome the Dutch invasion of Bahia in 1624 and that the Dutch occupation of Pernambuco (1630–1654) weakened the position of the *New Christian* merchants in Portugal. These circumstances would help explain why Portuguese *New Christians* shifted their business to Spain. The Portuguese rebellion in 1640 worsened the position of the *New Christian* merchants in Portugal even further and when Conde Duque de Olivares died and the Portuguese merchants lost their protector, large scale relocation/migration occurred among *New Christians* from Seville, Madrid, and Antwerp to Amsterdam and within a decade (1646–1655), Amsterdam became the center of the Portuguese New Christian and Jewish world. See Israel, "Spain and the Dutch Sephardic," 1978, pp. 48–49, Swetschinski, "Conflict and Opportunity," 1982, p. 229.

In the forward position of illegal trade was the port of Bayonne in southwestern France in which trade with the English and the Dutch via their intermediaries, the Portuguese merchants, was conducted and from where some Sephardic merchants engaged in the tobacco trade operated.[64] As much of this trade was contraband, the state had little control over import or export or consumption of tobacco. Nonetheless, states in Europe at various times in the seventeenth century tried to impose fiscal regulations on tobacco in order to control the trade and gather revenue. The imposition of import duties and consumption controls in various European states increased the price of tobacco and substantial profits could be made by smuggling cheaper tobacco across the French border into Spain via the Pyrenees Mountains and the Portuguese merchant networks.[65] As a consequence of differential tariffs on tobacco imposed, Sephardic merchants drew an increasingly larger share of the tobacco supply from elsewhere including Tidewater Virginia and Maryland where Dutch merchants traded alongside English merchants and transported substantial amounts of tobacco directly to European markets.[66] Over time and in order to expand tobacco supplies, Amsterdam merchants also began to invest in home grown production in the provinces of Utrecht, Gelderland, and Overijssel for distribution to other parts of Northern Europe. While the legal portion of the Atlantic trade from Spanish America was freighted on ships of the Spanish *Carrera de Indias* with as destination Seville, the contraband or illegal trade carried out by Dutch and Sephardic merchants was mostly routed to non-Iberian ports like Bayonne, Nantes, Bordeaux, Antwerp, Amsterdam, London or Hamburg. Estimates are that the contraband trade was substantial at perhaps half of the total but variable due to the changing geopolitical landscape and, by its nature, difficult to quantify. At the end of the Twelve Years' Truce when embargoes were re-imposed the trading situation changed once more and the next 25 years was a time of great uncertainty for all parties involved during which time the contraband trade continued to thrive.[67]

---

64 Carsten L. Wilke, "Contraband for the Catholic King: Jews of the French Pyrenees in the Tobacco Trade and Spanish State Finance," in Rebecca Kobrin and Adam Teller (eds.), *Purchasing Power: The Economics of Modern Jewish History* (University of Pennsylvania Press, Philadelphia, 2015), pp. 46–70.

65 Stanley Gray and V. J. Wyckoff, "The International Tobacco Trade in the Seventeenth Century," *Southern Economic Journal*, vol. 7, no. 1, July 1940, pp. 1–26.

66 The European markets (including Spain and Portugal) greatly expanded in the first half of the seventeenth century. Tobacco became particularly popular in Northwestern Europe. Norton, *Sacred Gifts*, pp.141–172.

67 Jonathan I. Israel, "A conflict of Empires, Spain and the Netherlands, 1618–1648," *Past and Present*, No. 76, August 1977, pp. 32–74.

During the seventeenth-century expansion of tobacco cultivation and trade, increased tobacco consumption was the driving factor.[68] As the consumption of tobacco increased, more and more European states introduced tariffs or monopolies in order to control consumption and gain revenue income which engaged government officials assigned to collect the fees and enforce the regulations. In some instances tax-farmers were installed to work on consignment for the government and collect the revenue.[69] In most instances, the state prohibited or restricted domestic consumption or colonial cultivation to keep firm oversight. In the case of Spain, which introduced the Royal monopoly in 1636, all tobacco shipments had to be sent to Seville along with other colonial staples where import duties were levied and regulations were imposed.[70] In the course of the seventeenth century several other European states imposed import duties and monopolies on tobacco cultivation and trade and as a result there was a patchwork of rules and regulations and a growing corruption and contraband trade developing as consumption increased. As a consequence, Sephardic merchants in Amsterdam were well positioned to take advantage of the circumstances under which the tobacco trade developed as they had well-established trade networks in place and were gaining market share in the European market.

Administrating and negotiating tobacco tax schemes and monopolies involved various layers of government and intricate merchant networks in which Sephardic merchants and their New Christian or Portuguese trade partners in Spain, Portugal, and southern France were active participants. They had already developed and maintained complex commodity chains and their readiness to exploit new business opportunities was an asset.[71] In addition, their tradition to migrate and relocate and their previous experience in colonial trade made them the premier candidates to be sought after to help administer the tobacco monopoly and be assigned as tax farmers. As Norton (2008) and Studnicki-Gizbert (2007) document, New Christian Portuguese merchants were actively engaged in the Spanish tobacco monopoly and tax-farming schemes, collecting import duties and fees and

---

68 Norton, *Sacred gifts* (2008), pp. 148–161.
69 Arthus W. Madsen, *The State as Manufacturer and Trader: An Examination Based on the Commercial, Industrial and Fiscal Results Obtained from Government Tobacco Monopolies* (Fisher Unwin, London, 1916).
70 Stanley Gray and V.J, Wyckoff, "The International Tobacco Trade in the Seventeenth Century," *Southern Economic Journal*, vol. 7, no. 1, July 1940, pp. 1–26.
71 Swetschinski, "Conflict and Opportunity," 1982, pp. 212–240.

financing the Spanish Treasury at the same time.[72] Most of the tax collectors of the Royal Tobacco Monopoly of Castile were Portuguese New Christians who in turn engaged tobacco wholesale merchants who imported tobacco from New Spain, Portuguese Brazil, or *Tierra Firme* and distributed tobacco in various forms to retail shops and consumer outlets through established merchant networks. Some of the Portuguese New Christian tax collectors were later persecuted by the Inquisition as 'Judaizers' but other families managed to negate these circumstances.

As Portuguese New Christians associated in trade with Sephardic merchants they lived a precarious life as illustrated by Wilke (2015) who researched a Sephardic community in Southwestern France involved in cross-border contraband trade with wide ranging ties to the tobacco monopoly lease holders in Spain.[73] A concession or lease assigned to an individual or a group of people (*Arrendadores*) was the standard way to administer tax collection at the state and local level. In the fall of 1636, shortly after the tobacco monopoly was introduced, the Spanish Crown announced a public auction at which the best bid would be granted the lease. State officials negotiated the terms and payments for the lease and in return allowed the individual or group of merchants the exclusive right to process, distribute and sell tobacco in the assigned region for an assigned period of time. The lessee was allowed to subcontract and employ a team (usually family members or close associates) to administer the lease terms but the contracts dictated that all the tobacco, processed, bought, and sold, had to be channeled through the lease holder. The contracts also mandated that the lessees' agents in port cities were responsible for registering all imported tobacco in order to guard against contraband.[74] The winning bid in 1636 went to Antonio de Soria, a Portuguese New Christian merchant who was well established and had been a regional tax farmer previously. In the ensuing years, other merchants and tax farmers (most all New Christian merchant families) bid and out-bid each other to obtain a lease and sub-lease. Among each other the *arrendadores* began to control the tobacco processing, wholesale and retail distribution and became a major source of financing for the Spanish Crown.[75]

---

72 Norton, *Sacred Gifts* (2008), pp. 210–223; pp. 211–212; Studnicki-Gizbert, *A Nation Upon the Ocean Sea* (2007), pp. 152–157. See, also, Wilke, "Contraband for the Catholic King," 2015, p. 48.
73 Wilke, "Contraband for the Catholic King," 2015, pp. 46–70.
74 Norton, *Sacred Gifts* (2008), pp. 209–210.
75 Norton, *Sacred* Gifts (2008), pp. 212–213.

It is hard to imagine that Portuguese New Christian merchants would have been offered the opportunity to organize and carry out tobacco tax farming schemes if they had not also been the merchants who controlled the supply trade. Thus, the most likely reason why Portuguese New Christian merchants came to the forefront of the Spanish tobacco monopoly was because they held control over the Atlantic tobacco trade and the European distribution trade networks. At the same time they were associated with and protected by Count-Duke Olivares who managed affairs for the Habsburg Empire in Brussels, in the Southern Netherlands. Olivares had courted New Christian merchant-bankers to help finance the affairs of state for the Spanish Crown in waging war against the Dutch Republic and the English state and to secure territory in Spanish America.[76] As state conveyors and tax-farmers, New Christian merchants were offered *Indulto* or state pardon by the Crown which allowed New Christians in Portugal suspected of "Judaizing" tolerance under the rules of the Inquisition and gave permission for Portuguese New Christians to reside in Castile and partake in trade with Spain's overseas Atlantic colonies. The privileged position the Portuguese New Christians were offered resulted in a return in favor of a substantial loan payment to help fill the coffers of the Royal Spanish Treasury and pay for war expenses.[77] As the Portuguese merchants held control over the slave trade, they also underwrote the development of tobacco plantations which in turn allowed them to enter the marketing of tobacco in Europe.[78] So, as Portugal resided under Spanish rule at the time (1580–1640) and Portuguese New Christian merchants were in the vanguard of collecting, marketing and distributing tobacco for the Spanish Crown in which Portuguese New Christian and Sephardic merchants with ties to the Amsterdam market became involved, the circle closed.[79] Typically,

---

[76] Jonathan I. Israel, "Olivares and the Spanish Netherlands," in *Empires and Entrepots: The Dutch, the Spanish Monarchy and the Jews, 1585–1713* (The Hambledon Press, London, 1990), pp. 163–188.

[77] James C. Boyajian, *Portuguese Bankers at the Madrid Court, 1626–1650* (Rutgers University press, New Brunswick, NJ, 1983), pp. 17–24; and Studnicki-Gizbert, *A Nation Upon the Ocean Sea*, (2007), pp. 112–129.

[78] Studnicki-Gizbert, *A Nation Upon the Ocean Sea* (2007), pp. 117–118.

[79] See also, Marcy Norton and Daviken Studnicki-Gizbert, "The Multinational Commodification of Tobacco, 1492–1650," in Peter C. Marcall (ed.), *The Atlantic World and Virginia, 1550–1624* (University of North Carolina Press, Chapel Hill, 2007), pp. 251–273. The Duke of Mantua (Italy) was the first to introduce a tobacco monopoly where a private merchant for a fixed payment handled the monopoly of import and sale of tobacco.

the cargo was shipped through a variety of ports and some of it passed through ports along the Atlantic coast of Portugal and Galicia, Spain, but some was transferred in the Canary Islands and Bayonne in Southwestern France or other ports along the Eastern Atlantic Seaboard or was smuggled across the border into Spain.[80] Ironically, it was the contraband trade that had enticed the Spanish Crown to declare tobacco a royal monopoly, and as a consequence of the New Christian and Sephardic merchant networks in existence, it were the Portuguese merchants who were put in charge to carry out the tax schemes. As Portuguese New Christian merchants controlled the slave supply and the tobacco trade network, Portuguese merchants and Amsterdam's Sephardic merchants remained the primary merchant groups distributing tobacco to the Northern European or more specifically, Amsterdam's market. As they continued to operate their trade network and simultaneously began to administer customs duties as assigned by the state contracts, they were in a most favored position to thrive in tax farming and contraband schemes.[81]

Thus, existing trade relationships and networks, including Sephardic and Portuguese New Christian merchants, created and maintained a link between the tobacco supply regions in Spanish America and consumers in Europe despite wars, embargoes, monopolies and tax schemes. These merchants exercised extreme caution in an effort to circumvent the border checks imposed by the Spanish officials while being prepared to pay off customs officials. As soon as illegal cargo was unloaded, the goods were channeled through the Portuguese New Christian and Sephardic merchant trade networks among the *Arrendadores* of the tobacco monopoly. As the tobacco distribution system was organized by interconnected merchant networks, lessee assignments followed the same pattern. As a result, the Spanish state tobacco administration depended on a far-flung long-distance trade network in which various warring parties participated and contraband became an essential part of the operations while simultaneously engaging the same merchants in state tax schemes. And thus, in the 1620s and the decades thereafter when embargoes had been re-imposed and war

---

80 See Carsten L. Wilke, "Contraband for the Catholic King: Jews of the French Pyrenees in the Tobacco Trade and Spanish State Finance," in Rebecca Kobrin and Adam Teller (eds.), *Purchasing Power: The Economics of Modern Jewish History* (University of Pennsylvania Press, Philadelphia, 2011), pp. 46–70.
81 Israel, *Empire and Entrepots* (1990), p. 374.

with the Dutch Republic had resumed, Portuguese New Christian and Sephardic merchants of Bayonne involved in the trade of tobacco from South America and the Caribbean islands were able to ship substantial amounts of the tobacco to the Dutch Republic some of which was recorded by Notary Public offices in Amsterdam.[82] To document and analyze the relationships between Portuguese New Christian and Amsterdam's Sephardic merchants in the tobacco trade in the late sixteenth and early seventeenth centuries, I will next turn to analyzing selected documents from the Engel Sluiter Historical Document Collection which forms the main source of information for research on the contraband or illegal tobacco trade in this study.

---

82 Ella M. Koen and Wilhelmina C. Pieterse, "Notarial Records Relating to the Portuguese Jews in Amsterdam up to 1639," *Studia Rosenthaliana*, 33, no. 1, 1999, pp. 81–82, no. 3457; 34, no. 1, 2000, pp. 87–88, no. 3544; 35, nos 1–2, 2001, 67, no. 3546, 78, no. 3589, 79, no. 3593, 88, no. 3631. See also Norton, *Sacred Gifts* (2008), p. 212.

Chapter 3

PORTUGUESE MERCHANTS AND THE TOBACCO TRADE WITH *TIERRA FIRME*

3.1 Contraband and Trade Rivalry in the Eighty Years' War

As described in the first two chapters, Dutch–Spanish and Dutch–Portuguese trade relations in the early seventeenth century were determined to a large extent by the ebb and flow of battles, embargoes, and trade protection measures in effect during the Eighty Years' War when the Dutch were at war with Habsburg Spain from 1568 to 1648 the time at the end of which the Dutch established hegemony in the Atlantic economy. Only during the Twelve Years' Truce between the warring parties from 1609 to 1621 did some order of normalcy return to Iberian-Dutch commercial exchange but trade with *Tierra Firme* and the Spanish Caribbean islands remained off limits to Dutch merchants as Spanish trade and navigation rules and prohibitions remained in effect. For much of the time, trade rivalry between Habsburg Spain and the Dutch Republic continued unabated and sea battles occurred at regular intervals. At entry points to major rivers where the Spanish held sway over self-declared territorial rule, embargoes and blockades were imposed by both parties and thus trade and navigation was regularly obstructed. Along the coasts of *Tierra Firme* and the Caribbean islands Dutch merchants tried to undermine Spanish control and intrude upon Spanish territory with some resolve but often only temporarily. Brazil was a Portuguese possession but as Portugal was united with Spain from 1580 until 1640, Spanish territorial control and trade restrictions affected Brazil as well even though Portugal continued to trade on a semi-autonomous basis. In any event, all Dutch trade as well as trade conducted by Sephardic merchants resident in the Dutch Republic was illegal trade as far as the Spanish were concerned and therefore, typically, not recorded contractually. So, in effect, we have only incidental evidence of the Dutch–Spanish and Dutch–Portuguese tobacco trade from official freight records in the Notary Public records in the City Archive of Amsterdam for the early seventeenth century as discussed in the previous chapters.

Dutch mariners were trespassers and illegal merchants in the Iberian colonial world and in the traditional carrying trade with the Iberian Peninsula, including Portuguese ports, which were officially blocked from 1580 until the start of the Twelve Years' Truce (1609–1621). In the Eighty Years' War, Dutch vessels were often attacked at sea and at entry points to trading posts. Absolute restrictions were in effect from 1595 until 1609 during which time Dutch mariners and merchants sailed out to the Caribbean region to secure salt and sugar, commodities in which they had established trade and market interest prior to the embargoes imposed and were now unable to obtain at Portuguese ports. Meanwhile, and as they sailed more frequently to Brazil and the coasts of *Tierra Firme*, they engaged in bartering with coastal populations for tobacco, pearls, and other trade goods, and raided Spanish coastal settlements. Some carrying trade via the traditional Portuguese merchant networks with Portuguese ports was restored in 1609 but when war with Habsburg Spain resumed in 1621, Dutch and Sephardic merchants once more began to venture out across the Atlantic and this time tried to establish colonies under auspices of the Dutch West India Company (WIC) which was founded for the purpose of harassing the Spanish at sea, establishing control over Spanish and Portuguese colonial supply areas, and securing Dutch commerce.[1]

Instead of conducting trade with Spain and Portugal, as they had traditionally done when peaceful conditions prevailed, in the period after 1621 when war resumed, serious efforts were made by the Dutch to establish a foothold in Portuguese Brazil and in the Spanish Caribbean region. Dutch engagement with the Spanish included the capture of the Spanish Silver Fleet in the Battle of the Bay of Matanzas off the coast of Cuba in 1628 and the capture and attempt at settlement of Tobago off the coast of Trinidad in the same year. The Dutch, under guidance of the WIC, also tried to capture territory and control sugar shipments from Salvador (Bahia) in Portuguese Brazil in 1624 but this effort failed as the Portuguese took back control a year later.[2] In 1630, a second attempt by the WIC at securing the Brazil sugar supply was successful and the province of Pernambuco became a Dutch colony. In Punta de Araya where salt winning and shipments led to contact with coastal communities in *Tierra Firme* or at La Margarita Island and Cumana nearby where the pearl fisheries drew Dutch mariners ashore, tobacco gradually entered into the trading circuits as the analysis presented in this chapter will show.

---

[1] Wim Klooster, *The Dutch Moment: War, Trade, and Settlement in the Seventeenth-Century Atlantic World* (Cornell University Press, Ithaca, 2016).

[2] Christopher Ebert, *Between Empires: Brazilian Sugar in the Early Atlantic Economy, 1550–1630* (Series: The Atlantic World, Volume 16, 2008).

As discussed in the previous two chapters and as some documentary evidence and explorer chronicles illustrate, Amsterdam's tobacco trade involved besides Dutch merchants also Sephardic merchants and other merchants of the Portuguese Nation.[3] The small Portuguese Jewish merchant community that had emerged in Amsterdam in the late sixteenth century had direct links to the sugar trade originating in the Portuguese Atlantic Islands of Madeira, São Tomé, the Cape Verde Islands and Brazil but offered additional opportunities in the trade of other colonial staple products. At that time, during the last decade of the sixteenth century, Portuguese and Antwerp merchants were transferring their business to Amsterdam as alternating Dutch and Spanish embargoes and blockades of the Scheldt River obstructed commerce. Fairly quickly, a notable amount of colonial staple goods including sugar and tobacco were traded, processed, and distributed via the Amsterdam market. As in the case of the sugar trade, the tobacco trade involved contacts with Portuguese merchants engaged in trade or exchange in Spanish America and Portuguese Brazil. Some of this trade was directly with the Iberian Peninsula, but in other instances and in particular when contraband or illegal commerce was conducted, exchange took place via Atlantic ports in France, England, or the Dutch Republic, notably Amsterdam, or Hamburg in Northern Germany. Wim Klooster (1998), among others, has documented these illicit trade connections occurring later in the seventeenth and in the eighteenth century.[4] In this chapter, I will draw attention to the circumstances that explain the start and early development

---

3 Israel recognizes that war with Habsburg Spain had a great influence on the structure and character of Sephardic merchants' strategies in dealing with trade opportunities. See Jonathan I. Israel, "A Conflict of Empire: Spain and the Netherlands 1618–1648," *Past and Present*, no. 76, August 1977, pp. 34–74; and, Jonathan I. Israel, "The Changing Role of the Dutch Sephardim in International Trade,1595–1715," in J. Michman (ed.), *Dutch Jewish History* I (Jerusalem, 1984), pp. 31–51. Israel divides the period from 1595 to 1648 into roughly three periods: 1595–1608, the phase of economic warfare in the Eighty Years' War; 1609–1621, the years of Truce with Spain; and 1621–1648, with the resumption of war with Spain, and colonial strive with Portugal over control of Brazil. See also, Jonathan I. Israel, "Spain, the Spanish Embargoes, and the Struggle for the Mastery of World Trade, 1585–1660, in Israel, *Empires and Entrepots* (1990), Chapter 8, pp. 189–212; pp. 197–201; and Jonathan I. Israel, *Diasporas within a Diaspora: Jews, Crypto Jews, and the World Maritime Empire, 1540–1740* (Brill, Leiden, 2002).

4 Wim Klooster, *Illicit Riches: Dutch Trade in the Caribbean, 1648–1795* (KITLV Press, Leiden, 1998); See also, Linda M. Rupert, *Creolization and Contraband: Curacao in the Early Modern Atlantic World* (The University of Georgia Press, Athens and London, 2012), and Jesse Cromwell, *The Smugglers' World: Illicit Trade and Atlantic Communities in Eighteenth-Century Venezuela* (University of North Carolina Press, Chapel Hill, 2018).

of illicit Dutch trade in the late sixteenth and early seventeenth centuries by focusing on the Engel Sluiter Historical Document Collection which illustrates the commercial rivalry between Habsburg Spain and the Dutch Republic with respect to the trade in tobacco and other goods along the coast of *Tierra Firme*. As discussed in Chapter 2, and referred to as ESHDC in the footnotes, the Engel Sluiter Historical Documents Collection offers a unique insight into the trade rivalry between Habsburg Spain and the Dutch Republic and the officials and merchants involved in the commercial strife and documents how the illegal or contraband trade was conducted.

Most of the documents in the Engel Sluiter collection analyzed for the purpose of this study concern the origins of tobacco smuggling and relate to the question of the threat of foreign merchants involved in illicit trade as perceived by the Spanish authorities. The foreign merchants included Portuguese merchants who were often suspect in the eyes of the Spanish officials reporting on trade matters. Although Portugal was united with Spain at that time, in the reports sent by the *Audiencias* about conditions along the coast of *Tierra Firme* repeated reference is made to the contacts that existed between Portuguese resident merchants and English, French and Dutch explorers and mariners. The documents include chronicles about Dutch, English, French, Spanish, and Portuguese voyages to the New World as well as documents illustrating smuggling efforts and contraband trade among English, French, and Dutch merchants and mariners and members of the Portuguese Nation which included Portuguese New Christian and Sephardic merchants.[5] Economic and fiscal documentation predominates the collection covering both the rise to commercial prominence of the Dutch Republic and the intricacies of Spanish and Portuguese trade and navigation in the Americas as well as Spanish Crown revenues and expenditures including records from the *Contaduria* section of the Archives of the Indies in Seville and import and export duties on goods from America. In addition, the collection contains transcribed accounts of payments to Spain by foreign resident merchants and various reports from the *Audiencias* about the threat of foreign merchants upon Spanish territories and interests in *Tierra Firme*.

---

5 The collection is kept at UC Berkeley, Bancroft Library. For an overview of the collection see Chapter 2. For a description of the documents included in the collection see Julie van den Hout, *Listing to the Engel Sluiter Historical Documents Collection* (Collection number BANC MSS 98/79 z) completed 2016. In the footnotes specific items from the collection are referred to in the abbreviated form ESHDC (Engel Sluiter Historical Document Collection), followed by a title, date and year, and carton and folder number. The footnotes in this chapter contain several quotes from Sluiter's notes included in the specific items referenced.

The documents in the collection relate mainly to the Dutch Republic, Spain, and Portugal. Copies of unpublished manuscripts are included in the collection and the majority are in Spanish, transcribed and provided with notes in English by Engel Sluiter. Many of the documents in the collection derive from Seville's *Archivo General de Indias* and contain information about contraband in tobacco and other goods and recommendations provided by Spanish officials and administrators on ways to prevent illegal exchange. The documents allow for an analysis of the different parties involved in the tobacco contraband trade and the measures taken by Spanish officials to counter the situation. Despite concerted efforts, Spanish control measures were not terribly effective and failed to stop the tobacco contraband trade conducted by the various members of the Portuguese Nation and Dutch merchants in which, as we will see or as implied, Sephardic merchants were involved (Figure 3.1).

One of the first sets of documents in Sluiter's collection on Portuguese merchants and merchants of the Nation engaged in trade with *Tierra Firme* and Hispaniola derives from reports presented in 1601 by witnesses at an incident involving a slaving vessel from Guinea, West Africa. The vessel had delivered slaves to Cartagena and thereafter had sailed to Santo Domingo, Hispaniola, after which it was captured by the English on the return voyage.[6] One witness, a native of Sicily who had been aboard the vessel, stated in front of the Spanish court in Cartagena that the vessel had sailed from Florence via Seville to Guinea in West Africa and had then set course to Cartagena. The owner of the vessel was Italian and had a license from the magistrates of Seville and had carried slaves as cargo for, among others, Portuguese merchants in Cartagena. Another witness revealed that officers of the *Casa de Contratacion* in Lisbon had a factor in Seville who had granted licenses and had authorized sailing vessels to sail to Guinea in service of the Spanish King. In still another witness report reference is made to Leghorn (Livorno) in Italy where the Florentine owner kept his vessel.[7] The purser of the vessel reports that various items were loaded on the vessel including beads, ale, wine, and sundry which were exchanged in Guinea for 265 slaves after which the vessel sailed to Cartagena to deliver the slaves from where the vessel sailed to Santo Domingo, Hispaniola, in ballast. At Santo Domingo, various merchants shipped hides along with tobacco, ginger,

---

6 ESHDC, September 12, 1601, Carton 1, Folder 1-5.

7 Livorno was a well-known transit shipment point in the trade network between the Mediterranean and Portugal in which Sephardic merchants participated. See Francesca Trivellato, *The Familiarity of Strangers: The Sephardic Diaspora, Livorno, and Cross-Cultural Trade in the Early Modern Period* (Yale University Press, New Haven, London, 2009).

Indian pepper, sugar, and other merchandise. On the return voyage, the vessel was captured by the English for reasons not made clear. The witness reports illustrate that there were many parties engaged in trade with the Spanish possessions and that Portuguese merchants were involved in farming licenses and authorizing shipments as well as trading slaves to the Spanish territories permitting contraband to be shipped on the return voyage.

From 1600 onward reports sent to Spain by officials and administrators about intrusions by French, English and in particular Dutch privateers were regular occurrences. In the reports, recommendations were made to meet the foreign threat by improving the frequency at which the Spanish fleet would sail and supply the forts and towns along the coast of *Tierra Firme* with needed provisions and improve the conditions whereby coastal communities would be able to exchange products and earn income to sustain themselves. One of the foremost Spanish officials engaged in dealing with the economic conditions and the threats of foreign merchant intruders in Spanish America was Luis de Fajardo, General of the Spanish Armada at the time. He recommended meeting the foreign threat by sailing the Armada more frequently and by better coordinating the naval force to counter the threat imposed by Dutch, English, and French smugglers. His ideas met with broad support and in the reports sent by Francisco Coloma, Commander of the *Armada de Barlovento*, we learn that the fleet scheduled to sail to *Tierra Firme* would leave in September, earlier than was normally the case, so that residents would receive provisions sooner and that merchants would have enough time to dispose of their goods and that thereby colonial residents would have no need to trade with foreigners.[8] The document suggests that Cartagena was a smugglers hideout alongside a slave market and that the local population was engaged in contraband trade.

---

8 Francisco Coloma states: "[...] it is desirable that the Armada and warships to the Indies sail together until the beginning of November and keep company until about Trinidad island. Then one squadron sweep along the *Tierra Firme* coast to clear it of smuggler-corsairs reaching Santa Marta at the end of March or mid-April and staying there until the fleet picks up the silver at Porte Bello and Cartagena and then joining the silver galleons outside Cartagena harbor so as to sail together to Havana." In an aside he states, "[...] the stay over at Santa Marta has advantages of providing meat supply for the squadron and avoids the possibility that goods for trade go secretly on the squadron, and, [...] Cartagena is not to be entered!" Quote from Sluiter's Research Notes attached to the translations of the documents referred to. See ESHDC, 1600, Museo Naval, Navarette Collection, vol. 23, Carton 1, Folder 3.

THE TOBACCO TRADE WITH *TIERRA FIRMA* 69

Figure 3.1 Historical map of Terra Firma, Guiana, and the Antilles Islands ca. 1732.

Source: Wikimedia Commons in the Public Domain: Instituto Geografico de Venezuela Simon Bolivar.

Trinidad Island appears to be the take-off point for the incoming fleet where vessels sailing in convoy to service *Tierra Firma* and the Spanish Caribbean islands dispersed in different directions while Hispaniola served as staging point for the return voyage. In March 1601, a report is sent to the King by the President and Judges of the *Casa de Contratacion* of Seville with details about the *Armada de Barlovento*, including recommendations about the routes to be sailed and the ports where she would be stationed to be most useful. The report also gave details about how the fleet was to be provisioned, and how the soldiers and sailors were to be paid.[9] The report was accompanied by opinions of the generals who were consulted in the matter. Various opinions (*pareceres*) were expressed but all agreed that a port at windward (La Margarita Island, Cumana, or Puerto Rico) was essential for the fleet to be stationed because it would allow news about the enemy passing by to be passed on to leeward locations and

---

9 See ESHDC, March 13, 1601, Notes, Navarrete Collection, v. 23, f. 97r-127v, Box 1, folder 4.1. The *Casa de Contratación or Casa de la Contratación de las Indias* was established by the Crown of Castile in 1503 in the port of Seville as a crown agency for the Spanish Empire. It functioned until 1790, when it was abolished in a government reorganization. The *Armada de Barlovento* was also known as the Windward Fleet.

thus be more effective. Supplies would have to come from Spain including rigging, sailcloth, cordage and masts as well as armaments. New Spain would provision food and other necessities. Some of the generals' suggestions are quite specific with reference to where the threat of foreign intrusions were most immediate and where the fleet should be refitted, provisioned, and overwinter. One report specifically mentioned Puerto Rico along which coast most corsairs lie in wait for the ships which arrived unescorted from Spain and the Canary Islands en route to Santo Domingo, Hispaniola. Other locations under threat were La Margarita Island, Caracas, Cumana, and Maracaibo.

3.2 Salt Winning, Pearl Fishing, and Tobacco Smuggling at *Tierra Firme*

Sluiter (1948) suggests that the kind of trade the Dutch merchants and mariners were engaged in, in the early seventeenth century, invited smuggling and raiding for food supplies and water as well as tobacco for the crew working in the salt pans.[10] As the salt trade at Punta de Araya was illegal, the intrusion by Dutch mariners on *Tierra Firme* aroused acute concern of the Spanish governors and there are repeated reports sent by the administrative officials raising the issue of tobacco and pearl smuggling alongside the salt trade as a serious attack on Spanish territorial security and commercial interests. The pearl beds of La Margarita Island, Cubagua Island, and Araya Bay were worked in rotation every three years and during the season of 1600–1601 when pearl diving occurred off Cubagua Island, 16 kilometer north of Araya, a large share of the pearls were carried away by the Dutch.[11] It was at the small settlement of Nueva Ecija de los Cumangotos not far from Cumana where Amerindians resided, that most of the tobacco smuggling occurred. In 1603 residents there harvested thirty thousand pounds of tobacco most of which disappeared (i.e., were smuggled). In 1605, the town was referred to as a market fair where tobacco was exchanged for contraband goods with foreign mariners.[12] In 1606, the Council of the Indies admitted that tobacco growing at Nueva Ecija had increased substantially as the smuggler demand had expanded. This was the time when the salt hauling at Punta de Araya was at its height and when many mariners ventured out to

---

10 Engel Sluiter, "Dutch-Spanish Rivalry in the Caribbean Area, 1594–1609," *The Hispanic American Historical Review*, vol. 28, no. 2, May 1948, pp. 165–196.
11 Engel Sluiter, 1948 , p. 181, with reference to Suarez de Amaya, governor of Cumana, who wrote to the King in 1603 that the royal *quinto* was down to three thousand pesos and the following year to sixteen hundred ducats; not sufficient to cover the governor's annual salary.
12 Andres de Rojas, to the King, La Margarita, December 16, 1605, Audiencia de Santo Domingo, referred to by Sluiter (1948), pp. 182–183.

trade or barter for provisions and tobacco. We assume that part of the cargo was carried back to the Dutch Republic where a growing consumer market for tobacco was developing in the early seventeenth century.[13]

The untenable situation developing at the salt pans of Araya continued to be the main concern expressed by the governors and administrators and was brought to the attention of the King and Council of the Indies at Seville repeatedly. A reconnaissance of Punta de Araya made in 1604 by an Italian engineer with the task to make recommendations to the King and Council if it would be possible to fill in the salt pans to prohibit further salt hauling by the Dutch turned up negative results but the suggestion to instead inundate the area received a more favorable response and received the backing of the *Junta*. However, the lack of funds and time considerations prohibited the plan to go forward. In 1606, Dutch salt merchants were still very active and only a direct attack by the Spanish fleet under the command of Luis de Fajardo broke the Dutch ongoing attempt at gaining access to the salt pans, needing provisions, and obtaining tobacco supplies in their effort to harass the Spanish officials and to trade with coastal communities. On August 14, 1607, an English merchant at Lisbon reported to London

---

13 George A. Brongers, *Nicotiana Tabacum: The history of tobacco and tobacco smoking in the Netherlands* (H. J. W. Becht Uitgeversmaatschappij, Amsterdam, 1965), pp. 19–20. See also, Wim Klooster, "The Tobacco Nation: English Tobacco Dealers and Pipe-Makers in Rotterdam, 1620–1650," in Laura Cruz and Joel Mokyr (eds.), *The Birth of Modern Europe* (Brill, Leiden, Boston, 2010), pp. 17–35; pp. 21–22. Klooster notes that English and French students at Leiden University were found smoking tobacco in 1590 and that perhaps contact with Spanish troops during the Eighty Years' War may have introduced Dutch residents to tobacco consumption. Reported tobacco import into Seville had increased dramatically during the first decade of the seventeenth century (see Marcy Norton, *Sacred Gifts, Profane Pleasures: A History of Tobacco and Chocolate in the Atlantic World* (Cornell University Press, Ithaca and London, 2008) Figure 7.1, p. 143. Klooster (2010) acknowledges that two Jewish tobacco brokers were in business in Amsterdam by 1620 and that they were engaged in tobacco processing as well (see Chapter 1). We also know that Portuguese merchants were the crucial link in bringing tobacco to market in Europe in which Norton recognizes that the merchant networks in existence between Portuguese New Christians and Sephardic communities along the Atlantic seaboard were the mechanism by which tobacco was traded and transferred. Norton (2008, p. 154–155) also records a case in which Dutch merchant bankers investing in a voyage to the Caribbean hired a Portuguese "pilot" to serve as master on one of their vessels and employed other Portuguese mariners to serve as crew and interpreters. See also, Marcy Norton and Daviken Studnicki-Gizbert, "Imperial Rivalries and Commercial Collaboration: Portuguese and English Merchants and the Formation of an Atlantic tobacco Trade, 1492–1609," in Peter C. Mancall (ed.), *The Atlantic World and Virginia, 1550–1624* (University of North Carolina Press, Chapel Hill, 2007), pp. 253–273. Please note that Norton and Studnicki-Gizbert focus primarily (or exclusively) on English merchants.

that a huge Spanish Armada had been outfitted at SanLucar in southern Andalusia equipped with eighty vessels and sixteen thousand men.[14]

Truce negotiations between the Dutch Republic and Spain began in 1607 which resulted in more circumspect activity of Dutch merchants and smugglers along the coast of *Tierra Firme* including the salt shipments from Punta de Araya. During 1606 and 1607 a hectic correspondence across the Atlantic between the *Junta de Guerra de Indias* and the King and Council had taken place and recommendations and options were weighed concerning flooding and defending Araya and how to pay for it. Similar to concerns about tobacco cultivation and smuggling in *Tierra Firme* with the Cumanagotos Indians and along the Guyana Coast with the Caribs, salt mining and smuggling at Araya was of great strategic concern during the truce negotiations and so was pearl fishing and smuggling at La Margarita Island. In all instances, local populations were involved and implicated in the transactions.[15]

The Truce in effect from 1609 until 1621 resulted in a revival of Dutch salt hauling from France, the Cape Verde Islands, and Setubal in Portugal as had been the case before 1595 but the reasons for smuggling and contraband trade on the part of resident colonial populations, namely the scarcities of European provisions and the lack of markets for tobacco, was not eliminated by the Truce conditions.[16] In fact great uncertainty and economic decline set

---

14 ESHDC, August 14, 1607, in Brazil Collection, PRO, SP 89/3; Hugh Lee at Lisbon to Earl of Salisbury, London. The reporter states: "[…]they go for the West Indies by reason of daily reports that come from thence of the great commerce lately increased there by the English, French, and Dutch, that it is feared that except it be speedily remedied, it will hazard the Indies. The news is lately come from there that the Indians are all removed from the sea side far up into the country, from trading with any stranger, and proclaimed upon pain of death that no tobacco by hereafter planted there for that there was a great trade for the same with the Indians. If this armada goes for those parts, it is with a resolution to put to death all the strangers of what nation so ever that they shall there take in any kind of trade whatsoever[…]".

15 See Notes ESHDC, September 10 and September 30, 1606, and January 4 and February 18, 1607.

16 Engel Sluiter (1948), pp. 189–193. For a resumption of the salt trade from Setubal and Aveiro, Portugal, see Catia Antunes, "The Commercial Relationship between Amsterdam and the Portuguese Salt-Exporting Ports: Aveiro and Setubal, 1580–1715," in *The Articulation of Portuguese Salt with Worldwide Routes: Past and New Consumption Trends* (University of Porto, Porto, 2008) pp. 161–181. See also, Jonathan I. Israel, "Spain and the Dutch Sephardic, 1609–1660)" *Studia Rosenthaliana*, vol. 12, no. 1/2 (July 1978), pp. 1–61; pp. 5, 19, who refers to Setubal as the main salt shipment port and Sephardic merchants as the predominant merchant group engaged in the salt trade during the Twelve Years' Truce from 1609–1621. See also Jonathan I. Israel, *Dutch Primacy in World Trade, 1585–1740* (Oxford: Clarendon, 1989), 38–79, and Jonathan I. Israel, *Empires and Entrepots: the Dutch, the Spanish Monarchy and the Jews, 1585–1713* (London: Hambledon Press, 1990), 135–141.

in after 1607 along the coast of *Tierra Firme* when Spanish officials prohibited tobacco cultivation and depopulated areas where tobacco growing had occurred. Smuggling was seriously reduced but at the expense of economic well-being and with severe negative outcomes for coastal populations affected. To drive the enemies and "heretic" Protestant Dutch and English mariners out, the ecclesiastical powers pressed to install the Inquisition at Santo Domingo, and in November 1607, the Council of the Indies recommended that a branch of the Holy Office be set up in Hispaniola. Ultimately, Cartagena became the seat of power of the Holy Office. From the records it is not clear if depopulation of the coastal communities and prohibition of tobacco cultivation and trade caused the economic recession or if truce negotiations between Spain and the Dutch Republic starting in 1607 explain the decline of smuggling activities with Dutch and Portuguese merchants. Whereas salt hauling at Punta de Araya diminished as Dutch and Portuguese merchants resumed their trade with Setubal and Aviero during the Twelve Years' Truce (1609–1621), smuggling of pearls and tobacco from the area seems to have continued unabated at least according to Sluiter's record collections.

The pearl fisheries of La Margarita had been in existence since the 1580s according to reports from factors and officials on the island reporting to the King. Between 1580 and 1584, 300,000 pesos worth of pearls were sent to Spain.[17] In 1584, the *Contaduria* at La Margarita Island reported on cargo from the island delivered to Cartagena in 1582 and 1583 when galleys from Cartagena picked up the royal *quinto* of pearls but no report of arrival had been received.[18] While, by then, pearl fishing had been conducted for some time it was poorly organized, handled by corrupt officials, and under threat from pirates. In 1602, the then Governor of La Margarita Island Pedro Fajardo wrote to the Crown, about the *Alcabala* (royal sales tax) as introduced per royal order in 1601.[19] This document provides very interesting information about the commerce of the island including how the pearl trade is conducted,

---

17 ESHDC, La Margarita, *Contaduria*, Records related to pearl industry, slaves, and taxation, 1577–1644; October 31, 1584, British Museum, Add.MSS 36, 314, Adrian de Padilla, (factor) to the King. (Carton 3, Folder 3-19).
18 The factor, Adriano de Padilla, complains that his salary was to be paid in *Tierra Firme* from the customs duties on pearls but since no payment had been received from the royal *quinto*, he had not received a salary. He recommended that a galley be stationed at La Margarita Island and suggested that the Crown could collect revenue from other sources such as a levy (*demora*) on 3,000 Indians residing in the area, duties on export of pearls, or rent payments in Araya on the mining of salt. The same could be done at Hispaniola and all the revenue together could support two galleys.
19 ESHDC, La Margarita, Contaduria, Records related to pearl industry, slaves, and taxation, 1577–1644; June 22, 1602, Pedro Fajardo, Governor of La Margarita to the Crown. AGI, Santo Domingo 180. (Carton 3, Folder 3-19).

the number of Spanish vessels that arrive each year, and the goods they bring. From the data presented it is clear that substantial profit margins are in effect and that sometimes wholesalers, retailers or shopkeepers on La Margarita Island mark up prices over 40 percent above the price they pay to merchants who deliver the goods from overseas. The goods include cloth, wines and fruits from the Canary Islands, and flour, biscuits, bacon, tallow, sugar, cassava, and maize from Caracas, Cumana, Puerto Rico, and Guyana. Furthermore, slaves are brought in from Guinea which are paid for in value of pearls. In a side note Fajardo recommends that pearl fishers should remain exempted from the *alcabala* for five years and be allowed to buy slaves.

Fajardo also reports on Portuguese merchants active on the island in smuggling activities and he recommends the Portuguese to be expelled along with foreigners who had settled on La Margarita Island in the previous years. In fact, Fajardo thinks that no foreigners and Portuguese should be allowed to remain on La Margarita Island and he expresses concern that every foreign vessel that arrives in port carries Portuguese mariners and pilots. He is also aware and expresses concern that local residents on the island have contact with the mariners and communicate with them about smuggling opportunities.[20] Fajardo notes that he had written in many letters to the King about the smuggling between La Margarita islanders and foreigners and thinks that the remedy was to make it a matter of concern for the Inquisition. He states that smuggling takes place in clear daylight and he reports on a vessel under the command of Antonio de Anaya who left with pearls from La Margarita Island for Cartagena. According to orders he had to sail directly to Cartagena and surrender his bills of lading. On board were four foreigners expelled from La Margarita Island in compliance with the royal *Cedula*. After clearing customs Antonio de Anaya sets sail for Punta de Araya contrary to the orders given where privateers lie at anchor and where the foreigners were released and where further smuggling took place. In the same letter Fajardo states that the *alcabala* had not yet been imposed at Cumana and he thinks that some sales are made there in order to escape paying *alcabala* on La Margarita Island and he urges *alcabala* to be introduced in Cumana.

---

20 See footnote above, ESHDC, La Margarita, Contaduria, Records related to pearl industry, slaves, and taxation, 1577–1644; June 22, 1602, in which Fajardo expresses his opinion: "... for no ship of Englishmen or pirates comes here that do not carry Portuguese, and some have a Portuguese pilot, ... and it is impossible to prevent them from communicating with those (i.e., the Portuguese?) of the island, both for smuggling and to get such information as they may want,"...and, "...the foreigners here are many and they do not defend the island from enemies in time of emergency." He then suggests that "...if your Majesty wishes that they remain on the island, it will be possible to obtain over 8,000 pesos in naturalization fees from them."

In an endnote Fajardo makes reference to Manso de Contreras who will be his successor in *residencia* but who later accused Fajardo of misconduct and corruption. The two men are more than suspicious of each other. In a letter from Manso de Contreras to the King from La Margarita Island sent on November 28, 1603 a report was made that great abuses in the pearl fishery had occurred and that he brought charges against 150 persons and that fines were made in the amount of 54,500 pesos. A total of 236 charges were issued against Pedro Fajardo and Manso de Contreras suggests that there were complaints about a close friendship between Fajardo and the Bishop of Puerto Rico and that few *quintos* had been paid in pearls and that the Bishop had a parcel of the best fisheries.[21]

Similar situations occurred at nearby locations along the coast of *Tierra Firme*. Depositions taken by Suarez de Amaya, Governor of Cumana in 1601, notes that many privateers along the coast of *Tierra Firme* were suspected of and probably were involved in the contraband trade and that the task of the officials was to prevent that. Suarez de Amaya reports that two vessels had been anchored off the coast near the inlet of the Bordones River at Cumana along the mainland a short distance from La Margarita Island, and that he had ordered that Captain Domingo Cervantes with some soldiers be sent to inquire who they were.[22] Returned from his mission of inspection, Captain Cervantes made a deposition on April 21, 1601, that they were merchants from Venice and that they were Catholic, that they had come directly from Venice to sell merchandise and that there were Spaniards among the crew, and, that they were en route to Hispaniola. Captain Cervantes told them that if they had no permit from the King of Spain they should leave and they replied that they would go to La Margarita Island in order to sail to Hispaniola. The same day Suarez de Amaya decided to personally visit the two vessels to find out more and asked the Spaniards to talk to him upon which he found out that they had sailed from Genoa with merchandise destined for Venice and on the return from there had stopped at Naples where they took on more cargo and sailed to the West Indies. Suarez de Amaya then asked if the government of Genoa or Venice had given them a license to sail to the Indies and they answered that they had not but that the principalities of Genoa and Venice had given them license to trade in the Canary Islands and Brazil but that they had

---

21 See Notes Engel Sluiter, ESHDC, La Margarita, Contaduria, Records related to pearl industry, slaves, and taxation, 1577–1644; November 28, 1603, Lic. Manso de Contreras to the King, La Margarita. (Carton 3, Folder 3-19).

22 See Notes Engel Sluiter, ESHDC, Cumana, Nuevo Andalucía, Audiencia de Santo Domingo, Records concerning investigation of two Italian vessels; April 19, 1601. (Carton 3, Folder 3-20).

come to the Spanish Indies to make a profit and that they carried silks and cloth. Others made depositions that in addition to silk and cloth, the vessels also carried olives, oil, soap, and raisins and that they had sold merchandise at La Margarita Island in the amount of almost 10,000 ducats and that they had collected pearls. Asked if they had loaded salt they said they had not. Another deposition referred to contacts the crew had at La Margarita Island and that they had been well received, and that they had many friends there who treated them as if they were in their home country. In addition they stated that they were subjects of his Majesty and carried bulls of the Holy Father and that they were Catholics. The insistence on the latter suggests that they may have been Portuguese New Christians as they seemed well connected through the merchant networks of the Portuguese Nation.

That the problems with contraband trade at La Margarita Island and Cumana was not resolved is clear from a report sent by the *Consejo de Indias* after examining letters sent from Don Luiz Fajardo and the Governors of Cumana and La Margarita Island and others in 1605.[23] The *Consejo* recommends Cumanagoto to be evacuated because of tobacco smuggling. Cumanagoto was an Amerindian settlement where, as the reports suggest, the indigenous residents were planting nothing but tobacco and which is reputedly the place to which the smugglers have the most occasion to resort to. The recommendation to evacuate the population refers to both "*colonials*" (i.e., Creole and Portuguese) and "*naturales*" (indigenous Indian population) and suggest that they should be relocated to Cumana and be given houses and land to cultivate. At the same time, the planting of tobacco in the province (presumably in all of Nueva Andalucia) and the Barlovento or windward islands (presumably La Margarita Island and Trinidad Island) is to be prohibited for a period of ten years so that, "[…] the reason they have for smuggling with enemies may be taken away, and so that they instead may turn to other occupations and the production of other agricultural products of more advantage to the subjects of his Majesty and to the King's taxes and income." The *Consejo* suggests that the plans be communicated to the *Audiencia* of Santo Domingo for forwarding to Cumana and the islands referred to for comment and if there are no objections and no inconveniences noted, then the recommendations are to be put into effect and a report be made to the *Consejo*. If it does offer disadvantages, the plan is not to be put into effect and substitute measures are to be taken to stop the smuggling problem and to encourage general cultivation.

---

23 Notes Engel Sluiter ESHDC, February 13, 1606, *Memo of the Consejo*. (Carton 3, Folder 3–20). Luiz Fajardo (c. 1556–1617) was a Spanish naval officer in service of the Spanish Crown.

3.3 The Canary Island Connection

That indeed foreigners engaged intrusively in trade with *Tierra Firme* in the early seventeenth century is clear from reports sent from SanLucar, Spain, on November 26, 1607, about the conditions of transfer of goods at the Canary islands.[24] In the report, mention is made of the order of safe passage given by the King to allow Spanish vessels on the way to the Spanish territories unobstructed transfer of goods in the same way allowed Portuguese vessels sailing to Brazil and Angola. From the report it is evident that not only official Spanish and Portuguese vessels passed by the Canary islands for safe passage to Brazil and *Tierra Firme* but that vessels from the rebel territories of the Dutch Republic, more specifically from the provinces of Holland and Zeeland, sailed to and from the Canary islands with both Dutch and Portuguese and likely Amsterdam Sephardic merchants on board who held shares in cargo transported to and from *Tierra Firme* and carried goods to and from the Canary islands to the provinces in the Dutch Republic. In the report presented to the King of Spain, the official notes that all the profits end up in rebel territory.[25]

The Canary islands held a special strategic position in the Atlantic trade network. As the Spanish Crown clamped down on foreign trade, local trading communities throughout the Spanish and Portuguese realm

---

24 See Notes Engel Sluiter, ESHDC, Pedro Albarez Noua to King: San Lucar de Barrameda, November 26, 1607. (Carton 1, Folder 1-6): in which he reports: "[...] Sire: I cannot refrain from again reporting to your Majesty, as I did from the Canaries, and to let you know all that goes on there, [...] for no year passes that four or five ships *de arribada* (goods arriving) come to said Canary Islands and not a ship arrives with less than 200,000 ducats and some come loaded as in this past year (1606)." Albarez Noua goes on to say: "[...] this year, 1607 in March, two came, one from La Florida, and the other from Puerto Rico, [...] money, ginger, hides, sarsaparilla from Caracas, and sugar, and all this was sent to France and it was loaded on a French ship called San Luis, the royal duties of *Averia de armada* and the rest were lost thereby, and they do not declare [cargo] to your Majesty nor to the *Casa de Contratacion* in Seville." In the report Dutch and Portuguese merchants are mentioned in one breath, when he states: "[...] although they claimed they were going to Brazil and Angola, they were going *arribada* to the Spanish Indies." suggesting participation from among members of the Portuguese Nation.
25 The report referenced above states: "[...] And many times they have sent ships from rebel Holland and Zeeland, and they carry Hollanders aboard with them. Shares in the said ships, and make two voyages [round trip?], [...] and return to take them to their provinces [Dutch Republic]." "[...] and, all the money which comes from the Indies passes to the rebel Netherlands, France, and England, and the ships carry much cloth, [...] and those who do this are Francisco Dias Pim. ta [Pimentel?], citizen of La Palma, and Juan del Ballesteros de las Muñecas."

protested and argued that the King was undermining their livelihood. Confronting the growing restrictions on trade due to the economic and military war with the Dutch Republic, interested parties and officials in Portugal petitioned the Crown to reopen trade routes and ports and to lift embargoes on trade with Northern Europe. The King and Council complied and the Canary islands benefitted from the more tolerant trade policies and merchants on the islands developed intricate systems to avoid paying duties by ignoring to take out licenses to trade beyond the islands. As a staging point to the Caribbean region the islands provided supplies and fresh water but also offered opportunities for illegal trade. As trade from Spain and Portugal to the Canary islands was free and unencumbered and extended to include Flemish, Breton, Scottish and English merchants (arranged by treaty or because the subjects were from vassal states), the islands became an entrepot for contraband. Whereas there was little oversight by the Spanish Crown on the Canary Islands, merchants often declared that they were trading with merchants on the islands but in actual fact they sailed on to the Caribbean region or *Tierra Firme*. On the island of Tenerife, according to the report just referred to, it was obvious that Canary islanders were collaborating with Dutch and Portuguese merchants engaged in trade with the Dutch Republic and *Tierra Firme*.[26] As reference is made to several Portuguese Canary islanders, it appears that Dutch mariners and Portuguese and Sephardic merchants formed partnerships and it is likely that Amsterdam Sephardic merchants were involved. A report sent by the *Junta de Guerra de Indias* to the King in 1609 confirms the situation as it had developed.[27] To quote from Sluiter's translation of the document:

"[…] The commerce of foreigners in the Indies has always been odious to the laws and the good government of those provinces, and therefore great precaution has been taken that they and their goods do not go in the regular Indian fleets." "[…] the inconveniences (or harm) of their trade increases greatly in the case of individual traders (trading ships) which leave Cadiz or Seville without being registered (and licensed and inspected), in the first place because they drain off the products

---

26 See ESHDC, November 26, 1607, Box 1, Folder 1-6, Pedro Alverez Noua to King: San Lucar de Barrameda; Pedro Alverez Noua, the official submitting the report to the King about conditions at the Canary islands, refers to Dias Franco, Luis Lorenzo, and Andres Lorenzo, among others engaged in smuggling with merchants from the Dutch Republic.

27 See Notes Engel Sluiter, ESHDC, September 7, 1609; *Junta de Guerra de Indias* to King, Madrid.

of the land and thus slacken the trade of Spain and also in the name of commerce they create hostility, corrupting the fleets of your Majesty, providing arms etc., to the Caribs, and in the second place because along the way they sow their depraved customs and errors with great detriment to our religion and our temporal affairs." "[...] for this reason they are considered and punished as pirates found and caught beyond the Canaries."

It would seem that the junta report is referring to Judaizing and to Portuguese New Christian merchants operating outside of the Spanish trade regime but in the same report there is also a reference made to: "[...] the ships from the North, [...] and the faith being contaminated by the obstinacy and rebellion of the subjects of the church in that region, [...]" referring obviously to the Dutch Republic and Protestantism. In the report the groups referred to above are providing or trading arms with the Caribs suggesting that they are engaged in exchange with Amerindian groups in coastal areas. Among them are the Cumangotos, resident Indians near Cumana, in an area where tobacco cultivation was expanding and exchange markets or fairs were developing.

From notes in the Engel Sluiter collection it appears that contraband cargo was indeed shipped via the Canary Islands to La Margarita Island. In 1608 report is made by a letter of Juan Hurtado y Vernal the *Contador* (Treasurer) on La Margarita Island about Francisco Gonzales de Lugo, *Depositario general* (Custom custodian) and *Tenedor de Bienes de Difuntos* (Spanish official in charge of estate matters) who was engaged in a shipment of goods including contraband cloth originating in the Dutch Republic or England consigned to his house on La Margarita Island. [28] Gonzales de Lugo was from La Palma in the Canary islands and had his contacts there. When Hurtado Y Vernal was made aware of the shipment and took steps to seize it, he was told by Fadrique Cancer, the Governor of La Margarita Island, to keep quiet and that there was no remedy. As it was, there were several merchants engaged in the contraband trade which included shipments from Guyana and Trinidad. The report includes names of several other suspect members of the plot; the *contador* or book keeper, Migual Rubio, Captain Torrico, Benito de la Cruz, Bartolome Rastroxo, and Luis Lopez de Aflaro who were all present at Gonzalez de Lugo's house when Hurtado Y Vernal paid a visit and asked about goods at his residence. Gonzales de Lugo answered in presence of all the members of the party there that: "[...] Fernando de Oruna, the Governor of Guyana, had

---

28 Notes Engel Sluiter, ESHDC, June 11, 1608. Juan Hurtado Y Vernal to King. (Carton 3, Folder 3–17).

sent him a shipment of cloth for a certain amount of money he owed him, and in order to be paid he had accepted the cloth, and that if I paid him I would receive all they brought him, even though it came from the Netherlands or England."[29]

3.4 Depopulation and Prohibition of Tobacco Cultivation

The junta reports referred to give three main reasons for the frequency of North European intrusions in the Caribbean: (1) the good reception they received from the inhabitants of the region due to the fact that the goods they brought were cheap, abundant and in demand, (2) the safety with which salt could be loaded at Punta de Araya, and, (3) the profits they made from smuggling pearls and tobacco. In the reports, mention is made of Santo Domingo (Hispaniola), La Margarita Island and Cumana, Trinidad and Guyana, and Venezuela; locations where removal of coastal populations were proposed and where punishment was meted out to the corsairs and their abettors, the Amerindians and other coastal residents. Several reports, however, cast doubt on the removal plans and if the steps to be taken are sufficient to combat illegal trade. The *Junta de Guerra* thus recommends the stationing of regular forces based in Puerto Rico or windward of all the islands and coastal areas.

From the Sluiter collection of records it is not clear if consideration of depopulation of coastal communities and control over salt shipments and tobacco cultivation and trade in *Tierra Firme* set in due to truce negotiations between Spain and the Dutch Republic starting in 1607 or if smuggling activities engaging Dutch, Portuguese, and Sephardic merchants was strictly a local affair unaffected by negotiations occurring in Madrid and the Hague. Whereas salt hauling at Punta de Araya diminished when Dutch, Portuguese, and Sephardic merchants resumed their trade with Setubal and Aviero during the Twelve Years' Truce (1609–1621), smuggling of pearls and tobacco from the area seems to have continued unabated at least according to Sluiter's document collections. In any event, it seems that at the beginning of the Twelve Years' Truce in 1609 the stage was set on *Tierra Firme* and the nearby Spanish islands in the Caribbean for a serious intent by Spain to combat intrusions by Dutch pirates and their collaborators—Portuguese

---

29 In a note from testimony by Atilano Bernardo de Quiros, Royal Treasury *Contador* on the vessel la Asuncion, on January 25, 1611, it was declared that Fransisco Gonzalez de Lugo was the most powerful man on the island and that he carried China goods without registry or without declaring them. These goods arrived under the name of Gaspar Diaz, his nephew.

New Christian and Sephardic merchants—some of whom came along on merchant vessels from Amsterdam. As the report from the Junta to the King stated, the purpose of this Armada is the guarding and defense of the islands and coasts of New Spain and *Tierra Firme*. In August 1606, a Royal *Cedula* had been issued prohibiting the growing of tobacco for 10 years on the island of La Margarita, the province of Cumana, and the province of Venezuela.[30] The *Cedula* reads (Sluiter translation):

> The King: [...] "Through letters from Luiz Fajardo, Captain General of the Atlantic Squadron (*Armada del Mar Oceano*), and from my Governor of that island (La Margarita) and of the province of Cumana, and from other qualified persons zealous in my service, it has been understood that to various parts and ports of the windward islands there ordinarily come many ships of rebel Dutch, English, and French to smuggle for tobacco, of which there is a great abundance since it is the principal industry which the natives (*naturales* and *coloniales*)[31] have because they thus find a market for it; being much esteemed and sought by said nationalities, my governors not having been able to find a remedy for this, which besides the damage suffered in my royal revenues because of the communication and trade, which from some of said ports and parts occurs with smuggled cloth and goods which the enemies carry in, to Peru and by the merchants who go there from this Kingdom with merchandise, produces many inconveniences worthy of remedy, for the trade and industry of tobacco the natives make and consider the chief one, whereas they could occupy themselves in others of great value, cultivating the land and sowing other crops and working gold mines, of which there are many in those parts. This having been seen in my Council of the Indies and a recommendation having been made to me, it has seemed desirable to me to prohibit the planting of tobacco in said islands (and areas) for 10 years, in order that as a result the natives may work mines and engage in other industries of greater utility and benefit for them, and for my revenues and royal duties."[32]

---

30 See Notes Engel Sluiter ESHDC, August 26, 1606, *Audiencia* Santo Domingo, 180 and 193. Two copies of the same *Cedula*, one addressed to the Governor of the province of La Margarita, and the other to the Governor of the province of Venezuela. (Carton 3, Folder 3–17).
31 *Naturales*; indigenous Indian population and *Colonials*; descendents of Spanish and Portuguese settlers, Creoles among them. New Christians or crypto-Jews are referred to as Portuguese.
32 Notes Engel Sluiter in ESHDC (above), August 26, 1606.

"...And, in order that this may be put into execution in that island of La Margarita and province of Venezuela, I have thought well to send you this by which I order that as soon as you receive this you issue order that henceforth no tobacco be planted in all that island of La Margarita and province of Venezuela for said 10 years. If no important considerations appear to you to militate against this, for if they do write and inform me in detail your views, and the manner in which said smuggling and cultivation and development of the land may be handled. If no inconveniences present themselves, execute this *Cedula* and publish it [...]"[33]

3.5 Smuggling as a Way of Life on Trinidad Island

The fact that smuggling, corruption, and contraband trade was a way of life is also evident from a letter sent by Pedro Suarez Coronel, Governor of Cumana to the King, from Coche Island (part of the jurisdiction of the La Margarita island group), on September 2, 1609. The report concerned the conduct of Don Fernando de Berrio who was appointed Governor of the province of Guyana residing in Trinidad. Fernando de Berrio had succeeded his father Antonio de Berrio as governor who had died in 1596. Following in his father's footsteps he explored the inland regions of Guyana in search of El Dorado and founded the city of Santo Tome near the mouth of the Orinoco river. De Berrio tried to develop a tobacco plantation but failed. To compensate for his losses he began to engage in tobacco smuggling with English and Dutch merchants.[34] Pedro Suarez Coronel reports that at Lent in the spring of 1609, four ships had arrived and that the men on board disembarked and entered the town and were received by monks of the convent of San Francisco and by the Governor. Coronel goes on to say that in all of the Caribbean provinces smuggling had been stopped but that in Trinidad smuggling had continued and that other provinces along the coast were affected. Without having the means and unable to prevent smuggling, an English vessel came from Trinidad and arrived at Cumanagoto where she was attacked and where some of the crew were killed. Coronel reports furthermore that residents of Caracas, Cumanagoto, Cumana, and La Margarita Island were going to Trinidad to trade and that Don Fernando de Berrio had a *patache* which, it was rumored, was obtained by smuggling

---

33 To the La Margarita copy is appended the following ministerial directive: "[...] La Margarita, the Governor to his Majesty, March 29, 1611: The Governor of la Margarita asks whether it would be for the royal service to discontinue the *Cedula* prohibiting the planting of tobacco on that island [...]" The Venezuela copy indicates copies made of the above *Cedula* at Caracas, September 8, 1612.

although he—de Berrio—claimed that he had seized her and had sold her to the local officials. Coronel claims that this was just an excuse to bring illegal merchandise on shore and therefore, he recommended that the King remedy the situation. He goes on and recounts numerous other incidents in which de Berrio was implicated and participated, to then conclude that a force of sixty men with boats are necessary to deal with the situation and that the Governors of La Margarita and Cumana provide Guageries and other Amerindian groups to supplement the force. From the report it also appears that Don Fernando de Berrio bartered goods for captives from Trinidad and Guyana (Santo Tome) to sell as if they were Guinea slaves. Coronel states that the Cumanagoto Indian settlement has need for defense and that the site is surrounded by Indians and attacked daily by the enemy. Furthermore, Carib Indians appear to be on the prowl and continue to threaten the coastal towns. Implied in the report is the capture of smugglers kept under Coronel's supervision as he states that they will not be pardoned until the situation at Trinidad and Santo Tome is remedied. In 1610, Diego Nunez Brito, a capellan on La Margarita Island, complains to the King that Don Bernardo de Vargas Machuca, the newly appointed Governor of La Margarita Island, replacing Pedro Fajardo, acts as an autocrat who interferes in ecclesiastical jurisdiction and spies on him (Nunez Brito) and that he (Nunez Brito), obtained 32 Indian slaves in exchange for smuggled cloth and goods in a bribery deal with Don Fernando de Berrio, which he refers to as Governor of "El Dorado."[35]

---

34 Notes Engel Sluiter, ESHDC, *Audiencia* de Santo Domingo, 100, September 2, 1609; Pedro Suarez Coronel to the King (Carton 3, Folder 3-18). The following report submitted by Pedro Suarez Coronel to the King in 1609 summarizes the events:

"Sire: As to the province where Don Fernando de Berrio is stationed, I have already informed your Majesty that he is within my jurisdiction, for your Majesty gave Trinidad Island to Domingo de Vera (Adjudant of Don Antonio de Berrio) in order to penetrate El Dorado and Guyana and therefore it belongs to this government in the part where he is settled and so far he has not found, nor will find, El Dorado by that route, and there is no reason for him to be stationed in this province, for he uses it only to support open smuggling with enemies, which your majesty has ever tried to stop in these parts, and this proceeds so openly that, as alleged, he is the one who does the trading and makes the agreements, and who divides the cloth with his companions, and whom they pay." Concerning English tobacco contraband trade in Trinidad and Guiana, see Joyce Lorimer, "The English Contraband Trade in Trinidad and Guiana, 1590–1617," in Kenneth R. Andrews et.al., *The Westward Enterprise: English Activities in Ireland, the Atlantic, and America, 1480–1650* (Wayne State University Press, Detroit, 1979).

35 Notes Engel Sluiter in ESHDC, March 24, 1610, British Museum, Mss, 36, 319. (Carton 3, Folder 3–18).

In 1611, Bernardo de Vargas Machua, then Governor of La Margarita Island wrote to the King about pearl fishing in the province whereby he called attention to the lack of tobacco for the divers: "[...] being as it is their chief support and protection, and, [...] that in order to obtain it they seek it at great distance from there [the pearl beds] and pay very high prices." Upon inquiry, the Governor was told that since tobacco cultivation was prohibited in the province, they (the divers) had to travel inland. In the letter to the King, Machua expresses surprise that nobody seemed to know why tobacco cultivation on the coast was prohibited but referring to the *Cedula* of 1606 prohibiting tobacco cultivation he believed that the enforcement of the order should be discontinued reporting the special circumstances under which the pearl fishermen labored: "[...] the Negroes who work in the pearl industry are many and, [...] without tobacco they work much less, and, [...] with greater risk to their lives through sicknesses which happen to them because they live almost all day below the water, [...] it is very necessary and convenient for the service of your Majesty that these Negroes have tobacco, [...] the more so since in this island there are no gold mines nor other industry, only the pearls," and he continues, "[...] for that reason, [...] it would be very much for the service of Your Majesty that tobacco be grown in this island at all times." He then requests that the owners of the canoes engaged in pearl fishing, the *Senores de Canoas*, be given permission to grow tobacco, but adds, " [...] but no one else in order to obviate the disadvantages which arise from not growing it here." In good order he says: "[...] for indeed, through the mercy of God, smuggling has entirely been eradicated."[36]

In August, 1612, Vargas Machuca sends another report to the King and reports that English and Dutch smugglers have returned to Guyana and Trinidad Island and that some ten or twelve vessels passed by La Margarita Island in mid-June and that in August, French vessels came by trying to capture the pearl fishing canoes. The Governor presents a report that the French smugglers were pursued and that some were captured. Then follows his recommendation:

> "[...] It is for the good of the royal service that for the present no tobacco be planted in Trinidad and Guyana until the enemy forgets that trade and region, for the damage that may come to us who govern to leeward of these places is great." At the end he states that he is well aware that to deny tobacco planting has a detrimental impact on the livelihood of a settlement

---

36 ESHDC, March 29, 1611, Audiencia Santo Domingo 100, Bernardo de Vargas Machua, Governor of La Margarita, to King. (Carton 3, Folder 3–18).

but that it would be advised to prohibit planting for a certain period of time, nonetheless, "[...] as during the interim the enemy will desist from coming to that island, seeing he gets no profit."[37]

3.6 Unintended Consequences

The drastic measures taken by the officials to counter attempts made by foreign merchants to engage in the tobacco contraband trade had many unintended consequences. Protests and objections from local coastal populations and concerns expressed by some officials about the economic decline it would cause meant that ultimately very little changed and that illegal trade continued throughout the rest of the seventeenth century. The opinion expressed by the *Consejo* to the Governor of Cumana to depopulate the town of Cumanogote and move the residents to the city of Cumana forms a case in point.[38] The opinion reads:

> "[...] I have been informed that many rebel Dutch, English and French smuggling ships are accustomed to gather at the city of Cumanogote, [...] to barter for the tobacco which is very abundant, as it is the principal enterprise of the natives. With regard to its export, it is very highly valued and sought after by the said nations, [...] and neither the preceding governors nor their lieutenants have been able to remedy this situation nor the damage to the taxes belonging to me, due to the contraband trade which is carried on by the enemy from there to Peru, and the loss suffered by merchants taking goods from these kingdoms (Spain and Portugal), and the many difficulties that arise [...]"

The report suggests that it would not be too difficult to depopulate Cumanogote since there are no more than thirty houses in the town and the place is useless as there is no gold, no silver, no pearl fishing, and no agricultural production, and no profit to the Royal Treasury. So, the order reads that all the settlers should be removed to Cumana which is the capital of the province and the Governor's residence. By destroying shelter and protection in Cumanogote and by removing the residents (*naturales* and *coloniales*) and relocating them to Cumana, the governor will be better able to resist the enemies when they come to take on water at the river for there is no

---

37 ESHDC, August 26, 1612, Audiencia Santo Domingo 193, Bernardo de Vargas Machua, Governor of La Margarita, to King. (Carton 3, Folder 3-18).
38 ESHDC, San Lorenzo el Real, by order of the King, our Lord, Juan de Ciriza, signed by the members of the *Conserje*, August 26, 1606. (Carton 3, Folder 3-20).

other river they can go to in the district. So, the double benefit of taking away access to tobacco and access to fresh water would keep the smugglers at bay, seems to be the suggestion.

But, reality was different as noted by Pedro Suarez Coronel, Governor of Cumana, written to the King on April 28, 1607.[39] Suarez Coronel argues that depopulation of Cumanogote is not a good idea for reason that it will not stop the smuggling efforts. He presents the King with the fact that more than twelve thousand Indians live inland and without Spaniards at Cumanogote there would be no defense against smugglers as foreigners would conduct their contraband enterprise directly with the Indians who are hostile towards Spanish rule. The other reason was that all the Indians of Caracas in neighboring Venezuela would side with the other Indians inland from Cumanogote and therefore Caracas would have to be also depopulated. Another fact is presented by Suarez Coronel, namely, the Spanish depend on the Indians in trade and support and alienating and relocating Indians would cause more friction, and would only encourage the Indian tribes to flee inland and, "[...] further, the negroes of the pearl fishery would flee at once to the Indians of Cumanogote and they could not be recovered." In other words, depopulation and relocation of Indians at Cumanogote would have a domino effect on other groups in the area and open up more instead of fewer opportunities for smuggling. Suarez Coronel goes as far as to state that, if the area is depopulated and no Spanish presence remains in Cumanogote, then the road along which cows and bulls are herded to feed the population at La Margarita Island and Cumana would not be safe. Also, local residents from Caracas, Cumana, and La Margarita would continue to smuggle with the Indians inland as they would not be noticed. Here the question is who are the local residents; Creoles, Portuguese, along with indigenous Indians, enslaved Africans, Mestizos and Mulattos? And, who would provide the labor to cultivate or mine and provide for the Spanish overlord to make ongoing administration worthwhile? In other words a scenario of depopulation would create a bleak future for *Tierra Firme*.

On June 10, 1608, another letter from Pedro Suarez was sent from Cumana to the King to argue the case for better defenses of the Punta de Araya salt pans.[40] He also states that all the measures to limit smuggling ordered by the King had been implemented and that from October 1606 to June 10, 1608 no enemy ships had come to the salt pans but to ensure that defense is guaranteed he requests supplies and manpower to build a fort and station

---

39 Notes Engel Sluiter, ESHDC, April 28, 1607, British Museum Add. Mss. 36 319.
40 Notes Engel Sluiter, ESHDC, June 10, 1608, AGI, Santo Domingo 191.

soldiers at Araya.[41] In the letter he states that the Indians of the provinces are in revolt and mentions that in Nuevo Andalucia, including Guyana, more than 140 thousand Indians are un-pacified and adds that he had stopped the growing of tobacco in all the provinces but mentions that in Trinidad tobacco is grown and that it is traded shamelessly and secretly and that the residents there obtain a great quantity of cloth, and that, "[...] never foreign ships are lacking." In other words, the good with the bad. In his letter he suggests that the culprit for smuggling is the Governor of Trinidad and Guyana, Don Fernando de Berrio, who on excuse of being charged to find El Dorado is given certain privileges to allow the tobacco trade with English and Dutch merchants to proceed in the state of Bolivar, present day Venezuela, of which Trinidad was part. Obviously, this was a controversial matter and as proof of the situation he includes a memo sent to him written by Captain Prado and concludes by proclaiming that what goes on in Trinidad and Guyana needs to be corrected because otherwise the measures taken in Cumana, Caracas, and Hispaniola to depopulate the areas where tobacco was cultivated and traded would serve no purpose and would only lead to economic decline. He claims that ten thousand Amerindians who resided along the rivers and inland in Guyana had been forcefully removed, sold, and relocated (made into slaves presumably) to other parts to cultivate tobacco against the orders of the King. In addition to the report sent to the King he also sends a report to the *Audiencia* at Santo Domingo. How urgent the situation had become is clear from a letter sent by Pedro Suarez Coronel to the King on March 14, 1610 in which he states that unless permission to trade is restored, the province will go into further decline.[42] He argues that since the need of this land is so great because no vessel comes directly from Spain with cloth and no one wishes to ship on the vessels which your Majesty has given permission to come trade, it appears that no ship had arrived for over three years and therefore great scarcity had resulted and he reports that he has given permission to charter a vessel and bring cloth separately from the regular scheduled *flota*. In the letter he says: "[...] if your Majesty grants this favor this province will have what it needs and it will cost them half as much." The letter traveled by way of Caracas.

In 1611, a Royal Order was issued to do a court inquiry or *Residencia* of Don Fernando de Berrio, Governor of Trinidad and Guyana, and his ministers and other officials of state and to investigate the smuggling charges and punish the culprits. Sancho de Alquica is put in charge and

---

41 Note, this is the period when Notarial records show evidence of 'illegal' tobacco cargo shipped to Amsterdam!
42 Notes Engel Sluiter, ESHDC, March 14, 1610, AGI, Santo Domingo, 191.

sets out from La Margarita with three *lanchas* or launches, one *piragua* or small boat, thirty Spaniards, and some 100 Indian and Negro rowers on December 14, 1611. He is ordered to go to San Joseph de Oruna on Trinidad, and from there to Santo Tome de Guyana along the Orinoco, back to Trinidad, and finally back to La Margarita. He writes reports on all his visitations and details on his findings in a document sent to the King on June 14, 1612.[43] De Alquica arrived at San Joseph de Oruna in Trinidad on December 29, 1611 and found that the town had 32 houses of thatch and some 40 men. He offers his commission before the *Cabildo* and soon receives a confession from the towns' residents that they have engaged in smuggling during the period 1604–1611 with French, Dutch and English *corsairs* and "other nations" (i.e., Portuguese?). Their confessions taken, De Alquica asks what their excuse was and they tell him that "[…] they had lacked many necessities and to obtain them they had been forced to this step." De Alquica spent 30 days in Trinidad and then moved on to Guyana where he arrived on February 8, 1612. In San Tome he led the *Interrogatorio General* in *Residencia* of Fernando de Berrio during which it became clear that Don Fernando de Berrio was gravely implicated in smuggling which had been permitted to go on during the time designated (1604–1611). During his stay in Trinidad, De Alquica had learned that there were eighteen smuggling vessels and that several had sailed from Trinidad up the Orinoco and thus upon arrival at San Tome he verified that that was the case. His visit to San Tome lasted sixty days during which he conducted his investigation. He reported on the town and took testimony from the residents which included thirty-eight charges of smuggling filed against Don Fernando de Berrio to which he consented. In addition to smuggling, de Berrio was also charged with enslaving Indians. In self-defense, de Berrio alleged that although he had confessed to smuggling, he had done so out of necessity as supplies and provisions were lacking during the sixteen years of his governorship from 1597 until 1612. De Berrio was found guilty of smuggling and a money fine was imposed and he was never to hold office again. In addition *alcaldes* (mayors) and *regidores* (town council members) were implicated.

In March 1612, the *Junta de Guerra de Indias* in Madrid sums up the situation in the following way (in English translation by Engel Sluiter):[44]

---

43 Notes Engal Sluiter, ESHDC, December 14, 1611–June, 1612, Sancho de Alquica to the King, La Margarita, June 14, 1612. A *Residencia* is usually conducted for a 70-day period by a specially commissioned judge to examine the conduct of retiring high officials like a governor.
44 ESHDC, *Junta de Guerra de Indias* to the King, April 6, 1612.

"Sire: It having been learned by various routes that at Trinidad Island there came a great number of enemy ships of different nations, and particularly, Hollanders and Englishmen, to smuggle with the citizens for the products of the land, and especially for tobacco which is the thing they want most, and that this was done with such liberty that ordinarily there are present there 10 or 12 hulks, and that besides the great injury which results from this to the royal treasury and the trade of the Indies, the thing that causes much worry is the spreading of those parts of the books of their sects carried there by the heretics, besides that fact that they have the plan to make themselves strong in some port of that island, which lies to windward, and later to capture entirely."

The recommendation is given that the silver fleet be sent out the next year to pass by Trinidad and capture the hulks. The *Junta de Guerra* goes into great detail about how many galleons, *pataches* and *barcos luengos* should be launched and involved in the attack but also expresses the concern that if the silver galleons are damaged or destroyed in the raid, then it would affect the annual voyage to Puerto Bello. The concern that this could happen was not unwarranted because according to one source the Dutch were known to blow up their ships when attacked and thus could set fire to the galleons. The King, after considering all the options, orders the fleet to pass by Trinidad Island and sends notice of his decision to Francisco de Varta, President of the *Casa de la Contratacion* on April 6, 1612.

In February 1614, the situation had further deteriorated in *Tierra Firme* and Pedro Suarez Coronel as Governor of Nueva Andalucia reports to the King and Council on behalf of the ecclesiastical and other leading citizens in Cumana about the public welfare of the town and declares that in light of the concerns about the declining conditions of the province and the great need experienced by the population that the Crown should provide support to finish the construction of the church and to pay for lamp oil and wine for the curates to celebrate mass.[45] They also refer to the importance of helping build new settlements along the road inland to explore for gold and silver. Since the province lacks the resources including labor provided by Indians as they were relocated and the land was depopulated, the Governor makes the request that the pearl industry be permitted to reissue the use of labor provided by the native population and to restart the cultivation of tobacco, because as stated: "[...] for in all the surrounding provinces it is grown,

---

45 Notes Engel Sluiter, ESHDC, February 4, 1614, AGI, Santo Domingo 190.

and that the permission (to plant tobacco) continue until his Majesty orders otherwise." He also makes the observation that (translation Sluiter):

"[...] in the Islands de Barlovento (the Windward islands), Dominica, and others, there are many Negro slaves in the power of the Caribs, obtained from ships wrecked there which sally forth to do damage and that therefore they ask his Majesty to let the city have, in order to aid in building the church, and to assist, all those Negroes which they can catch from said islands, and that to achieve these ends and to have trade and commerce in this province in as much as tobacco, brazil wood, and some hides are produced that they be allowed to load some ships of this city directly (to Spain) which will have the result that many will come to become citizens in this fertile land to make plantations, cattle ranches, etc." and that "[...] his Majesty design to order that to this province be sent some (Negro) slaves in order that they may be divided among the citizens of this city on credit for a certain period of time of payment in order that with them they may make sugar mills and make sugar since this land is good for it." He asks for the favor that: "[...] on the products of the land they pay no duties as was granted to the neighboring province of Caracas."

The antagonistic relationship with the Caribs came to a head in 1612 when Sancho de Alquiza, Governor of Guyana and Trinidad, reported to the King that the island of Trinidad was in a constant state of war with the native population of the area. He recommends that the Caribs be captured and enslaved and that Trinidad and Guyana and La Margarita Island coordinate their efforts to rendezvous and bring an *armada* together to combat the Caribs. He recommends that local residents man the *armada* as they have the experience to deal with hostile Carib Indians.[46] He also points out that an aid in the war against the Caribs would be the Arawak who live on the mainland and states: "[...] they will go on the expedition with great gusto because of the great enmity they have with the Caribs in order to revenge themselves for the many killings they have done among their relatives and by eating them [...]" He explains to the King that the fleet could be financed from proceeds made from selling Negro slaves captured or rescued from shipwrecked vessels.

---

46 ESHDC, February 11, 1612, Sancho de Alquiza to the King, San Joseph de Oruna, Trinidad.

In 1614, a report was issued about the state of affairs in both *Tierra Firme* and Guyana during the period July 10, 1613– June 30, 1614.[47] The report illustrates the extent to which Carib and Arawak Indians were involved in the illegal tobacco trade. At the end of June, 1613, a report was made by the Mayor of Trinidad that several enemy vessels were threatening the island and that another corsair ship had arrived whose crew were trying to land. In a letter dated June 25, 1613, Antonio de Muxica, lieutenant of San Tome de Guyana request enforcements to expel the English settled on the river banks in company of the Caribs who are planting tobacco for the Netherlanders and who are robbing the friendly Indians and carried them off to their settlements to use them in the growing of tobacco. Report has it that along the Corentyne River more than 50 Netherlanders had settled who committed robberies and insults. Captain Andres Garcia is sent to La Margarita Island to collect soldiers and munitions to combat the situation. On July 10, 1613, Don Bernardo de Vargas, then governor of La Margarita Island, reports that in the province of Arawak on the mainland coast, some English had settled with the favor of Carib Indians for the purpose of planting tobacco and he petitioned the King to give him permission to send a lieutenant there to subdue the Caribs and expel the English. In the same year, on July 12, 1613, Don Bernardo de Vargas reported that the English were planting tobacco in Trinidad Island and on the coast of San Tome de Guyana and that it would be expedient to expel them from there before they could fortify themselves. He recommends that the galleons scheduled to sail in 1614 go via Trinidad and deposit 50 soldiers with arms and munitions there to defend the island and recruit another 50 soldiers from among the local population to attack the English on land. Antonio de Muxica, lieutenant of Guyana sends a letter dated May 30, 1614, that because of the threats and evil conduct of the Netherlanders and Caribs against the Arawak Indians he had sent an attack force to the settlement along the Corentyne River and had set fire to the fort the Dutch had built. Again, the recommendation is made to clear the land along the coast from the Rio Maranon to the Orinoco as another three or four foreign settlements had sprung up, all of them trading products collected and cultivated along the tributaries upstream.[48] Don Juan Tostade, who through absence of Sancho de Alquiza governs Trinidad, writes in a letter dated June 16, 1614, that they hanged several Netherlanders who had been captured and

---

47 Notes Engel Sluiter, ESHDC, October 7, 1614: Caribbean, British Museum, Add. Mss., 36,320: "Report of the State of things on Trinidad Island": July 10, 1613– June 30, 1614.

48 Another letter was sent by Antonio de Muxica on July 24, 1614 which describes the Dutch fort captured and its lay-out.

that this had stopped smuggling on Trinidad but that upstream the Orinoco River, smuggling continued unabated and that earlier in the month, along the south coast of Trinidad, local Indians had seen a number of Carib *piraguas* alongside Dutch vessels which reportedly were taking on tobacco that had been cultivated near the Dutch fort along the Corentyne River. Don Juan Tostade states that: "[...] it appears from the deposition of six witnesses how that island (Trinidad) is usually surrounded by and landed by Netherlanders and Caribs, and that therefore the citizens live short of many goods for they cannot go out to obtain them for the Caribs come to rob up to the very town itself and this because of the close alliance they have with the Dutch [...]." Juan Diaz de Mancilla, curate and vicar of Trinidad in a letter of June 30, 1614 reports that he has confirmed intelligence that from the Guayapoco to the Orinoco rivers there are four Dutch settlements.

In the meantime, the situation in Cumana is deteriorating further and it is recognized that unless the town can offer goods to trade by restoring tobacco cultivation or by introducing sugar production, it will be difficult to secure the future well-being of the town's population. In the context presented, it is clear that the relocation of Indians and the depopulation of coastal communities had created serious hardships for Cumana and that unless labor was provided by capturing Negroes from neighboring states and islands, as the prohibition of enslaving Amerindians had led to labor shortages, the situation would not be rectified. In 1615, Pedro Suarez Coronel is replaced by Juan de Haro who writes to the King that arms and munitions are in great need as rumors have it that: "[...] the Hollanders are outfitting a goodly number of ships with the design of founding and settling three or four colonies on the shores and in the ports of the Western Indies."[49] He says that he has a great shortage of weapons and that he had to ask the Governor of La Margarita Island for kegs of powder and harquebuses (tripod guns) in order to defend against enemies including the Caribs. He claims that his predecessor had made the request initially for arms and munitions but that the *Casa de la Contratacion* of Seville had taken the money and spent it on other things.

3.7 Summary and Conclusion

In 1615, a *Cedula* was issued under which permission was given to send annually a large ship to Cumana with supplies from Spain for a six-year period ending in 1621. At the end of 1616, a *Cedula* orders the *Audiencia*

---

[49] Notes Engel Sluiter, ESHDC, June 7, 1615, British Museum, Add.Mss 36, 320 (AGI Santo Domingo 54-4-9).

of Santo Domingo to show why they impede the Indians from going pearl fishing. A *Cedula* dated April 28, 1618 asks if it is desirable to place a curate and sacritan in Cumana under the authority of the Bishop of Puerto Rico. Another *Cedula* dated April 28, 1618, requested the Governor of Cumana to report if the tobacco harvested in Cumana province paid duties or not.[50] Apparently tobacco cultivation had resumed. A *Cedula* dated September 15, 1618, ordered the Governor of Cumana to raise men in the Province of Venezuela to punish the rebel Indians of the Cumanagotos. Also on September 15, 1618, a *Cedula* ordered *encomiendas* vacant in Cumana to be given to deserving persons, and on September 18, 1618, a *Cedula* ordered pacification of the Cumanagoto and Carib Indians. Then followed some undated *cedulas* granting the town of Cumana the revenue of 2 1/2 percent paid on merchandise imported from Spain and a *Cedula* by which the Crown gave Cumana the revenue from judicial fines the latter also reports that arms were sent to the province, dated October 11, 1618. Five *cedulas* are ordered to outfit 40 settlers to whom the King gave permission with their households and family to colonize the province. The Agent under whose direction the *cedulas* were ordered was Lorenzo Lopez de Ycurrategui. He also was an agent for Trinidad and Guyana during the time. For Trinidad he obtained exemption from paying *alcabala* and *almojarifazgo* in Sevilla on the tobacco they transported from the island and he also received munitions and obtained permission for a *patache* to go yearly to the province of Trinidad - Guyana.

From a Royal *Cedula* (translated by Sluiter) issued in Madrid in June 1620 by the King to the Governor of New Andalucia it is clear:[51]

"[...] Experience having demonstrated that the tobacco which is grown and harvested in many coastal and Mediterranean places of my Indies, islands and mainland of the Atlantic, is one of the chief attractions for corsairs and pirates of various nations who go to barter for it with the planters who have this crop because of the great profit which they draw from it as far as Asia and Persia where it is sold at excessive prices and that en route these corsairs do great damage and robberies among the ships, barks, and other vessels of my subjects who with products of their areas navigate from one place to another with continual fear and danger. Although I could order prohibiting the planting and growing of

---

50 Notes Engel Sluiter, ESHDC, July 22, 1619, AGI, Santo Domingo, 179, "Powers of Agency" for the period from September 1, 1615 until July 22, 1619.
51 Notes Engel Sluiter, ESHDC, June 10, 1620, Royal Cedula, Madrid in AGI Santo Domingo 190.

said tobacco in all the said Indies in order to take away the opportunity for enemies to go to barter and trade there, yet, considering the poverty and necessity of the citizens and natives of that land, and that if I take away this business and trade they would receive much prejudice, I have agreed and resolved that for the account of my royal treasury there be bought in that province 4,000 *arrobas* of said tobacco per year at the most reasonable price possible in order that it may be carried to the city of Cartagena and be stored and from there, with the remaining quantities which for my account are to be bought in other parts of the said Indies, it may be carried annually to the *Casa de la Contratación* of Seville in the galleons of my Royal Armada of the Indies."

He appoints Diego Pinelo to be in charge and gives orders on how to proceed with the purchase of tobacco.

"[...] I order you that as soon as he arrives in the province, you call together all the citizens and planters of the places where it is grown, and with the assistance of said Don Diego Pinelo hold an open *Cabildo* and proclaim this my *Cedula*, and having done this, learn from said growers what quantity of tobacco has been harvested in the past, and at what price they have sold and traded it, and, whether they can supply each year the said 4,000 *arrobas* or more, and at what prices, and according to what conditions you find, you will draw up papers and records necessary with said planters for each planter's share [...], assuring them on my part that what this amounts they will be paid from any income I may have in that land, and not having it anywhere there, [...] they will be paid in Cartagena from any funds which may be in my royal treasury [...], and that in ample time you try to bring together and have ready the said tobacco in the place where it is to be embarked on the ships which will come for it, which is to be the one which my general of the fleet of the Indies will send to La Margarita for the pearls, [...] and if it seems better to you that they be remunerated for their tobacco with cloth, supplies, and other common necessities, [...] tell Diego Pinelo to report this to my Council of the Indies,"

Clearly, by 1620, the King and his officials on *Tierra Firme* had come to terms with the fact that tobacco was there to stay and it was better to accommodate than to punish local residents and depopulate the coastal regions. In doing so, they introduced "regulated trade" and in effect imposed a state monopoly. One characteristic of tobacco cultivation and trade is in fact regulation, either in the form of controlling trade and imposing state monopolies or by restricting consumption. In both instances, taxation and revenue collection were the instruments by which this was accomplished. As the Spanish saw the potential for revenue collection in tobacco, they sought to participate and dominate in both the cultivation and the trade of tobacco. But, as the government tried to do so, illegal trade became more prominent and engaged several parties all of which one way or another profited from the trade.

In the history of the development of tobacco cultivation and trade, Portuguese New Christian merchants played an important role from the very beginning. As tobacco entered the mercantile Atlantic circuit as a commodity, Portuguese merchants were in the vanguard of providing slave labor and developing tobacco plantations along the coast of *Tierra Firme*.[52] At the receiving end of the supply chain were Dutch mariners and among them were Sephardic merchants from Amsterdam who were allied to Portuguese New Christian merchants through networks of contact that had existed for a period of time prior to the engagement of Portuguese merchants in *Tierra Firme*. The first reports in Engel Sluiter's collection about smuggling by Dutch mariners in rivalry with the Spanish Habsburg date from the time when the first Portuguese New Christian merchants relocate from Portugal and Antwerp to Amsterdam in the late sixteenth century to form and develop the Amsterdam Portuguese Jewish community and it stands to reason that Amsterdam's Sephardic merchants participated in the trade network.[53] By the early seventeenth century, the Portuguese merchants dominated the tobacco trade in the Caribbean region. As evidence from the Engel Sluiter collection makes clear, in the development of tobacco for export from *Tierra Firme*, Amerindians played an important role. They held market fairs at regular times of the year when the merchant vessels passed by and the Cumagoto Indians in the area were directly involved in trade with the Dutch. From the evidence presented by Sluiter's Historical Documents Collection, the early smuggling of tobacco was related to the salt winning at Punta de Araya. The needs of the crew onboard salt vessels while at anchor at Araya Bay dictated that fresh water and food had to be procured nearby which brought Dutch mariners on shore to exchange supplies with the Amerindian population and barter tobacco. For the purpose of exchange, Portuguese merchants residing along

---

52 Studnicki-Gizbert, *A Nation Upon the Ocean Sea* (2007), pp. 118–119.
53 In fact, we have evidence that they did from the records collection for Hispaniola (Audiencia de Santo Domingo) for 1596. See Chapter 1; the case of Simon the Herrera along with Manual Cardozo and Juan de Riberos who carried two passports, one Dutch and one Portuguese. See Engel Sluiter, "Dutch-Spanish Rivalry in the Caribbean Area, 1594–1609," in *The Hispanic American Historical Review*, volume 2, May 1848, pp. 165–196; 174.

the coast became essential as they served as pilots or, as described by Cromwell (2018) served as *practicos*. As experienced coastal traders with connections to Spanish officials and members of the *Audiencias* and as go-between at various strategic locations including the Canary islands, Trinidad and Hispaniola, Portuguese pilots played an important role as we will see in the next chapter.

Sustained success in the tobacco trade required a diverse and well-connected array of conspirators or allies and also required a regular supply of slave labor. As the Portuguese merchants were well connected in the slave supply trade and as contractors for the Spanish colonists, they often served a double function in the import-export trade by supplying labor and purchasing tobacco. In addition, and by contracting with Dutch merchants, Portuguese pilots were often useful in delivering the needed supplies of textiles, tools, and hardware which stimulated tobacco planting. As go-between they were also crucial for Dutch merchants to trade tobacco and smuggle pearls from the fisheries off the coast of *Tiera Firme*. Thus, a well-connected tobacco merchant sought security by taking Portuguese pilots onboard who would negotiate with residents of coastal communities, including indigenous populations, to deliver the goods at set times in set locations along the coast. Of course this required that the pilot was familiar with the coastal communities involved and at the same time could communicate with and have trust in the captain of the vessel and vice versa. From the Dutch captain or merchant's perspective, acquaintance with a member of the Portuguese Nation or a Sephardic merchant onboard would be an asset.[54] Although contractual evidence of Portuguese merchant networks operating alongside Dutch merchants engaged in the tobacco trade along the coast

---

54 The documents in the Sluiter collection often refer to both Dutch and English mariners along the coast of *Tierra Firme*. At the time, when both the Dutch and the English were at war with Spain, there was close collaboration between the two, both militarily and in trade. Both countries had established trade relationships with the Iberian Peninsula via Antwerp and, in fact, signed a bilateral treaty in 1585; the Treaty of Nonsuch, by which England agreed to support the Dutch rebels against Spanish rule. We also know that the English alongside the Dutch were instrumental in introducing tobacco cultivation to Barbados. So, it is not surprising that the tobacco trade was an Anglo-Dutch enterprise and that leading Amsterdam tobacco merchants were engaged in the Chesapeake tide-water region when tobacco cultivation developed there; see Wim Klooster, "The Tobacco Nation: English Tobacco Dealers and Pipe-Makers in Rotterdam, 1620–1650," in Laura Cruz and Joel Mokyr (eds.), *The Birth of Modern Europe* (Brill, Leiden and Boston, 2010), pp. 17–35. There is however no sustained evidence of a joint enterprise between Dutch and English mariners or merchants engaged in the tobacco trade in the late sixteenth and early seventeenth century along the coast of *Tierra Firme* near Punta de Araya, Cumana or La Margarita Island.

of *Tierra Firme* is lacking from the documents, incidental evidence shows that Portuguese merchants were heavily involved in trade with the Dutch Republic as they formed a majority of merchants along the Atlantic Seaboard and were found in abundant presence in *Tierra Firme*, The Spanish Caribbean islands, and in Brazil in the seventeenth century and in the Atlantic trade circuit in general.[55]

The concerns expressed by Spanish officials and presented by Engel Sluiter in the Historical Documents Collection for *Tierra Firme* focus primarily on the tobacco contraband trade alongside the salt trade in Punta de Araya and by extension the smuggling of pearls in nearby coastal communities. The documents do refer to Portuguese merchants as the go-between in Trinidad and the lower Orinoco River and on the Canary islands. From the documents in the collection it appears that Dutch salt winning at Punta de Araya was the start of the relationship between Dutch merchants and tobacco and pearl smuggling around Araya, Cumana, and La Margarita Island. The Dutch salt trade at Araya started when embargoes imposed by the Spanish Habsburg rulers on the salt export from Portugal and the Cape Verde Islands in the late sixteenth century limited Dutch access to salt needed for the herring fisheries. Thus, in a round-about way and related to embargoes and blockages imposed during the Eighty Years' War between Habsburg Spain and the Dutch Republic, the tobacco contraband trade from *Tierra Firme* originated and developed alongside the Portuguese merchant trade in the coastal regions of the Caribbean. As a growing volume of tobacco reached European shores, Spanish officials became increasingly concerned about the Portuguese dominance in the tobacco trade and alerted the Crown of their suspicion of illegal contacts with Dutch and English merchants and mariners. In the next chapter on Hispaniola we will see more evidence of Portuguese merchants involved in the Dutch or rather the Amsterdam tobacco trade in the late sixteenth and early seventeenth centuries.

---

55 David Grant Smith, "The Mercantile Class of Portugal and Bahia in the Seventeenth Century: A Socio-Economic Study of the Merchants of Lisbon and Bahia, 1620–1690," (PhD dissertation, The University of Texas at Austin, 1975), Studnicki-Gizbert, *A Nation Upon the Ocean Sea* (2007), and the edited volume by Ida Altman and David Wheat, *The Spanish Caribbean and the Atlantic World in the Long Sixteenth Century* (University of Nebraska Press, Lincoln, 2019).

Chapter 4

PORTUGUESE MERCHANTS AND THE TOBACCO TRADE WITH HISPANIOLA[1]

4.1 Political, Economic, and Geographical Context

In *A Nation Upon the Ocean Sea*, Studnicki-Gizbert (2007) shows us repeated evidence of the role Portuguese New Christian merchants and their foreign partners played in smuggling activities and in bribing officials.[2] As members of the Portuguese Nation they promoted and conducted "free trade" and brought the wrought upon them by cultivating an elaborate system of working within the system and accumulating and circulating wealth outside the realm. Operating within and outside the Spanish system they extended partnerships with merchants in Northern Europe and the Mediterranean region and with the various merchant communities in the Spanish American colonies. In the 1620s, prominent members of the Portuguese Nation formed a key group in the efforts to install Count-Duke of Olivares as Prime Minister under King Philip IV of Spain who promoted the imperial commonwealth of Spain and Portugal. Within the realm the Canary islands and Hispaniola were integral parts of the inter-locking system of trade which merchants of the Portuguese Nation promoted and served. The islands were points of contact where cargo was transferred and where foreign merchants engaged in contraband trade thrived.

In a *World on the Move*, Russell-Wood (1992) reminds us of the connections, interactions, and movement of goods and people in the early modern Atlantic world. Perhaps more than any place Hispaniola exemplified that characterization and Portuguese merchants were the most prominent examples. Commercial success depended on regular and sustained personal

---

1 Engel Sluiter Historical Documents Collection, Carton 1: Espanola, folders 12–17.
2 Daviken Studnicki-Gizbert, *A Nation Upon the Ocean Sea: Portugal's Atlantic Diaspora and the Crisis of the Spanish Empire, 1492–1640* (Oxford University Press, Oxford, New York, 2007), Chapter 1, pp. 25–30.

contact and circulation of goods via the transatlantic networks of merchants and mariners which provided a steady stream of information about supply of products, market prices, routes to sail, and people to stay in contact with. The breadth of such merchant networks expanded significantly in the late sixteenth and early seventeenth centuries as Spain's imperial reach widened and engaged Portuguese merchants and bankers after the unification of 1580. However, the role of Portuguese merchants in the Atlantic trade had been evident for some time before the unification as evidence from the slave trade and sugar trade demonstrates. Furthermore, slaving and smuggling often went hand in hand and Portuguese merchants were omnipresent where slaves were in demand, plantations emerged, and export of staple goods became the life blood of the colonial administration.[3] The situation in Hispaniola forms a good example of this.[4]

In *Islanders and Empire*, Ponce Vázquez (2020) details how contraband trade came to define the political, economic and geographical situation in seventeenth-century Hispaniola (today, Haiti and the Dominican Republic) and how over time the island's multi-ethnic resident population gained control over governing institutions. In the sixteenth century, Hispaniola's colonial role was defined by its functioning transfer trade and the sugar economy. As Hispaniola's original Spanish population turned their attention to greater wealth in Central America and re-routed the imperial fleet to Veracruz in Mexico in the course of the sixteenth century, a rapid decline of the sugar economy set in turning Hispaniola into a periphery. The remaining islanders' resistance to decline and to Spain's mercantile system became legendary. In response to royal neglect and indifference, Hispaniola residents increasingly turned governing institutions into vehicles to advance their own self-interests and turned their attention to smuggling to survive and by engaging in trade with Spain's enemies and rivals. Ponce Vázquez describes how some isolated parts of the island and remote ports became thriving centers of illicit commerce. Contributing to the political economy based on contraband trade were members of some indigenous Indian tribes, African slaves and former slaves, Portuguese, Mestizos, and various other groups creating elaborate social networks that included foreign

---

[3] A. J. R. Russell-Wood, *A World on the Move: The Portuguese in Africa, Asia, and America 1415–1808* (Carcenet, Manchester, 1992). Stucnicki-Gizbert, *A Nation Upon the Ocean Sea* (2007); Ida Altman and David Wheat (eds.), *The Spanish Caribbean and the Atlantic World in the Long Sixteenth Century* (University of Nebraska Press, Lincoln, 2019).

[4] Juan José Ponce Vásquez, *Islanders and Empire: Smuggling and Political Defiance in Hispaniola, 1580–1690* (Cambridge University Press, Cambridge, 2020).

agents and merchants of rival European powers. These circumstances gave structure to the island's precarious political situation and defined the contours of the island within a broader trans-Atlantic context. In fact, the actions of residents operating outside the law continuously challenging Spanish imperial authority turned Hispaniola into a trans-imperial center of the Atlantic world. Hispaniola thus became a hub for a contraband trade that provided its poorer residents with a livelihood and its political elite with increased authority and greater access to European and regional markets.

Hispaniola (or *La Española* in Spanish) was the first Caribbean island to be occupied by Spanish forces. The island was discovered by Columbus in 1492 and became one of the most important transfer points in trade between Spain and the Caribbean region in the sixteenth century. For a brief period of time, Hispaniola constituted the center of Spain's discovery, conquest, and colonization of America. Immigrant settlers had arrived from the Canary Islands in the early sixteenth century and it was in Hispaniola where Europeans first came in contact with indigenous Amerindian populations who were taken captive and put to work.[5] For Spanish settlers, gold mining was the main attraction but through the spread of diseases a large number of the native-born Indian population died and the workforce was decimated. When the gold mines did not yield what was expected many settlers moved on to other parts of Spanish America leaving Hispaniola in decline.[6]

Due to the abandonment and neglect by the Spanish Crown and the depopulation that followed the decline in gold mining in the early sixteenth century, foreigners or "interlopers" followed to fill the gap and supply the island with needed provisions or to raid and trade with the native population and bribe the Spanish officials for favors. Soon contraband trade was established between coastal populations, including Portuguese merchants, and French, English, and Dutch privateers and mariners.[7] In 1563, the King complained to the *Audiencia* of Santo Domingo that cargoes from Portugal and other foreign countries were received in Hispaniola and elsewhere in the West Indies and exchanged for gold, silver and a variety of colonial products. Meanwhile, sugar had been introduced as a plantation crop in the second half of the sixteenth century. Sugar cane was introduced from the Canary Islands and African slaves were imported from West Africa to provide labor. In 1562–1563 John Hawkins delivered 300 slaves to the colonists of Hispaniola and

---

5 Carl Ortwin Sauer, *The Early Spanish Main* (University of California Press, Berkeley and Los Angeles, 1966), pp. 70–103.
6 Ponce Vásquez, *Islanders and Empire* (2020), Chapter 1.
7 Clarence H. Haring, *Trade and Navigation between Spain and the Indies in the Time of the Hapsburgs* (Yale University Press, New Haven, 1917), pp. 115–116.

100 more as a "deposit" with the authorities in Santo Domingo in return for hides.[8] For some time, Hispaniola was the principal source of the West Indian supply of sugar for the Spanish market but production began to decline when the Brazil sugar production and trade proved to be more profitable. Towards the end of the sixteenth century the provisioning and supply trade conducted by English, French, and Dutch privateers had replaced the sugar trade and corruption and bribery thrived.[9] In fact, the island became best known for the contraband trade in hides and tobacco.[10]

The first known direct Dutch contact with Hispaniola was in 1595 when several merchants from the provinces of Holland and Zeeland through contacts with their trading partners in Santo Domingo purchased trade goods which were later taken by force and carried off by an English vessel.[11] In 1596, the case of Simon de Herrera referred to in Chapter 2 was recorded by the *Audiencia* of Santo Domingo. In the court case that followed his arrest, Simon Herrera's documents included evidence which implicated him with Dutch interests and contacts as he was offered safe passage to Holland or Zeeland in the Dutch Republic.[12] Quite likely, the Portuguese Jewish merchants mentioned in the case, Simon de Herrera, Manuel Cardozo and Juan de Riberos, as their names appear in the documents, were the factors referred to by Engel Sluiter in his article published in 1948.[13] In 1597, a squadron of four vessels from the Dutch Republic sailed to the Caribbean region to trade and they took a Portuguese master along with a dozen of his compatriots to serve as interpreters.[14] Thus, in the late sixteenth and early seventeenth century, Hispaniola and its smaller neighbor Tortuga, had become regular transfer points for Dutch and likely English and French

---

8 On the history of slavery and slave trade in the Spanish Caribbean and Hispaniola see, Marc Eagle, "The Early Slave Trade to Spanish America: Caribbean Pathways, 1530–1580," in Altman and Wheat (eds.), *The Spanish Caribbean and the Atlantic World* (2019), pp. 139–160.

9 Genaro Rodriguez Morel, "The Sugar Economy of Espanola in the Sixteenth Century," in Stuart B. Schwartz (ed.), *Tropical Babylons: Sugar and the Making of the Atlantic World, 1450–1680* (University of North Carolina Press, Chapel Hill, London, 2004), pp. 85–114; p. 103.

10 See, Escudero A. G. "Hispaniola's Turn to Tobacco," in Aram B., Yun-Casalilla B. (eds) *Global Goods and the Spanish Empire, 1492–1824* (2014, Palgrave Macmillan, London), pp. 216–229.

11 Engel Sluiter, "Dutch-Spanish Rivalry in the Caribbean Area, 1594–1609," *The Hispanic American Historical Review*, vol. 28, No. 2, May 1948, pp. 165–196; 174.

12 Sluiter, 1948, p. 174.

13 Sluiter, 1948, p. 174.

14 Sluiter, 1948, p. 175.

privateers engaged in the tobacco and hide trade. Most of the smuggling took place along the northwest coast of Hispaniola, furthest removed from Santo Domingo, the seat of power of the Spanish administration (the *Audiencia*) (Figure 4.1). By 1606, the harassment and smuggling activities had become so blatant that the Crown prohibited the cultivation of tobacco for ten years and ordered residents along the northwest coast to be relocated along with their cattle and belongings to the southeast coast of the island closer to Santo Domingo so that they could be supervised in order to diminish or eliminate smuggling activities which, in the case of Hispaniola, centered on the trade of hides but included ginger, tobacco, and other goods. The reports that were exchanged between the governors, the *Audiencia*, and the Spanish Crown at this time attest to the fact that the intermediaries in the smuggling activities were Portuguese resident-merchants on Hispaniola.[15]

The principal town on the island was Santo Domingo on the southeast coast of the island. Santo Domingo along with San Juan (Puerto Rico) and Cartagena (Colombia) served as supply center and political center for

Figure 4.1 The Island of Santo Domingo or Hispaniola ca. 1723.
Source: John Carter Brown Library, Public domain, via Wikimedia Commons.

---

15 See also, Studnicki-Gizbert, *A Nation Upon the Ocean Sea* (2007), Chapter 4, pp. 92–121.

Hispaniola and *Tierra Firme* and housed the *Audiencia* through which most of the administrative tasks were coordinated. While Spain tried to administer its affairs from Santo Domingo, the Dutch, the English and the French tried to undermine Spanish commercial and military control by repeatedly attacking the Spanish fleet along the northwest coast of Hispaniola and the southeast coast of Cuba and by trading with the buccaneers who had established themselves on the island and nearby.[16] Herds of wild cattle and horses, first brought by Columbus, roamed the island which attracted an array of intruders who settled on nearby Tortuga which became known as a hide-out for buccaneers in the early seventeenth century. Besides the Dutch intrusion upon the Spanish realm of Hispaniola during the Eighty Years' War (1568–1648), the English pursuits during the Anglo-Spanish War (1585–1603) and the French pursuits were equally disruptive.[17]

As smuggling became a way of life, Portuguese merchants were attracted to reside along the north coast and on nearby Tortuga. In *A Nation Upon the Ocean Sea*, Studnicki-Gizbert (2007) refers to more than 200 Portuguese residents on the island in 1535 as reported by officials in Santo Domingo. He also suggests that the Portuguese residents held the monopoly in the slave trade for the island as well as in the trade in sugar; the island's primary export commodity in the sixteenth century.[18] By the mid-sixteenth century, Hispaniola reputedly had more Portuguese than Castilian settlers (*vecinos*) and reports were referring to coastal concentrations of Portuguese residents throughout the region.[19] It was common for Portuguese migrants to first establish residency in Castile and then travel to the Spanish Indies. In addition, the Crown had actively encouraged Portuguese migrants to settle in Hispaniola when concerns about depopulation and lack of development called for resettlement of the island. For instance in 1565, 150 Portuguese

---

16 The term buccaneer derives from the French word *boucaniers*, named so for their lifestyle of living off the cattle they herded and the grilled beef (*boucan*) they subsisted on off the coast of Hispaniola. The term is specific to the seventeenth century Caribbean. Another term used in the Engel Sluiter documents is corsair which is a French term to describe privateers. The term corsair is traditionally more specific with reference to the Mediterranean.

17 See, I. A. Wright, "The Dutch and Cuba, 1609–1643," *The Hispanic American Historical Review*, Vol. IV, no. 4, November 1921, pp. 597–634. See also K. R. Andrews, "English Voyages to the Caribbean, 1596–1604: An Annotated List," *The William and Mary Quarterly*, vol. 31, no. 2, April 1974, pp. 243–254.

18 Studnicki-Gizbert, *A Nation Upon the Ocean Sea* (2007), pp. 26–27.

19 Brian Hamm, "Between Acceptance and Exclusion: Spanish Responses to Portuguese Immigrants in the Sixteenth-Century Spanish Caribbean," in Altman and Wheat (eds.), *The Spanish Caribbean and the Atlantic World* (2019), pp. 113–135.

families were recruited to settle on the island. The Royal *Cedula* specified that the new settlers were to be *labradores* in farming but practice taught that many became engaged in commerce or smuggling instead.

Throughout the sixteenth century, collaboration with French, English and Dutch corsairs or buccaneers were reported and many Portuguese sailed aboard foreign vessels as pilots or *practicos*, leading to hostile response from Spanish officials.[20] In the reports, the Portuguese were often referred to as *Luteranos*, a term used to describe Protestant heretics, as they were associated with and accomplices to French, English, and Dutch privateers. The association with foreign merchants or *contrabandistas* is what defined the Portuguese but was also the reason why they were sought after as they had the experience of the sea and had proven themselves valuable participants in Spanish expeditions, explorations, and conquests starting with Columbus voyages to the Americas. By the early seventeenth century, Portuguese residents and mariners were more specifically associated with the Portuguese Nation and were suspected of collaborating with foreigners as they and their associates, the Dutch in particular, were viewed as undermining Spanish interests by collaborating with the enemy. Furthermore, they were suspected of trading with Jewish or crypto-Jewish merchants. Starting in the early seventeenth century the Inquisition tried many Portuguese residents in Spanish America and from testimony that emerged the ties with Portuguese and Jewish merchants abroad became increasingly clear.[21]

4.2 Portuguese Resident Merchants and Foreign Intruders

In his article on Dutch-Spanish rivalry in the Caribbean, published in the *Hispanic American Historical Review*, Engel Sluiter (1948) gives only scant notice of Portuguese merchants and the tobacco trade but the documents he collected and research notes he attached suggest that the Dutch and English smuggling activities on Hispaniola were significant and that tobacco was among the products traded or exchanged and that Portuguese residents

---

20 The term *Practico* is described by Jesse Cromwell in *The Smuggler's World: Illicit Trade and Atlantic Communities in Eighteenth-Century Venezuela* (University of North Carolina Press, Chapel Hill, 2018), pp. 131–132 as a experienced coastal trader whose business contacts may be consider legal by the authorities as he may have obtained licenses to trade. Often, in the eighteenth century, a *Practico* was hired by foreign merchant privateers to make contacts on shore and to have goods delivered. In fact, a *Practico* could be defined as a factor or correspondent.
21 Hamm, "Between Acceptance and Exclusion," (2019), p. 128.

on the island were the go-between.[22] As example of the magnitude of smuggling, Sluiter refers to a report from January 1605 when seventeen foreign vessels were noted in the Bay of Gonaives along the north coast of Hispaniola while thirty-four smuggling ships bound for *Tierra Firme* and the Spanish Islands were reported to have sailed from the Dutch Republic in the same year. In 1606, Admiral Juan Valvarez de Aviles fought a battle with thirty-one vessels intent on smuggling off the coast of southeast Cuba and of these twenty-four were Dutch, six were French, and one was English.[23] The Spanish report corroborates the claims made by the Dutch in 1608 that their trade in hides with Cuba and Hispaniola employed twenty vessels of two hundred tons each annually and that the value of the cargo of hides and other commodities was estimated at eight hundred thousand florins. Like in the previous chapter where reports made reference to, "and other merchandise", and the fact that tobacco was considered an illegal trade good it was typically not accounted for in ships freight lists or other public records.

In January 1605, the King had ordered the creation of the *Armada de Barlovento* to combat the onslaught of foreign intruders. The fleet to be created was to consist of ten large and small vessels totaling twenty-three hundred tons of shipping. A year earlier, Governor Antonio Osorio of Hispaniola had been ordered to carry out the depopulation of the north and west coasts of the island but to offer amnesty to all residents affected by the *Cedula* in the spring of 1604. The fate of the Portuguese residents is not clear from the orders given. In August 1604, the city council (*Cabildo*) of Santo Domingo issued a report to the *Audiencia* about on-going smuggling activities which stated that the relocation of the northwest coastal population was unrealistic and that the reason why foreign smugglers frequented the coast was because Spain failed to provide adequate food and supplies and opportunity to trade because of the Seville monopoly that governed trade relationships with the island. The *Cabildo* opposed the forced evacuations for reason that it affected the livelihood of the common inhabitants (*gente comun*) consisting of poor Spanish settlers, Portuguese merchants as well as Mestizo, Mulatto, and residents of African descent who would resist being moved and would flee inland to join others who had fled and they would continue to smuggle goods and coastal ports would, in that case, more likely be occupied by foreigners. A reason given similar to the one authorities had issued for *Tierra Firme*.

---

22 As in the case of *Tierra Firme*, Portuguese was the term used to describe *Converso* and Crypto-Jewish merchants.

23 See, Engel Sluiter,1948, pp. 183–184. See also, I. A. Wright, "The Dutch and Cuba, 1609–1643," in *The Hispanic American Historical Review*, vol. 4, no. 4, November 1921, pp. 597–634.

The *Cabildo* also questioned the wisdom of relocating large herds of cattle that had been the primary source of income for the coastal residents engaged in smuggling but had to be driven to Santo Domingo on the south coast.[24]

Nonetheless, the orders were carried out and 150 soldiers were sent from Puerto Rico to enforce the edict. In August 1605, the governor traveled to the region and read out the Royal Order (*Cedula*) and the evacuation began. Local residents were commanded to trek to the south with their cattle and other goods and almost immediately a revolt broke out which was answered by repressive measures. In the chaos, fires were set to dwellings, churches and convents and cattle were let loose and most of the inhabitants took to the hills or took refuge on board of foreign vessels at Gonaives Bay. Some fled to Cuba and only a small group of residents and cattle moved to settle near Santo Domingo. By the mid-seventeenth century the Spanish settlement and economy on Hispaniola had become extremely unstable and unprofitable and was consequently neglected by the Spanish Crown. Coupled with the fact that gold and silver had been found in Mexico and Peru and that the Spanish Crown was bankrupt, the importance of Hispaniola as the Spanish center of the New World had severely diminished. In 1668, without much opposition from King and Council, the French began their occupation of the western side of Hispaniola of what is now Haiti and in 1697 the Ryswick peace agreement granted territorial rights to the French. Sluiter (1948) concludes: "Spain's deliberate act of 1605, for which the Dutch in no small degree provided the immediate provocation, virtually abandoned the western half of Hispaniola and thus set up the conditions for the thriving of the buccaneers, the entry of the French settlers and flag, and ultimately for the emergence of the linguistically and culturally diverse Black Republic of Haiti."[25]

It is against this background that I will present evidence from the documents Sluiter collected, translated, and annotated for Hispaniola. Sluiter's Historical Documents Collection includes a significant portion of documents which include reference to Portuguese merchants alongside Dutch, French, and English smugglers in pursuit of obtaining hides and tobacco. In addition, the documents present evidence of involvement of Portuguese Jewish merchants engaged in the smuggling trade. The six file folders reviewed for the case study and quoted in the following pages range in time from 1589 to 1605, coinciding more or less with the majority of documents reviewed for *Tierra Firme*.[26]

---

24 Engel Sluiter, 1948, p. 187.
25 Engel Sluiter, 1948, p. 188.
26 ESHDC, Carton 1, Folders 12–17 (see Julie van den Hout's index listing of the documents collection).

The first document in Engel Sluiter's collection with notice of smuggling by Portuguese merchants along the coast of Hispaniola came from a witness testimony in a case involving the capture and confiscation of a Portuguese vessel by an English sea captain. The case occurred in 1586 when a smuggling ring involving Lisbon merchants and London residents were implicated.[27] The case was tried in Mexico in 1589. The persons in question were Pedro Freire, a merchant from Lisbon, and Hector Nuñez, a physician from London.[28] In the case, Antonio Freire de Lima served as witness. As a merchant from Lisbon, he (Antonio Freire de Lima) had been in partnership with the two suspects and had been a factor for Pedro Freire and Hector Nuñez and two other Lisbon merchants (Antonio Brandon and Ambrosio de Tith). In 1586, their vessel set sail for Angola where various goods including slaves had been loaded to be carried to Brazil. According to the testimony, the ship had run into trouble due to foul weather and had been forced to drop anchor off the north coast of Hispaniola. Here, goods were exchanged for 3,290 hides consigned to Pedro Freire and Hector Nuñez with destination Seville. The document refers to *arriba maliciosa*, suggesting smuggling.[29] En route from Hispaniola the vessel was captured by the English and taken to Plymouth where the cargo was confiscated. In order to avoid difficulties with custom officers, Hector Nuñez' name had not been entered on the bill of lading as he was a resident of London according to Melchior de Acosta, the owner of the Portuguese vessel, who was also a witness in the case. The case shows how consignment of goods to foreign merchants within the context of the rules and regulations of Atlantic trade in the late sixteenth century at time of war was problematic.

---

27 See ESHDC, October 11, 1589, Carton 1, Folder 12–1. *Archivo General de la Nación Universidad*.

28 Hector Nuñez was a leader of the crypto-Jewish community in England. A distinguished physician and successful merchant, Nuñez was born in Portugal and arrived in London at around 1550. He was admitted a Fellow of the Royal College of Physicians and of the Royal College of Surgeons in 1554. His large-scale trading activities in the Mediterranean enabled him to provide information for the government, and it was he who brought Sir Francis Walsingham, whose friendship he enjoyed, the first news of the arrival of the Spanish Armada at Lisbon. His wife, was Leonara Freire, who subscribed to the upkeep of the secret synagogue in Antwerp. Obviously, Pedro Reire and Antonio Freire de Lima were related through marriage. *Encyclopedia Judaica*, 2008.

29 Often vessels with intent to smuggle claimed that bad weather or shortage of provisions had forced them to seek shelter offshore where they planned to deliver goods or take cargo onboard.

Apparently, towards the end of the sixteenth century the regular provisioning and supply trade from Spain was in sharp decline and most of the trade was conducted by English, French, and Dutch privateers. In August 1593, a request (*consulta*) was made by the *Consejo de Indias* to the Crown on behalf of the residents of Hispaniola through their procurator (*procurador general*) in Madrid, Melchor Ochoa.[30] As agent of the residents of Hispaniola, Melchor Ochoa asked that private vessels with supplies for Hispaniola be allowed to supply the island in addition to the regular scheduled fleets (*flotillas*) which sailed from Spain on an annual basis. He also asked that one thousand negroes be sent on credit to stimulate the economy in both mining and sugar production. He claimed that sugar mills had been abandoned due to labor shortages. He suggested furthermore, that proper defense be provided and that munitions and powder be sent to Hispaniola since the galleys of the regular fleet had already left. Obviously, the *Consejo* was well aware of the problems associated with the colonial economy and recommended that in order to encourage gold mining in Hispaniola, the *quinto* for gold be cut to five percent for a period of five years.[31] Of great concern expressed in the request made by the *Consejo* was the situation with respect to foreign privateers. Mention is made that a royal edict of 1529, issued by Charles V, had allowed foreigners unlimited access and residential rights in order to sustain the development of the island and that many resident aliens of Hispaniola had taken advantage of the *Cedula* and had ties to the Atlantic trading networks. He (Melchor Ochoa) made the observation that a large proportion of the foreign residents were Portuguese who had lived on the island for a long time and were conducting trade with enemy smugglers. Consequently, the *Consejo* had ordered an investigation and asked for a report to be sent on the conditions on the island. On March 4, 1594, a report was sent from Fray Nicolas Ramos, Archbishop of Santo Domingo to the King.[32] Fray Nicolas Ramos writes to the King with the following (Sluiter translation):

> "Sire: This island is rapidly going to ruin, as at six or seven ports, English and French heretics come regularly and the citizens of those ports and even many of this city (Santo Domingo) trade with them, buy and sell, and often eat meat with them on forbidden days, both parties being in their cups and the heretics mocking the authority of the Pope and ridiculing the sacraments of the Holy Mother Church."

---

30 ESHDC, August 20, 1593–February 15, 1594, Espanola, Santo Domingo, 1575–1594: See Notes Engel Sluiter, Folder 1–12.
31 Note that the products entering Seville from Hispaniola were normally charged 7.5 percent.
32 ESHDC, March 4, 1594, Folder 1–12. It is not sure if the report sent was to conform to the request of the *Consejo*.

He goes on to state that the evil has spread to all parts of the island and that even Catholics buy and sell and smuggle and deal with the heretics. He claims that the *Oidores* in Hispaniola had put several coastal residents in prison who had "corresponded" with the foreign heretics whom they gave food and gifts in order to assure that their ranches and sugar mills would not be burned or ransacked.[33] The Archbishop demands their surrender alleging that they fall under his jurisdiction as abettors, defenders, and receivers of heretics and because of the strong suspicion as to the lack of orthodoxy of the abettors he suggests that the Church prosecutes and excommunicates them. Implied is the suspicion that the coastal population are New Christians and crypto-Jews. He declares himself "Ordinary Inquisitor" and asks the King that if the *Audiencia* disputes his jurisdiction then he, the King, should back him up. He goes on to say: "[…] as to the other smugglers, the previous archbishop here had a *Cedula* from your Majesty stating that he alone was to have jurisdiction in the crime of smuggling with heretics as an inquisition case under which he made judicial inquiries and proceeded to punish." Apparently, with the previous archbishop's death all the papers were lost while the *Audiencia* claims that the *Cedula* applied only to the predecessor. As Fray Nicolas Ramos, the Archbishop in writing of the document states: "[…] It is not desirable that the *Audiencia* have jurisdiction over this business for they give permission for smuggling to those they wish and tolerate others." He seems to be convinced that the commissioners care little about the faith as long as they receive their salary and he suggests that bribery is widespread among the local officials as they buy smuggled goods and sell hides to the heretics. He claims that the situation has gone so far that in some of the ports they accept heretics as godfathers when they baptize their sons. So he begs the King: "Your Majesty, for the love of God, should remedy this for the faith of many Catholics who deal with such heretics must be as thin as a thread of silk […]"

4.3 Bribery and Corruption among Officials and Administrators

On March 22, 1594, Francisco Alonso de Villagra wrote to the King as representative of the Council of the Indies (*Consejo de las Indias*) from Santo Domingo. He had written to the King earlier about the conditions in Hispaniola on November 13, 1593, presumably in reply to the concerns

---

33 An *Oidor* was a judge of the Royal *Audiencias* and *Chancillerías* for the Spanish King. The *oidores* of the overseas *audiencias* functioned not only as judges of the *audiencia*, but also as magistrates overseeing trade disputes and marriage disputes.

expressed by the *Consejo* on August 20, 1593. He introduces himself as a special investigator for the Governor, the *Audiencia* of Santo Domingo, and the Treasury. As a reporter he claims that the body of judges, the *Oidore*, had been engaged in investigations and that disputes had emerged.[34] In the report dated March 22, 1594, he states that there were abuses in the office of the *Regidor* at Santo Domingo and that some members were corrupt and engaged in suspicious behavior as merchants and not as true representatives of the islands. In that context he is referring to the Archbishop who had had a dispute with the *Audiencia* concerning the handling of an English corsair, Captain Langton, who had been smuggling and robbing in La Samana and Punta de Cayzedo and was still lingering off-shore with two vessels and two sloops. In fact, as he states, the corsairs were a continual menace and that unless the King were prepared to send a pair of galleys to clear the coast of corsairs and burn three or four sugar mills where the enemies get fresh meat, cassava, sugar and other provisions, the problem will not be solved. He intimates about the dispute that emerged with the Archbishop and says at the end: "Being on the point of closing this letter there occurred a dispute of jurisdiction between the Archbishop and the *Audiencia* owing to the English corsair," and acknowledges that many citizens of Santo Domingo have become implicated and have smuggled with the enemy and that regular communication between the parties on shore and aboard ships have occurred. He is obviously aware of the letter the Archbishop sent to the King about inquisitorial jurisdiction but states that the *Audiencia* has been opposed to the measures proposed by the Archbishop.

Some of the accused of smuggling with the enemy heretics had fled for refuge to the *Audiencia* and the Archbishop had threatened excommunication for those involved in offering protection. Upon further investigation it turned out that some members of the investigation team and the judges (*Oidores*) were implicated in collaborating with the smugglers. Alonso de Villagra ends with stating that: "[...] the judges that had been sent out over the island to check the smugglers have themselves eaten with them and returned rich, presumably through bribes, and, in the end the smuggling continues and the guilty remain unpunished." In response to the requests made by *Consulta* in February 1594, Hispaniola had received permission to charge favorable custom rates for import and export for five years but were also reprimanded for smuggling. In all, foreign privateers formed a threat to the island and coastal populations were implicated in collaborating with the enemy

---

34 ESHDC, March 22, 1594, Folder 1–12. Lic. Francisco Alonso de Villagra to the King in his Council of the Indies. AGI, Santo Domingo. Members of the *Oidore* include Simon de Meneses and Pedro Diaz de Villar. A third member, Villafane had been dismissed but was reinstated in January, 1594.

merchants. He states that half of the population of Hispaniola is Portuguese and are rooted in the coastal communities by which they are implicated as the culprits.[35] In May, 1594, the *Consejo*, having received the King's reply makes the recommendation that the Inquisition should be established at Santo Domingo which, in actual fact, never happened. Acknowledging the problems of smuggling the *Consejo* expressed the opinion that the Cardinal of Toledo as *Inquisitor General*, should give inquisitorial power to the Archbishop of Santo Domingo and his successors to move against the smugglers and the Portuguese by means of the Inquisition.[36]

From September 1594 until March 1595, Miguel Aleman de Ayala, Royal, Public, and Municipal Notary in Santo Domingo and clerk of Dr. Simon de Meneses, *Oidor* of the *La Comisión de Rescates* (commission to investigate smuggling) is charged with the prosecution of those guilty of smuggling with the corsairs. In the commission statement (September 23, 1594) Aleman de Ayala, the clerk, summarizes the smuggling investigation and states that foreign merchants trade slaves and linen for gold, silver, and other goods from the island. Meneses had ascertained that during the previous years over 350 slaves had been smuggled, a claim in which Captain Alonso de Caceres Carabajal and Baltasar de Monesterio, among other residents from the island, were implicated. In exchange for slaves, hides were traded. In a note mention is made of Simon de Herrera referred to earlier, as one of the suspects.[37] The report is followed by a list of 278 persons in Hispaniola who were implicated or accused of whom 67 were being tried for smuggling with the enemy.[38] The *Oidor* of the case, Dr. Simon de Meneses summarizes the circumstances under which the events unfolded.[39]

From orders issued by Simon de Meneses in October 1595, it is clear that Hispaniola had become a major slave distribution center for the Western Caribbean where slaves were smuggled from overseas to the north coast and then taken under false papers to Santo Domingo for shipment to Cartagena and other port cities. Meneses orders to proclaim publicly that no person whatever his position may export slaves from Hispaniola to other locations without clearance or license from him, the *Oido*, on penalty of 500 ducats.

---

35 ESHDC, March 30, 1594, AGI, Seville, Santo Domingo 1. Recommendations (*consulta*) of the Council of the Indies to the King, Folder 1–12. Notes Engel Sluiter.
36 ESHDC, May 12, 1594, Folder 1–12, *Consejo* to King.
37 ESHDC, September 23, 1594 to March 4, 1595, AGI, Santa Domingo 51.
38 See ESHDC, April 8, 1595, AGI, Sevilla, Santo Domingo 51, Carton 1, Folder 1–13.
39 ESHDC, April 8, 1595, AGI, Sevilla, Santa Domingo 51, Carton 1, Folder 1–13. Simon Herrera was named on the list of suspects prosecuted for smuggling and convicted and punished for their crimes. See Engel Sluiter *Notes* summarizing events from September 24, 1594–April 8, 1595. The list with names is attached to the document.

With respect to other smuggled goods like linen cloth, sailcloth, woolens, and silks, he orders that no one can sell these goods unless they carry a seal with the royal arms and that shopkeepers are not allowed to mix smuggled goods with Spanish merchandise and will have to record all goods, the name of the buyer of the goods, the amount and kind of goods sold, and the date when sold. In January 1595, he proclaims that any person denouncing smuggled goods is to receive twenty percent of the value of what he denounces and that African slaves, when they denounce, will be given freedom and that the person denounced will be forced to pay the price of his freedom. In April of 1595, witnesses were heard with regard to the honesty and effectiveness of Dr. de Meneses as *Oidor* or special investigator and prosecutor of the *La Comisión de Rescate* at which time it was said that two-thirds of all the inhabitants of the island were implicated in smuggling. Witnesses, including Dr. Pedro Dias de Rivera, Dean of the Cathedral and bishop-elect of the city of Panama, testified that de Meneses had conducted a thorough investigation.[40]

In May 1595, the *Audiencia* of Santo Domingo reported to the King after royal orders were given to punish smugglers and to supervise owners of ships *arribadas*. The instructions included an order to investigate the *Audiencia*.[41] Obviously, members of the *Audiencia* were implicated in smuggling activities. The reply from the *Audiencia*, which included Dr. Simon de Meneses, was swift. The members of the Audiencia were greatly offended and stated:

"[...] This island, as we have innumerable times written to your Majesty, is in the final stage of poverty, misery, and need because it has suffered, and daily suffers, such ruinous sackings, losses, storms, hurricanes, and other misfortunes [...]" The *Audiencia* goes on to claim that they have condemned all ships *arribados* according to the law and if *arribados* were deliberate, if unavoidable and accidental, the ships were allowed to stay after paying the royal duties and posting a bond to show up with ship and crew before the *Casa de Contratacion*. Of most concern, as expressed, was the shortage of supplies of grain, wine and cooking oil as the population was in great need, and, unless these supplies were provided by the Spanish flotilla, they would be smuggled in. As to accidental circumstances as occurred en route to Brazil with provisions or with slaves, it made no sense to drive them off or force them to return to Spain or Portugal, they stated. Besides, as the *Audiencia* claimed, corsairs would easily take stranded cargo and thus it would be better to

---

40 ESHDC, April 13, 1595, AGI, Santa Domingo 51.
41 ESHDC, May 1, 1595, AGI Santa Domingo 51, *Audiencia* of Santo Domingo to the King, May 2, 1595.

collect the royal duties on such cargoes. Furthermore, as they expressed: "[…] for to think that the ships which come directly to the island with the fleets will suffice to support the land is a patent fallacy, […]" In fact, only two ships with supplies come to the island annually, if at all!

In August 1595, a new *Oidor*, Dr. Quesada, arrived at Hispaniola (to replace Dr. de Meneses?), and in October 1595 the president of the *Audiencia* of Santo Domingo, Lope de Vega Portocarrero, writes (Sluiter translation):[42]

"[…] it is going on six months that this city has been blockaded daily by the English and no ship can enter or leave, […] fifteen days ago, a ship en route to New Spain with 31 Augustinian friars for the Philippines arrived in sight of this port which ship was captured by an English *Pinnace* which is continually waiting outside this port […] the friars and sailors abandoned ship and fled ashore, […] she carried wines and other provision which have supplied the Englishmen."

The report makes further notice that ninety percent of the citizens of the island have smuggled and brought in ship *arribados* and if the laws of the Indies are to be executed against them, this island will be depopulated. The population from the north coast had fled to the mountains at this time to escape the "judge of smuggling," the *Oidor*, but smuggling had not stopped and the *Audiencia* claimed that only galleys from the Armada would be effective in stopping the smuggling. The treasury had dried up since no custom duties were collected from ships *arribados* and thus officials and judges of the *Audiencia* would not be paid.[43]

In October 1597 a special investigator-judge (*Oidor*) was appointed and sent to Hispaniola, Puerto Rico, Jamaica, and Cuba.[44] He, *Licendiado*

---

42 ESHDC, October 22, 1595, AGI Santa Domingo 51, Lope de Vega Portocarrero, President of *Audiencia* to the Crown.
43 Lope de Vega Portocarrero acknowledges receipt of two royal warnings that an English fleet is coming (i.e. Drake and Hawkins) and he says that he has done everything to help defend the port including laying an iron chain stretched across the entrance to the harbor.
44 See ESHDC, September 10, 1597, AGI, Santo Domingo. Notes Engel Sluiter. Varela arrived at Ocoa on March 27, 1595 and he carried a commission for 17 months during which time he sentenced smugglers and their henchmen but meanwhile, smuggling continued unabated and often insults and attacks on the investigator-judge were perpetrated by the resident population and ranchers who depended on income from smuggling activities. See for reports, ESHDC, November 20, 1598, Bancroft Library, F1911, R6, v. 2, 160–188.

Hernando Varela, presents testimonies of witnesses and reports on arrests made of smugglers and collaborators. Many of the smuggling activities take place between the town of Monte Christi and Manzanilla Bay, including the smuggling of tobacco. Implicated in the case are Francisco Jimenez, Cristobal Perez, his brother, and Antonio Lopez, his brother-in-law; ranchers and residents of Monte Christi, Bayaha, and several of their slaves, Mulattos and citizens of la Vega who collect cattle hides, ginger, and tobacco but also gold, silver and pearls is being carried as cargo to French ships anchored at the bay. The witness in the case states that any and all smuggling transactions are channeled through Jimenez, Perez, and Lopez. The witness also states that (Sluiter translation):

> "[...] during the last six years ships come and go throughout the year usually to said Morre of Monte Christi and Porto Manzanillas, one loading and another unloading, and ordinarily there are four, six, or eight ships, and at present there are six ships, four French, one Dutch, and one English, which Englishman, the witness knows and saw, enter the port of Bayaha and take the ship of Antonio Hernandez which was loaded with goods for Spain." This witness report goes on to say that ordinarily pack trains come and go and everything thus smuggled is brought to Santo Domingo for sale. Also, products of the land are loaded and transported from the towns of La Yaguana to Puerto de Plata and to the north coast ports on to Dutch, English and French ships for transport to Europe. Fransicso Jimenez, Christobal Perez, and Antonio Lopez and other *tangomangos* (slave dealers) from Monte Christi give the foreigners orders for the goods they want from Europe on the return voyage. The witness says that since there was a shortage of wine, a recently arrived vessel had delivered this commodity and that the ship was Dutch. Rumors had it that the wine was loaded at the Canary islands and that it too was contraband. He names several more people from Monte Christi implicated in the smuggling ring, including Diego Jimenez de Mesa, the sheriff and mayor of the town, who had been imprisoned. Several people were reportedly arrested for corruption and bribery and had bought their protection from Diego Jimenez de Mesa in order to be able to smuggle. One witness tells the story how the bailiff of Varely arrived, captured, and had arrested two negroes who were carrying hides to the ships for anchor at Manzanillo Bay and how, when a few days later Francisco Jimenez arrived, a fight had broken out, and Jimenez and his men were captured and imprisoned but not until he had ordered other townsmen to escape to the mountains.

4.4 Depopulation and Evacuation Ordered and Dismissed

In 1598, the first proposals were presented to depopulate the northern regions of Hispaniola.[45] The case is presented by Baltazar Lopez de Castro, *Escribano de Camara de la Cancillería* from Santo Domingo, who states that (Sluiter translation):

> "[…] the cause of this miserable situation is that a large part of the citizens for more than seventy years have smuggled and smuggle in some of the north coast port with foreigners, with Portuguese, who were the first to introduce this diabolic trade with Frenchmen, Dutchmen, and Englishmen, who all or almost all are Lutheran heretics, who carry annually to their home countries 80,000 cattle hides and up […] plus gold, silver, pearls, sugar, ginger, lapis lazuli, pepper, tobacco, guayacan wood, and other things to be found in the island, which in all are worth in Spain over 600,000 ducats."

He goes on to say that the foreigners rob the ships they meet on the coast of Spain, in the Canaries, Brazil, and elsewhere in the Atlantic, and they seize slaves from vessels they encounter which they then carry to the Spanish colonies to sell.

Implied in the transactions are Portuguese merchants who reside on the islands and coordinate efforts to smuggle with the foreigners who come onshore to trade. As Lopez de Castro notes, the smuggling activities have become so all consuming that no other productive activity is taking place in the north coast region where the mining of gold, silver, and copper was previously the major source of income and where ranches and plantations produced goods for the home market and other Spanish territories. But, since piracy and smuggling had become too prevalent, more profit is made from selling contraband import products and export of hides, tobacco, and other products from the land. Furthermore, contraband trade between the islands was becoming a very profitable enterprise. In the report the contraband traders are referred to as *coloniales* implying that they have become or are well established on the island. Reputedly, as *coloniales* dispatch goods from the island through bribing officials and agents of the royal administration and thus all enrich themselves, Santo Domingo conducts very little official trade and *Licenciado* Hernando has fallen into shortage of revenue

---

45 ESHDC, November 20, 1598, Two memorials on how to stop smuggling and suggestion to depopulate the north. Bancroft library, F1911m R6, vol. 2, 160–188. Notes Engel Sluiter, Carton 1, Folder 1–15.

to sustain the administration and defend the island. After Varela left, Dr. Morquecho and Martin Gonzalez, his Notary, prosecuted the smugglers and those among the *coloniales* implicated in smuggling activities but, from time to time, the *Oidore* were pursued and captured by the smuggling bands.[46]

Lopez de Castro, *Escribano de Camara*, who wrote the report, also writes the recommendation to depopulate the north coast and writes (Sluiter translation):

> "[...] These smugglers claim that they cannot live in said island without smuggling because they lack the major part of the things they need for sustaining life, and that it is legitimate that they try to get them, without considering that this is a grave error, for without the smuggling they could live, although not with such luxury as the pirates provide them."

He continues with the suggestion that since the area around Santo Domingo is mostly vacant, there would be room to herd and tame cattle which now mostly roam along the north coast or in the interior of the island where the smuggling occurs, and as he observes that the chief aim that forces foreigners to come to the north coast of Hispaniola is to collect the cattle hides and other goods. So, by taking away the possibility of smuggling and removing the population, the goal would be achieved.

He then recommends that all the inland cattle ranchers and first those that are known smugglers, bring their cattle to the vacant lands near Santo Domingo and that in those designated for them, "[...] graze and grow, establishing living huts, roundups, branding establishments, and corrals, foremen and cowboys they need from the slaves according to the cattle and capital each has [...]" and then, for a period considered proper, "[...] they are not to take away their slaves and servants from the said ranches, on penalty of confiscation, for it may be that even though they have moved their herds to said sites, they might take their cowboys to use them where they formerly had cattle and there to join with other cowboys either their own or belonging to others, and through the chase of wild cattle get the hides for smuggling, [...]." In other words, as cattle and cowboys are mobile, they can easily move back to the north coast and continue their smuggling activities. In his report of recommendations, he, Lopez de Castro, realizes that not all problems of goods smuggling can be solved by simply designating lands for cattle raising near Santo Domingo. Because the other products of the land including ginger, guayacan wood, sugar, and tobacco, along with gold, silver, pearls and piedra azul will still be available in other parts of the island. Thus,

---

46 See ESHDC, November 20, 1598, Notes Engel Sluiter, Carton 1, Folder 1–15.

the measures recommended will not be sufficient but since the smuggling of hides is the primary reason why the corsairs operate along the north coast, the rest of the contraband can be controlled, he believes, by supervising the cultivation and sale of the products in the market of Santo Domingo and by licensing and issuing certificates to those who are legally registered to sell ginger, guayacan wood, as well as pepper (pimienta) and tobacco. And, all the shops and markets where cloth, slaves and other goods for sale are kept and sold must be inspected for licenses and certificates.

Along with the first recommendation, Baltazar Lopez de Castro issues a second recommendation in which he expresses that he is well aware that the coastal residents and the refugee population of the interior may rebel and that the men in charge of defense may not be able to put down a revolt or riot. These circumstances would have several consequences not the least being a situation where the foreign pirates would land and occupy the north coast and together with the revolting population (the *Coloniales*, Creoles, Mulattos, and run-away slaves) would seize control. Or, that depravity may turn the local population, in due time, into smugglers again and, as outposts to the Crown in the coastal region may not receive the support and defense needed to control the situation that may occur, and thus, the areas would still be lost to Spain and benefit the foreign powers (i.e. Lutheran heretics). He therefore recommends that the town of Puerto de Plata, with thirty residents, the port of Bayaja with sixty residents and the town of La Yaguana with eighty residents be demolished and the population be removed and relocated to two settlements near Santo Domingo. Here, the new residents could be employed in mining, agriculture, and stock raising and all the products could be shipped through Santo Domingo to Spain or neighboring islands.

In August, 1603, a *Cedula* is issued by the King in which he recognizes the measures taken to combat smuggling but, acknowledging the hardships and punishments that had followed, he calls for kindness and clemency so that the removal and resettlement ordered would be more easily and more fully carried out and expecting that there will be improvement and that illicit trade will be stopped, and that those who for fear of punishment moved to the interior will return to their homes and plantations and will cultivate and settle down peacefully.[47] Several other *cedulas* are issued at this time instructing the Governor of Santo Domingo (Antonio Osorio?) to carry out the removal of the three settlements and to relocate the population and herding the cattle to their new settlements and grazing grounds near Santo Domingo. The Archbishop

---

47 See ESHDC, August 6, 1603, Bancroft Library, F1911, R.6, vol. 2; Notes Engel Sluiter. Carton 1, Folder 1–15.

is informed about the decision and told to see to it that the matter is carried out with dispatch and equity necessary and with the order to pardon those implicated in smuggling if indeed they move to their assigned new locations and that in case they do not move with their houses and goods to the new sites they will not enjoy the pardon. The Archbishop is instructed to pursue the order "[...] with great suavity and convenience for all."

On August 24, 1604, Lic. Nunez de Toledo (*Oidor* of *Audiencia* of Santo Domingo?) writes to the King (Sluiter translation):[48]

> "[...] The removal of the settlements of the north coast of this island to the vicinity of this city appears to me to be a deed worthy of the zeal, although it will be difficult to execute, for the majority of the smugglers of those and other places are vagrants whom the merchants of this city encourage and aid, buying merchandise they smuggle with no little secrecy and much profit by selling them mixed in with those they receive from Spain so that it is impossible to prove, making a profit of 200 percent whereby the merchants become rich and the smugglers are further encouraged to be smugglers."

From the letter it is also clear that the order had not been carried out or completed yet as he acknowledges that the order of the decision to do so and to execute it had been received.

In August, 1604, the *Cabildo* of Santo Domingo presented a position on the obstacles in carrying out the plan to evacuate on behalf of Don Francisco Pimentel the *Alcalde Ordinario* and Baltzar de Sepulveda, citizen and *Regidor* of the city.[49] In the position statement the *Cabildo* acknowledges receipt of *the Cedula* addressed to Antonio Osorio, President of the *Audiencia* of Santo Domingo, dated August 6, 1603, to demolish three coastal towns and resettle the population but the objection is clear and the members of the *Cabildo* representing the citizens of Santo Domingo state: "[...] in order that the King may know the disadvantages that could result from this, we present this memorial, so that, seen, the King may order what is best for his service [...]." They advance all the same reasons already expressed in previous communications and some more which include concern about survival of the cattle herd to be moved and

---

48 See ESHDC, August 24, 1604, Lic. Nunez de Toledo to the King, Santo Domingo. See Notes Engel Sluiter. Carton 1, Folder 1–15.
49 See ESHDC, August 25, 1604, see "Memorial" *Cabildo* of Santo Domingo, (published by E. Rodriguez Demorizi (ed.), Relaciones historicas de Santo Domingo, vol. II, Ciudad Trujillo, 1945), Bancroft Library, F1911, R.6, v. II. with Translation/Notes Engel Sluiter.

the likelihood that many cattle will stay behind and still be smuggled for their hides. The main concern in the document is about the inhabitants of the island's northern regions and the "common people", Mestizos, Mulattoes, and free or run-away slaves, who cannot afford to relocate and are not inclined to do so and given that they have little property will likely stay behind or move to the interior from where they will continue to smuggle in which case foreigners will likely occupy the abandoned ports. *Cabildo* suggests that the remedy of depopulating the north be given up and that a new approach be taken to rid the island of smuggling which include more frequent delivery of goods from Spain in return for goods from the island to be shipped to Spain on a regular basis. Also, they recommend to increase the number of galleys guarding the north coast, and to allow the chief residents to only trade and reside in Santo Domingo and that vagabonds be exiled from the island. The *Cabildo* still supports depopulating Monte Christi but recommends building up and fortifying Puerto de Plata and imposing very heavy penalties on smugglers.

On December 9, 1604, Antonio Osorio, President of the *Audiencia*, acknowledged that he had received a petition from the *Cabildo* of the town of Monte Cristi in which they asked to be given a six month reprieve from executing the order of removal. In the request they mention that there is no plan to cover the expenses of the removal order and that therefore the execution should be delayed until January 1605.[50] On December 15, 1604, from a letter Antonio Osorio sends to the King, we learn that the greatest impediment to carrying out the orders of removal and resettlement is the poverty of the population consisting of vagabonds (as referred to) who rather take refuge in the interior than resettle on the south coast. In the meantime, word has come that the Dutch and the English threaten to conquer Cuba. Osorio asks for extra defense of the island and states that he has appointed a captain with commission to raise a company of men to carry out the orders to resettle the population. He ends by confirming that Lic. Francisco Manso de Contreras will execute the royal orders and Baltazar Lopez de Castro, a Creole and native of the land, will accompany and assist him.[51] From a dispatch (*Consulta*) sent by *Consejo de Indias* to the King in March 1605, it is clear that there is great opposition to the measures taken to depopulate and resettle the coastal residents of Hispaniola as almost all the inhabitants had been implicated in smuggling activities.[52] Osorio had suggested that to carry out the plan the Spanish fleet should pass by the north coast and drop off two companies of select troops who would disembark and stay on the island

---

50 See ESHDC, December 9, 1604, AGI, Santo Domingo, 52.
51 See ESHDC, December 15, 1604, AGI, Santo Domingo, 52.
52 See ESHDC, March 10, 1605, Bancroft Library, F1911, R6, vol. 2.

4.5 Portuguese Resident Merchants and the "Nation"

On August 23, 1605, a report was made of an inspection of a vessel – a *patache* named *El Don de Dios* – arriving at Santo Domingo with the flotilla from Spain but without a license to trade and with Portuguese sailors on board who originated from the Dutch Republic and from London. The captain was a native of London named Francisco Pere Granilla, and had been sent to Spain by the President of the *Audiencia* of Santo Domingo but was refused license by the registry.[53] Upon inspection it was discovered that several of the mariners on board were foreigners and some were related to each other. The *Audiencia* and the *Oficiales Reales* (Spanish officials) ordered the vessel to continue her voyage despite protests from customs officials. From the report it is clear that Spanish officials in Hispaniola were in cahoots with smugglers and covered each other by allowing the vessel to proceed although recommendation was made that bond should be posted.[54] The list of passengers and crew was as follows:

Sailors (or mariner-merchants):
Francisco Lopes, boatswain (*contramaestre*), native of Lisbon[55]
Miguel Geronimo Rosado, sailor, native of Sevilla
Domingo de Guzeta, sailor, native of San Sebastian in NW Spain
Francisco Jimenez, carpenter, native of Carmona near Sevilla[56]
Bernaldo Ybanes, sailor, assistant to the pilot, native of London[57]
Tomas Ybanes, sailor, native of London
Esteban de Xibeas, sailor, native of Sluis, Zeeland, the Dutch Republic
Cosme Abalsamo, sailor, native of .....
12 Deckhands (Duarte, Portuguese, and others Spanish)
36 Passengers (Spanish?)

---

53 Genealogical records suggest that Francisco Pérez Granillo was baptized 19 April 1587, in Nuestra Señora de las Nieves, Nueva Galicia.
54 The fiscal officials state that they doubt if indeed a bond was posted! Deposition was taken of Francisco Pere Granillo and master Juan Francisco who were later imprisoned in Santo Domingo. The captain and master claimed that the patache was attached to the flotilla and that the cargo and passengers were registered on another ship. The patache carried 450 bottles of wine along with pitch and tackle. Was the cargo (wine) taken on board at the Canary islands?
55 Related to Antonio Lopez, referred to earlier in the text?
56 Same as Francisco Jimenez referred to earlier in the text?
57 Don Philepe Ybanes was a well-known English privateer: see *Privateering and Piracy in the Colonial Period: Illustrative Documents* (edited by John Franklin Jameson), p. 565.

The foreign sailors aboard include mariners from Zeeland, in the Dutch Republic, and from London from where many privateer merchants operated. The boatswain/counter master, Francisco Lopes was Portuguese and born in Lisbon according to the report. Along with Francisco Jiminez, listed as carpenter on board, he appears to be akin to a Portuguese resident merchant ashore engaged in tobacco smuggling. The two names are either the same or related to the suspects referred to. The cargo on board including 450 bottles of wine may have originated in the Canary islands from where frequent passages were made to the Spanish Caribbean. This example suggests that many parties were involved in smuggling activities and that officials and administrators of the Spanish Crown were engaged and likely profited from the illegal activities. The link to Portuguese mariners in London and the province of Zeeland in the Dutch Republic suggests that New Christian and Portuguese Jewish merchants were actively involved in the smuggling ring.

In addition, in August 1605, 47 more island residents are found guilty of smuggling in Hispaniola which list includes several known Portuguese merchants along with Mulattoes and slaves and run-aways.[58] It is evident that smuggling is ongoing and according to the records punishment was harsh. Simon de Herrera, the merchant found smuggling in 1595, is named in a document dated 1608 after he was caught and tried by the Inquisition in Mexico and put to death.[59] The document makes reference to the fact that Simon de Herrera had been a resident of the Canary Island and had been apprehended together with Manual Cardozo and Juan de Riberos who had also been apprehended for possession of multiple passports and having associations with both English and Dutch merchants and smugglers. As referred to earlier, they were captured in Hispaniola in 1596 and among Simon de Herrera's confiscated documents were account books, bills of lading, and letters which implicated him with foreign commercial interest.[60] He was taken to the Inquisition in Mexico for trial and executed in 1604 after it became known that he had tried to sell his vessel which routinely sailed from Santo Domingo to Castile to the enemy and then applied for safe passage to take him to Holland or Zeeland in the Dutch Republic. In 1608, Antonio Osorio, then President of the *Audiencia*, wrote:[61]

---

58 See ESHDC, 26 August, 1605, AGI Sevilla, Santo Domingo 52, Carton 1, Folder 1–17.
59 See ESHDC, 1608, Carton 1, Folder 1–17, AGI, Santo Domingo, 52, Antonio Osorio, President *Audiencia* to King, January 1608.
60 See Engel Sluiter (1948), p. 174.
61 See ESHDC, 1608, Carton 1, Folder 1–17, AGI, Santo Domingo, 52, Antonio Osorio, President *Audiencia* to King, January 1608.

"[...] Having in this *Audiencia* prosecuted Simon de Herrera, a Portuguese, for having sold a ship called *La Pava*, which left this port for Castile, to enemies, and because he had set for a safe conduct in order to go to Holland and Zeeland, and having it brought to him from Count Maurice (the Dutch Republic) and the Queen of England, and for other atrocious crimes, on July 6, 1604, he was condemned in this *Audiencia* to die by hanging and confiscation of goods, which sentence was confirmed after review on December 24, 1604, and on January 8, 1605, the sentence was carried out, of which hereby report is made to your Majesty as per *cedula* of March 4, 1607."

4.6 Summary and Conclusion

In this chapter I have explored some common themes related to the contraband trade in the early seventeenth century in the Caribbean region facilitated by resident Portuguese merchants engaged in trade with English, French, and Dutch mariners and merchants in which, by implication, Portuguese Jewish merchants participated. In both the case of *Tierra Firme* and Hispaniola, the onset of trade obstruction due to the blockades and embargoes imposed during the Eighty Years' War in effect in the mid 1590s, were the start of ongoing smuggling during the early seventeenth century. In the case of *Tierra Firme* salt mining at Punta de Araya was the main objective, in Hispaniola obtaining hides was a major incentive. In both cases tobacco was smuggled as well and in due time took on a more important role. Also, in both instances, the Spanish authorities took drastic measures to undermine the efforts made by Dutch and other foreign merchants and mariners.

Tierra Firme and Hispaniola were the first source regions in Spanish America where large scale tobacco smuggling occurred. Both were sparsely populated and on the periphery of the Spanish Empire. In both instances Amerindians present played a role initiating exchange but in due time Portuguese or crypto-Jewish resident merchants became the main go-between. Dutch as well as English and French mariners exchanged goods freely and conducted trade and barter with local coastal populations. From around 1595, Holland and Zeeland merchants and mariners made regular voyages to *Tierra Firme* and Hispaniola and from Sluiter's Historical Documents Collection we gain some insight into what extent tobacco was smuggled and what role Portuguese merchants played. In fact, from the documents analyzed we can draw some preliminary conclusions.

Whereas Dutch salt mining appeared to be the main reason why the Dutch were drawn to *Tierra Firme*, tobacco smuggling occurred alongside at Punta de Araya and Cumana and at Indian settlements at the mouth of the Orinoco

River. A similar situation occurred at La Margarita Island where pearl fishing took place and where Dutch mariners raided or bartered for pearls in return for cloth, ironware, and implements. In many instances where exchange occurred, Portuguese merchants were implicated and served as go-between. In the case of Hispaniola, access to cow hides for leather supply available for barter along the northwestern coast of the island was the main objective at the beginning, but due to circumstances and as a result of the extension of trans-Atlantic trading networks that developed, slaves and tobacco replaced hides in due time. In fact, in the course of the seventeenth century, tobacco replaced sugar as the major staple crop traded on the island of Hispaniola.

As noted and from evidence presented in the Engel Sluiter Historical Documents Collection, Portuguese merchants were the main culprit in illegal trade which suggests a link to Amsterdam's Sephardic merchant community with respect to trade and distribution along the Atlantic seaboard as Amsterdam became the main staple port for tobacco. Sephardic merchants formed part of the Portuguese Atlantic trading network known as the Portuguese Nation or the *Nação* and the various contacts across the "Ocean Sea" were instrumental in the development of the contraband trade and Amsterdam's tobacco history.[62] Hispaniola had a significant Portuguese merchant presence and many of them seemed to have been involved in smuggling activities. In the case of Hispaniola, Sluiter's collection revealed the connection between Portuguese and Jewish merchants and mariners from Holland and Zeeland. For Hispaniola we do know that Portuguese Jewish resident merchants were involved in smuggling with the Dutch Republic as the case of Simon de Herrera demonstrates. In both *Tierra Firme* and Hispaniola the Spanish decided to depopulate the coastal areas where tobacco smuggling occurred and to resettle coastal residents to areas where supervision was attainable. In both cases Portuguese merchants were implicated in smuggling activities and in both instances tobacco cultivation and trade were the culprit.

The main concern on the part of Spanish colonial administrators in the coastal and island territories were the threats posed by smugglers and corsairs with specific mention of mariners and merchants from the Dutch Republic with whom the Spanish were at war. In their efforts to raid and smuggle, Dutch mariners made contact with local populations including different Indian tribes, Creoles and run-away African slaves, and Portuguese New Christians. Quite often these contacts took place in rather remote locations away from the main ports the Spanish galleons frequented on their annual voyages.

---

62 The term "Ocean Sea" is borrowed from Studnicki-Gizbert, *A Nation Upon the Ocean Sea* (2007).

The smuggling trade with Portuguese or New Christian merchants included the slave trade. Frequently report was made of Dutch vessels lying at anchor delivering provisions or slaves or awaiting cargo to be loaded. Sometimes when ships were captured and hauled into port, a list of mariners, merchants, smugglers, port of origin, and voyage details were recorded and we thus occasionally find out the specifics of the merchant networks and the products exchanged. Concern about the frequency and extent of tobacco smuggling is often referred to in the reports sent to King and Council in Spain and resulted in plans to prohibit tobacco cultivation or to only allow cultivation with royal permission or, to offer a guaranteed set price for tobacco to the planters in order to motivate them to operate through the official licensed channels. The latter strategy was often suggested after Spanish officials in the territories expressed concerns about depopulation of specific areas as depopulation and evacuation could lead to severe hardship and unrest which would have a direct impact on economic prospects of the region and income for the Crown. In both the reports sent from *Tierra Firme* and Hispaniola we find evidence of these concerns and strategies.

Chapter 5

CONCLUSION

5.1 Introduction

In the last section of his 1948 article "Dutch-Spanish Rivalry in the Caribbean," Sluiter concludes that the policies implemented in 1606 by the Spanish Crown to inundate the Araya salt pans, to prohibit tobacco cultivation along the coast of *Tierra Firme*, and to depopulate coastal areas and relocate residents of Northwestern Hispaniola, were meant to choke-off the smuggling going on in their territories.[1] The documents analyzed in the previous two chapters illustrate the process by which this took place. In both *Tierra Firme* and on Hispaniola, Portuguese residents were key to the contraband trade with Dutch merchants who sailed along the coasts and up the rivers in *Tierra Firme* and along the shores of Hispaniola to drop anchor and to take tobacco on-board in exchange for cloth or woolen and silk goods, implements, and arms in high demand among coastal populations. From the documents presented we learn that among the crew on Dutch vessels were Portuguese merchants or pilots likely related to or linked in trade with Portuguese resident merchants on shore. In a *Cedula* issued by the Crown on October 28, 1606, the expulsion of all Dutch and Flemings was ordered in *Tierra Firme* and in the case of Hispaniola 10 merchants from the Dutch Republic were being rounded up.[2] On November 10, 1607, the Council of the Indies recommended and the King approved that a branch of the Holy Office be erected in Hispaniola which suggests that the Portuguese were suspected of Judaizing.[3] Sluiter (1948) does recognize that in the meantime the first negotiations for a truce between the Spanish and the Dutch had

---

1 Engel Sluiter, "Dutch-Spanish Rivalry in the Caribbean Area, 1594–1609," *The Hispanic American Historical Review*, vol. 28, no. 2, May 1948, pp. 165–196; pp, 193–196.
2 Antonio de Osorio to the King, *Audiencia* Santo Domingo, Santo Domingo, November 28, 1607. Referenced by Engel Sluiter (1948), p. 194, footnote 106.
3 Council of the Indies to the King, *Audiencia* Santo Domingo, Madrid, November 10, 1607. A year later Cartagena was designated as the new seat of the Holy Office. Referenced by Engel Sluiter (1948), p. 195, footnote 110.

begun and that ports of the Iberian Peninsula would open again for Dutch trade to resume which would take away the incentive to haul salt or tobacco, pearls, and hides from the Caribbean. So, the stick and the carrot approach was applied, apparently, but it did not end the contraband tobacco trade.

In fact, the ban on tobacco cultivation and relocation of coastal populations encouraged tobacco smuggling and invited mariners and merchants to come on shore and bribe officials and both the Dutch and English mariners continued to trade, raid, or barter.[4] As we saw from documents collected for *Tierra Firme*, Amerindians in the Province of Cumana were in revolt after the ban on tobacco cultivation was issued while in Trinidad tobacco was still grown and traded and cloth was exchanged in large quantities, and "[...] never foreign ships were lacking."[5] Here Fernando de Berrio, the Governor of Trinidad and Guyana, was the culprit and was given certain privileges to allow the tobacco trade with English and Dutch merchants to proceed.[6] Meanwhile, thousands of Amerindians were removed and resettled further inland where they were forced to work on tobacco plantations against the orders of the Crown. Obviously, these were contradictory and controversial matters and, reputedly, Spanish officials in charge of carrying out the *Cedulas* issued by the King were also engaged in smuggling activities. Widespread bribery was reported in Trinidad and Guyana and on Hispaniola, and officials argued that the situation needed to be corrected because otherwise the measures taken in Cumana and Santo Domingo would serve no purpose and would only lead to economic decline and revolt. In 1610, a report was sent from Santo Domingo which proclaimed that unless permission to trade is restored the economy will go into a deep decline.[7] In 1611, a Royal Order was issued to make a court inquiry of Don Fernando de Berrio and his ministers and other officials of state and to investigate the smuggling charges and punish the culprits. De Berrio alleged that, although he had engaged in smuggling, he had done

---

4 Joyce Lorimer, "The English Contraband Tobacco Trade in Trinidad and Guiana, 1590–1617," in K. R. Andrews et.al., *The Westward Enterprise: English Activities in Ireland, the Atlantic, and America, 1480–1650* (Wayne State University Press, Detroit, 1979).

5 Reference from ESHDC quoted in Chapter 3.

6 In 1611, a Royal Order was issued to make a court inquiry of Don Fernando de Berrio, Governor of Trinidad and Guyana, and his ministers and other officials of state and to investigate the smuggling charges and punish the culprits discussed in previous chapters.

7 Notes Engel Sluiter, ESHDC, March 14, 1610, AGI, Santo Domingo, 191, discussed in Chapter 3.

so out of necessity as supplies and provisions were lacking during the 16 years of his governorship from 1597 until 1612. De Berrio was found guilty and in addition several mayors and town council members were implicated.

In Hispaniola, in the meantime, something similar happened. Here, the trade of tobacco was clearly linked to the complex infrastructure that had developed among consumers and producers of tobacco which could simply not be undone by edicts of depopulation or removal of coastal populations. In an interesting way, tobacco replaced sugar as the main colonial staple cultivated and traded in Hispaniola in the seventeenth century but once established, tobacco cultivation and trade created a force of its own outside of the regulated Spanish trading circuit.[8] In fact, the remarkable take-off of tobacco on Hispaniola occurred after the royal edicts (*cedulas*) were issued and after residents were removed from the Northwest coast. Once the area fell into decline and Spanish settlers had moved on to more profitable destinations in Mexico and Peru, for the remaining population --including a remnant of Amerindians, poor Spanish, Mestizo, Creole, and run-away slaves, along with Portuguese merchants-- tobacco became essential in trade with English, French, and Dutch privateers in order to receive supplies and provisions and, as a result, the contraband trade in tobacco had its heydays.[9]

The cases illustrate that *Tierra Firme* and Hispaniola had deeply entrenched interests in smuggling activities of which the tobacco trade was the most pronounced. Spain had allowed some parts of *Tierra Firme* to develop the contraband trade outside of the legal Spanish trade circuits and then tried to reverse course which led to widespread adversity, bribery,

---

[8] Escudero A. G. "Hispaniola's Turn to Tobacco," Aram B., Yun-Casalilla B. (eds), *Global Goods and the Spanish Empire, 1492–1824* (Palgrave Macmillan, London, 2014), pp. 216–229. See also, Laura Nater, "The Spanish Empire and Cuban Tobacco during the Seventeenth and Eighteenth Centuries" in Peter A. Coclanis (ed.), *The Atlantic Economy during the Seventeenth and Eighteenth Centuries* (The University of South Carolina Press, Columbia, 2005), pp. 252–276.

[9] Jesse Cromwell, *The Smugglers' World: Illicit Trade and Atlantic Communities in Eighteenth-Century Venezuela* (University of North Carolina Press, Chapel Hill, 2018) describes how estrangement from the metropolitan center (Spain) resulting from a lack of support and provisioning which drove settlers and tobacco planters to engage in contraband trade with the Dutch, English, and French privateers (pp. 46–47). Marcy Norton, *Sacred Gifts, Profane Pleasures: A History of Tobacco and Chocolate in the Atlantic World* (Cornell University Press, Ithaca and London, 2008) describes how early Spanish and other European settlers and explorers became embedded in exchange with Amerindian societies in the sixteenth century along the coast of *Tierra Firme* and on the Caribbean islands out of necessity of obtaining food and access to fresh water as well as access to tobacco (pp. 90–102).

and revolt. The reason why Spain had permitted the illegal trade to occur was because of the lack of regular services and supplies being delivered to resident coastal populations after Spain's primary attention was directed towards gold and silver mining on the mainland. Once the illicit trade was in place and merchant networks depended on on-going contraband activity, it was very difficult to dislodge as we know from the historical record of illicit trade in the late seventeenth and eighteenth centuries.[10] From the start, the Spanish mercantile system depended on supplies and provisions from elsewhere in Europe, mostly Northwestern Europe, which engaged Dutch, English and French private merchants in the Iberian trade. Dependent on the ebb and flow of war and peace, Spain's trading partners were either favored or obstructed in conducting trade. Regardless, markets in Northwestern Europe absorbed a great deal of the Spanish or Portuguese colonial products brought into port as Spain and Portugal depended on supply goods and provisions from the Dutch Republic, England, or France.

Most transactions within the legal trading system benefitted powerful merchant groups or merchant houses in Andalucia (Seville), and Portugal (Lisbon). These merchant houses began to dominate the finances, logistics, and regulatory systems which dictated mercantile policies of the *Casa de Contratacion*. By determining who could trade and legally enter the Spanish and Portuguese American colonies, the system grew rigid and mostly closed-off which was one reason why smuggling traditions began to take hold. Over time, the strict schedule of the *Carrera de Indias* which serviced the principal ports at set times of the year, meant that there was little flexibility to adapt to changing market conditions. This created opportunities to manipulate prices by the major merchant houses and contributed to bribery and fraud on the part of customs officials. It was in this environment that Dutch, English and French merchants and corsairs were able to penetrate the system and engage in contraband trade. It was also in this environment that Portuguese merchants became involved in the various segments of the trans-Atlantic trade.[11]

---

10 Wim Klooster, *Illicit* Riches: *Dutch Trade in the Caribbean, 1648–1795* (KITLV Press, Leiden, 1998). See also Linda M. Rupert, *Creolization and Contraband: Curacao in the Early Modern Atlantic World* (The University of Georgia Press, Athens, London, 2012); Cromwell, *The Smugglers' World* (2018).

11 Cromwell, *The Smugglers' World* (2018), pp. 33–42; Daviken Studnicki-Gizbert, *A Nation Upon the Ocean Sea: Portugal's Atlantic Diaspora and the Crisis of the Spanish Empire, 1492–1640* (Oxford University Press, Oxford, New York, 2007), pp. 34–38.

5.2 The "Vast Machine" of the Portuguese Nation

The onset of trade among the members of the Portuguese Nation occurred during the second half of the sixteenth century and accelerated after 1580 with the unification of Spain and Portugal. As the European market for Atlantic and Caribbean colonial products expanded—sugar and tobacco in particular—Portuguese merchants of the Nation became well established in the Atlantic world and gained a foothold in Amsterdam. They also migrated to Andalucia (Seville and Cadiz) where they established themselves as banker-merchants financing a substantial part of the Spanish Court and its Administration and formed a link to Northern Europe connecting silver mines and sugar plantations to the manufacturing sectors of England, the Dutch Republic, and France. As Amsterdam developed as the most prominent staple market for colonial goods it became the main center for processing and distributing sugar and tobacco.[12] By extension, the Portuguese merchants also engaged in the slave trade as they had established relationships with West Africa and encountered a growing demand for slave labor in Brazil serving sugar plantations and on *Tierra Firme* and Hispaniola where tobacco plantations were being established. Along trade routes across the Atlantic they established links with transfer points in the Azores, Madeira, and in particular in the Canary islands and they embarked as crew on trading vessels of the *Carrera de Indias* as well as on Dutch, English, and French merchant vessels. Along the coast of *Tierra Firme* and on the Spanish islands they became resident merchants supplying the growing number of settlers and plantation owners and along the established route across the Caribbean region they became the factors and correspondents for Dutch, English, and French merchants. As Stucnicki-Gizbert in *A Nation upon the Ocean Sea* (2007) observed, a tight relationship had been forged between the Nation and the Spanish Habsburg Empire whereby Portuguese merchants shadowed the westward expansion of Spanish settlers and then alongside merchants of other nations organized the commercial infrastructure necessary for Spanish colonization.[13] However, after the 1580 unification with Spain, Portuguese merchants became more suspect. Having aligned with Habsburg Spain, the Portuguese were drawn into war with the Dutch Republic on the wrong side of trade. As Dutch merchants were prohibited to trade with the Spanish possessions and the Spanish Crown officially prohibited commerce of any sort

---

12 Jonathan I. Israel, *Dutch Primacy in World Trade, 1585–1740* (Clarendon Press, Oxford, 1989); Wim Klooster, *The Dutch Moment: War, Trade, and Settlement in the Seventeenth-Century Atlantic World* (Cornell University Press, Ithaca, London, 2019).

13 Studnicki-Gizbert, *A Nation Upon the Ocean Sea* (2007), pp. 38–39.

with their enemies during the Eighty Years' War, the Portuguese merchants became ever more important as go-between and ever more suspect in the eyes of the Spanish administrators. And thus the contraband trade was born which engaged Portuguese merchants and also Sephardic merchants from Amsterdam and smaller Jewish merchant communities in Hamburg and along the west coast of France.

Clearly, Dutch-Spanish and Dutch-Portuguese trade relations in the early seventeenth century were determined by the occurrences of battles, embargoes, and trade protection measures in effect during the Eighty Years' War. The Dutch engaged in war with Habsburg Spain for a good part of the sixteenth and first half of the seventeenth centuries from 1568 to 1648. Only during the Twelve Years' Truce from 1609 to 1621 did some order of normalcy return in trade with the Iberian Peninsula, but Dutch trade with *Tierra Firme* and the Spanish Caribbean islands remained off limits. For much of the time at war, battles were fought at sea and attacks occurred at various entry points of major rivers where the Spanish held sway over self-declared territorial hegemony in *Tierra Firme* and the Caribbean islands of Jamaica, Hispaniola, Cuba, Puerto Rico and Trinidad. Brazil was a Portuguese possession but as Portugal was united with Spain from 1580 until 1640, Spanish territorial control and trade restrictions affected Brazil as well even though Portugal continued to trade on a semi-autonomous basis. All Dutch trade as well as trade conducted by Portuguese and Sephardic merchants resident in the Dutch Republic was thus illegal and therefore usually not recorded contractually. In effect, we have only incidental evidence of the tobacco trade from the Spanish colonies in the Notary Public records of Amsterdam in the early seventeenth century as Dutch merchants, as well as Amsterdam Sephardic and Portuguese New Christian merchants resident in Amsterdam, were trespassers in the Iberian colonial world and the traditional carrying trade with the Iberian Peninsula, including Portuguese ports, was officially blocked prior to the years of the Twelve Years' Truce from 1609 to1621. Consequently, Dutch merchants and Amsterdam's Sephardic merchants ventured out to the coastal areas of South America and the Caribbean islands where they bartered or traded with indigenous coastal populations and resident Portuguese merchants for products in demand in the Dutch Republic, including tobacco.

In *Tierra Firme* salt mining at Punta de Araya was the initial driving factor which led to contact with coastal communities for food and fresh water and tobacco exchange with indigenous populations. The region was thinly populated and Amerindians alongside Creoles, Mestizos, run-away slaves, and Portuguese merchants as well as English, French, and Dutch mariners and merchants freely congregated and conducted trade along the coast.

In exchange with Hispaniola, cow hides were the initial attractions but soon tobacco was traded as well. As some documentary evidence and explorer reports illustrate, Amsterdam's tobacco trade or smuggling as the case may be, involved besides Dutch merchants also Sephardic merchants after a small but significant Portuguese Jewish merchant community had emerged in Amsterdam in the late sixteenth century which was linked to the sugar trade originating in the Portuguese Atlantic Islands of Madeira, São Tomé, the Cape Verde Islands, and Brazil. At that time, during the last decade of the sixteenth century, Portuguese and Antwerp merchants were transferring their business to Amsterdam as alternating Dutch and Spanish embargoes and blockades of the Scheldt River and the Flanders coast obstructed commerce. Soon a notable amount of colonial staple goods including sugar and tobacco were traded, processed, and distributed via the Amsterdam market. As in the sugar trade, the tobacco trade involved contacts with Portuguese merchants engaged in trade or exchange in Spanish America and Portuguese Brazil. Some of this trade was with the Iberian Peninsula (Seville and Lisbon), but in other instances and in particular when contraband or illegal commerce was conducted, exchange took place via the Canary Islands or the Atlantic ports in France, England, the Dutch Republic and North Germany; notably Amsterdam, Hamburg, London, and Bayonne in Southwestern France.[14]

From the analysis presented, the trade and smuggling that emerged can best be described as entangled as it shows evidence of interconnections between the Dutch Republic and the Iberian Peninsula and Spanish and Portuguese possessions and mutually reciprocal relationships between Portuguese New Christian and Sephardic Jewish merchants alongside Dutch, French, English, and German merchants that spanned the Atlantic and Caribbean worlds.[15] Often, the relationships were trans-national or trans-imperial and involved merchant groups at various points of contact that had traded with each other before.[16] Sometimes, the exchange took place on the periphery of empires or in coastal areas where imperial power was poorly represented

---

14 See, Carsten L. Wilke, "Contraband for the Catholic King: Jews of the French Pyrenees in the Tobacco Trade and Spanish State Finance," in Rebecca Kobrin and Adam Teller (eds.), *Purchasing Power: The Economics of Modern Jewish History* (University of Pennsylvania Press, Philadelphia, 2015), pp. 46–70.

15 Studnicki-Gizbert, *A Nation Upon the Ocean Sea* (2007). See also, and in particular, Jonathan I. Israel, "Jews and Crypto-Jews in the Atlantic World System, 1500–1800," in Kagan and Morgan (eds.), *Atlantic Diasporas* (2009), pp. 3–17.

16 Daniel M. Swetschinski, *Reluctant Cosmopolitans: The Portuguese Jews of Seventeenth-century Amsterdam* (The Littman Library of Jewish Civilization, London, Portland, 2000), and Jessica Vance Roitman, *The Same but Different: Inter-Cultural Trade and the Sephardic, 1595–1640* (Brill, Leiden, 2011).

as was the case in the early seventeenth century in *Tierra Firme* and on the Spanish Caribbean islands.[17] In still other instances, specific contacts between West Africa, *Tierra Firme*, and the Spanish Caribbean islands occurred in which Dutch, Portuguese, and Sephardic merchants engaged in both the slave and tobacco trade.[18] By the late sixteenth century, Dutch merchants made regular voyages to *Tierra Firme* and sailed up the Orinoco and Amazon rivers and their tributaries but from the ship logs that have survived we do not gain a clear picture as to what extent tobacco was deliberately planted and traded or if exchange was conducted mainly through barter.[19] Norton, in *Sacred Gifts* (2008), suggests that tobacco production for Atlantic trade initially occurred in the Eastern Caribbean which she describes as a colonial backwater in the late sixteenth century and alliances formed between semi-autonomous Amerindian communities and English and Dutch privateers, Portuguese merchants, and various Spanish coastal settlers.[20]

From all accounts researched for this project that was the case. *Tierra Firme*—along the coast between the Orinoco and Amazon rivers—and the Spanish Caribbean islands—Trinidad and Hispaniola in particular—were among the first regions where tobacco was cultivated and traded and where colonial officials collaborated with foreign merchants about which the *Audiencia* in Santo Domingo expressed constant and persistent concern. From archival records we know more about English privateers engaged in illegal exchange in the Eastern Caribbean region in the late sixteenth

---

17 Studnicki-Gizbert, *A Nation Upon the Ocean Sea* (2007), pp. 118–119; Swetschinski, *Reluctant Cosmopolitans* (2000), pp. 108–109.

18 Cata Antunes and F. R. D. Silva, "Cross Cultural Entrepreneurship in the Atlantic, Africans, Dutch and Sephardic Jews in Western Africa, 1580–1674," *Itinerario*, vol. 35, no. 1, 2011, pp. 49–76.

19 From archival records we know more about English privateers engaged in illegal exchange in the Caribbean region in the late sixteenth and early seventeenth century during the English-Spanish war from 1585 to 1604 than about Dutch or Amsterdam merchants engaged in contraband trade in the region at the same time. See K. R. Andrews, "English Voyages to the Caribbean, 1596–1604: An Annotated List," in *The William and Mary Quarterly*, vol. 31, no. 2, April 1974, pp. 243–254. The English language literature on tobacco exchange in *Tierra Firme* is almost exclusively related to English merchant explorers, see for instance Norton, *Sacred Gifts* (2008), Chapter 7, pp. 141–172, and Cromwell, *The Smuggler's World* (2018), pp. 52–58. According to George Edmundson, "The Dutch on the Amazon and Negro in the Seventeenth Century," *The English Historical Review*, vol. 18, no. 72, October 1903, pp. 642–663, the Dutch and English often collaborated in maritime adventures in the late-sixteenth and early-seventeenth centuries and explorer records often refer to encounters with both Dutch and English merchants.

20 Norton, *Sacred Gifts* (2008), "Introduction," pp. 1–12; Chapter 7: pp. 148–156.

and early seventeenth centuries during the English-Spanish war from 1585–1604 than about Dutch or Amsterdam merchants engaged in contraband trade in the region at the same time.[21] The Dutch and English merchants often collaborated in maritime adventures in the late-sixteenth and early-seventeenth centuries as they were both at war with Spain and evidence from the Sluiter collection of documents suggests that they delivered and received tobacco shipments from each other. We do know a great deal more about Dutch contraband trade during the second half of the seventeenth century and the eighteenth century, most of which was conducted via Curacao and nearby territories of what is now Western Venezuela: Coro and Maracaibo.[22]

Research on the early seventeenth century contraband trade is limited by the fact that very few public records exist due to the nature of the trade conducted and the geographical scope of the area where contraband trade occurred; in the backwaters of the Spanish and Portuguese colonial realms. Accessing the Engel Sluiter Historical Document Collection made me aware of that. Throughout the Engel Sluiter Historical Document Collection, smugglers and foreigners involved in illegal trade are referred to in the context of capture, corruption and bribery charges and policy strategies in dealing with illegal trade. Remarkable are the detailed considerations to inundate or to depopulate areas where smuggling occurred and tobacco was cultivated and exchanged. The collection on *Tierra Firme* and Hispaniola also describes involvement of indigenous Indian tribes, Creoles, run-away slaves, and Portuguese merchants in coastal areas where they had settled to conduct trade or engage with smugglers. There is ample evidence in the collection from records presented that Dutch merchants

---

21 See K. R. Andrews, "English Voyages to the Caribbean, 1596–1604: An Annotated List," in *The William and Mary Quarterly*, vol. 31, no. 2, April 1974, pp. 243–254. The English language literature on tobacco exchange in *Tierra Firme* is almost exclusively related to English merchant explorers, see for instance Norton, *Sacred Gifts* (2008), Chapter 7, pp. 141–172, and Cromwell, *The Smuggler's World* (2018), pp. 52–58.
22 See Wim Klooster, "Contraband Trade by Curacao Jews with Countries of Idolatry, 1660–1800," *Studia Rosenthaliana*, vol. 31, 1/2, 1997, pp. 58–73; Jonathan I. Israel, "The Changing Role of the Dutch Sephardic in International Trade, 1595–1715," in Joseph Michman (ed.) Proceedings of the Symposium on the History of the Jews in the Netherlands (1982), published in *Dutch Jewish History* (Jerusalem 1984), pp. 31–51, in which he emphasizes that after the Eighty Years' War had ended, Dutch Sephardic merchants conducted most of the carrying trade between Curacao and the Spanish American mainland often collaborating with Portuguese merchants at Cartagena and Maracaibo. See also Rupert, *Creolization and Contraband* (2012). Cromwell, *The Smuggler's World* (2018), Chapter 4.

were trespassers and not welcome in the colonial Iberian world of the late sixteenth and early seventeenth century.[23] Most of the evidence presented is from Spanish colonial administrators (*Audiencia*), who reported to the King and Council from territories administered about threats of smugglers with specific mention of Dutch and English mariners and merchants in contact with local indigenous or coastal populations. Quite often exchange contacts took place in rather remote locations away from the main ports which were the primary locations where the Spanish galleons frequented during their annual voyages. The smuggling trade with Portuguese or New Christian merchants included the slave trade. Frequently, reports were made of English and Dutch vessels lying at anchor delivering provisions and receiving pearls, hides or tobacco in return. Sometimes, when ships were captured and hauled into port, mariners or merchant smugglers were reported by name and their port of origin and voyage details were recorded and we thus gained some insight into the specifics of the merchants and products involved in smuggling activities. Of particular interest were situations where suspects were tried as was the case with Simon de Herrera, the Jewish merchant, who was persecuted by the Inquisition and whose goods were confiscated after he tried to sell his ship to the enemies, and who had sent for safe passage in order to escape to Holland or Zeeland in the Dutch Republic. He was eventually put to death when he was convicted. Another case concerned a Spanish governor, Don Fernando de Berrio, who pursued the search for El Dorado causing him great economic loss which he tried to compensate for by trading tobacco illegally with the English and the Dutch. He was denounced by the Council of the Indies in the province of Venezuela.

Concern about the frequency of tobacco smuggling is referred to in several of the reports and resulted, as we saw, in plans to prohibit tobacco cultivation or allow cultivation with royal permission only. In several instances, recommendations were made to undermine smuggling activities in specific coastal regions and depopulate specific areas. The records suggest that Portuguese merchant networks in trade with Bayonne, London, and Amsterdam were also implicated in tobacco smuggling activities. Furthermore, the salt pans of Punta de Araya, frequented by Dutch vessels to transport salt to the Dutch Republic were of particular concern as the Spanish administrators were well aware that besides salt, tobacco, pearls, and other trade goods were smuggled to Amsterdam and other ports in Holland and Zeeland.

---

23 For scope and content of the cartons and file folders see Listing Julie van den Hout, *Engel Sluiter Historical Documents Collection* (2016).

CONCLUSION

In Amsterdam, Portuguese New Christian and Sephardic merchants became the most prominent merchant groups engaged in the Atlantic staple trade, in particular in the sugar trade. In Chapter 1, I raised the question if the tobacco trade conducted by Portuguese and Sephardic merchants coincided with the sugar trade, and if so, did the same merchants participate in both trades or were they separate merchant groups conducting trade in different parts of the Atlantic world? From the accounts we have and have analyzed, we can draw a preliminary conclusion that Portuguese and Sephardic sugar merchants engaged in trade with Amsterdam focused their attention on Portuguese Brazil while tobacco merchants engaged in illegal trade with Spanish territories where the first tobacco barter exchange took place and where the first tobacco plantations developed, formed different trade networks. This does not mean that tobacco was not shipped alongside sugar from Bahia or Pernambuco, but most of the records in the Sluiter collection suggests that the tobacco trade occurred via different merchant networks. Swetschinski, in *Reluctant Cosmopolitans* (2000) concluded that by and large merchants exchanged whatever goods they could take along on board and sell for an acceptable price within a given circuit which suggests that colonial trade goods like sugar and tobacco may have been shipped and sold at various points along the routes of the Atlantic trade networks in Spain, Portugal, France, or Amsterdam and Hamburg as circumstances dictated. Evidence presented here suggests that this was the case. We do know that several Portuguese and Sephardic networks overlapped and that in due time different circuits developed in the Atlantic and Caribbean region and it is conceivable or likely that at transfer points in the trade networks some goods were loaded and unloaded and directed to different ports along the Atlantic seaboard or to different points of trade along the coast of South America and the Caribbean region. From all accounts, *Tierra Firme* and the Spanish Caribbean islands were among the regions where tobacco was first cultivated, traded, or bartered for and where the first plantations developed. This suggests that the slave trade along with the supply trade dictated that export of tobacco for Northern European markets originated in the same general areas. However, European efforts at colonization of the Wild Coast were mostly unsuccessful even though the Spanish, Portuguese, Dutch, English, and French all vied for control of the wide swath of mostly marsh land of *Tierra Firme*.[24] Considered the land

---

[24] Several attempts were made by Dutch explorers to settle specific locations along the Wild Coast but most of them failed.

of plenty and opportunity, and the land of gold (El Dorado), exploration efforts mostly failed and territorial gains more often than not were abandoned.[25]

As referred to, relatively few freight contracts drawn up by Notary Publics and archived at the City Archives of Amsterdam record tobacco shipments in the first few decades of the seventeenth century and few records of the first voyages to the Caribbean by Portuguese and Dutch explorers show specific evidence of tobacco shipments. Tobacco bartered for or traded in *Tierra Firme* and Hispaniola was illegal merchandise and therefore not recorded or accounted for but the fact that the Spanish prohibited tobacco cultivation and depopulated specific areas where tobacco contraband trade occurred suggest that smuggling was widespread. The reports sent by Spanish administrators to the King and Council document the contacts and collaboration between various groups and English, French, and Dutch smugglers and reveal the reasons why the Spanish officials participated in tobacco exchange and were bribed. In particular the role of Portuguese New Christian merchants in smuggling and bribery schemes seems evident.

It is within the context of these events that I analyzed the documents in the Engel Sluiter Historical Documents Collection. Whereas the connection between Portuguese merchants in *Tierra Firme* and Hispaniola and Dutch merchants and mariners is obvious, the connection with Amsterdam's Sephardic merchants and the tobacco market of Amsterdam is not directly evident from the documents and can only be implied. Here it is important to recognize the role first Antwerp and then Amsterdam played in trade with Portugal and the effect the unification of Spain and Portugal had on the Portuguese trade with Amsterdam after 1580. At the same time, a rapid increase in immigration of Portuguese New Christian into Spain and its territories occurred. The Dutch and the Spanish were at war with each other for most of the course of this study and were engaging in embargoes

---

25 William Usselincx, a Flemish merchant, was one of the major advocates of Dutch colonization of the Wild Coast which would also form a bulwark of the emerging Dutch Republic against Spanish domination in South America. In 1603 he petitioned to the States General in The Hague to promote Dutch settlement and the establishment of plantations. Others supported the idea but few Dutch immigrants volunteered to settle in the tropical and mostly inhospitable environment of *Tierra Firme*. For a review of the different failed attempts, see Jessica Vance Roitman, "Second is Best: Dutch Colonization on the 'Wild Coast'" in L. H. Roper (ed.), *The Torrid Zone: Caribbean Colonization and Cultural Interaction in the Long Seventeenth Century* (University of South Carolina Press, Columbia, 2018), pp. 61–205.

and blockades to obstruct each other's mercantile endeavors. The Dutch were prohibited or shied away from entering Iberian ports and at the same time they were blocking the entrance to Antwerp, then still a major staple market for Iberian and Baltic products. Between 1585 and 1595 the transfer of the staple market function for Northern Europe occurred between Antwerp and Amsterdam and in the process many Portuguese merchants—among them New Christian merchants—settled in Amsterdam where the opportunity was offered to safely practice the Jewish religion and gain a foothold in Dutch commerce at the same time.[26] According to Israel, in *Diasporas within the Diaspora* (2002), Dutch merchants first engaged in contraband trade with Spanish America via Portuguese New Christian contacts in Puerto Rico, Cuba, Hispaniola, and Cartagena but soon expanded their contacts along the coast of *Tierra Firme* where they engaged in the salt trade at Punta de Araya and meanwhile smuggled tobacco and pearls.[27] These contacts likely engaged Amsterdam Sephardic merchants as evidenced by one of the first records in the Engel Sluiter Historical Documents Collection, implicating Jewish merchants engaged in trade with Dutch merchants on Hispaniola in 1596. The Spanish, thereafter, imposed a ban on all Dutch trade with the Iberian Peninsula and kept a watchful eye on Dutch merchandise sold illegally in Spanish America. And thus the story unfolded.

The reports and documents collected by Sluiter and analyzed for the purpose of this study entail the period from roughly 1596 until 1607 (prior to the Twelve Years' Truce in effect from 1609–1621) when Dutch trade was severely undermined and trade with Spain and Portugal and their overseas territories was severely restricted. Sephardic merchants—resident in Amsterdam at that time—were or had been primarily involved in the trade of colonial staple goods among which sugar and tobacco from Portuguese Brazil and Spanish America were traded via Portugal. Under the circumstances of embargoes imposed and blockages occurring, Portuguese and Sephardic merchants ventured out alongside Dutch merchants to preserve or recapture their foothold in colonial trade. During the period of the truce from 1609 and 1621 trading opportunities with Portugal were restored but trade with

---

26 Jonathan I. Israel, "The Economic Contribution of Dutch Sephardi Jewry to Holland's Golden Age, 1595–1713," in *Empires and Entrepots: The Dutch, the Spanish Monarchy, and the Jews: 1585–1713* (The Hambledon Press, London, 1996), 417–447.

27 Jonathan I. Israel, *Diasporas within a Diaspora: Jews, Crypto-Jews and the World Maritime Empires: 1540–1740*, (Brill, Leiden, London, Cologne, 2002), "Introduction" pp.1–39; pp. 16–19.

the Spanish and Portuguese territories remained off-limits.[28] The ongoing negotiations between Spain and the Dutch Republic during the truce years to either establish peace or to resume war centered on commercial interests whereby Spain perceived itself to be in a disadvantaged position because Dutch trade with the Iberian Peninsula had resumed but Antwerp, in the Southern or Spanish Netherlands, remained off limit due to ongoing blockades of the Scheldt River which gave Amsterdam a clear advantage. Meanwhile, the Dutch contraband trade with the Spanish territories went on unabated and in 1621 war resumed.

In this context and by implication, it would seem that Dutch merchants and mariners connected with the Portuguese merchant networks of the Nation trusted that their established relationships at various points of contact along the Atlantic routes would allow them to circumvent blockades and embargoes. During the years of truce these network relationships were enhanced and reinforced and when Portuguese New Christian merchants became securely established in Portuguese Brazil and in Spanish America, Sephardic merchants conducting trade serving the Amsterdam market were able to fully integrate into the Atlantic merchant networks. So, whereas sailing under the Dutch flag prohibited commerce with Spanish and Portuguese possessions during the truce years, smuggling went on unabated. It is during the years of truce that a rapid growth in the sugar and tobacco trade focused on Amsterdam occurred and that members of the Portuguese Nation, as a result, moved in increasing numbers to the Dutch Republic from both Portugal and Antwerp, as well as from some other staple ports in Europe, including Rouen, Venice, and Livorno. In addition, several Portuguese or crypto-Jewish merchants from Brazil moved to Amsterdam where many re-converted to Judaism reinforcing the Portuguese and Sephardic trans-Atlantic trade networks.[29]

When hostilities between the Dutch Republic and Spain resumed in 1621, a new phase in trade relationship began and embargoes were re-imposed

---

28 See Jonathan I. Israel, "A Conflict of Empire: Spain and the Netherlands, 1618–1648," *Past and Present*, No. 76, August 1977, pp. 34–74. And, Israel, "Sephardic Immigration into the Dutch Republic, 1595–1672," *Studia Rosenthaliana*, vol. XXIII, Fall 1989, pp. 45–53. During the first decade of residency in Amsterdam, both London and Hamburg Sephardic merchants carried out much of the North-European trade with the Iberian Peninsula. Israel maintains that the truce years were a period of expansion of Dutch navigation and trade and a period of renewed immigration of Portuguese and Sephardic settlement in the Dutch Republic.

29 The London Sephardic community ceased to exist and all Jews were expelled by order of James I in 1609.

on Portuguese ports and the number of Jewish immigrants from abroad settling in Amsterdam was reduced.[30] Then, when Portugal regained independence from Spain in 1640, a brief period of restoration in trade relationships between Amsterdam and Portugal took effect, however, problems in Dutch Brazil in the mid-1640s spoiled the situation.[31] In the late 1640s when Spain and the Dutch Republic finally settled on a peace treaty and Spain lifted the embargoes on trade, a new influx of Portuguese immigrants to Amsterdam occurred and the trade in the Caribbean region via Curacao took hold. Meanwhile, a revolt by Portuguese planters in Brazil against Dutch rule and the eventual demise of the colony led to a return of Sephardic merchants to Amsterdam and a dispersal of Portuguese Jewish immigrants throughout the Caribbean region including emerging British and French colonies, the Dutch settlements in Suriname, Curacao and St. Eustatius, and some smaller Dutch settlements along the Wild Coast occurred.[32]

Thus, the "Vast Machine" referred to and discussed in detail by Studnicki-Gizbert in *A Nation Upon the Ocean Sea* (2007) consisting of mostly Portuguese New Christian merchants, established themselves alongside Spanish settlers in Spanish America and in Portuguese Brazil as members of the wide-spread Atlantic merchant network of the Portuguese Nation, engaged in the slave trade, the salt trade, the supply trade, and the trade in colonial staples. Evidence from the Engel Sluiter Historical Documents Collection supports that view but also demonstrates that connected to or integrated with the "Vast Machine" were Dutch and English merchants aspiring to become the merchants of the Atlantic world. Several of the records in the Engel Sluiter Historical Documents Collection, analyzed and discussed in chapters 3 and 4, show evidence that shipmasters, mariners and crew members were multi-national and derived from both the provinces of Holland and Zeeland and from London or other

---

30 Swetschinski, "Kinship and Commerce: The foundations of Portuguese Jewish Life in Seventeenth-century Holland," *Studia Rosenthaliana*, vol. XV, 1981, pp. 52–74; p. 62; Israel, "Sephardic Immigration into the Dutch Republic, 1595–1672," *Studia Rosenthaliana*, vol. XXIII, Fall 1989, pp. 45–53; p. 51.

31 Meanwhile there was an increase in the number of Sephardic resident merchants in Rouen, Hamburg, and Gluckstad, Denmark, and a return of Portuguese Jewish merchants to Antwerp which remained within the Spanish realm in the Southern Netherlands.

32 Israel, "The Changing Role of the Dutch Sephardim in International Trade, 1595–1715," referred to earlier, and Jonathan I. Israel, "Spain and the Dutch Sephardic, 1609–1660," *Studia Rosenthaliana*, vol. XII, no. 1/2, 1978, pp. 1–61.

ports in England besides pilots or merchants on board who were often Portuguese and likely New Christian and Jewish.[33]

The multi-national or cross-imperial nature of the tobacco trade is also evident in the trade with Virginia and Maryland in the 1620s and following decades.[34] England—like the Dutch Republic an up-start on the Atlantic scene—had challenged the hegemony of the Spanish Empire by attacking the Spanish at sea and raiding the shores of its colonial territories and by settling and occupying deserted or poorly defended islands and coastal regions and established Virginia as a tobacco colony in 1607. Norton and Stucnicki-Gizbert (2007) discuss how Virginia did not develop as a colony until two decades after tobacco plantations and trade on Trinidad had already engaged European merchants and planters. In their essay they suggest that Virginia was an off-spring of the trade network established earlier in the Caribbean region and along the shores of *Tierra Firme* in which English merchants alongside Dutch and Portuguese merchants took part. They point out that by 1606, tobacco smuggling was of such a magnitude that it invited *Cedulas* to be executed to prohibit the cultivation of tobacco and depopulate coastal areas in Spanish America and obstruct the contraband trade conducted by both English and Dutch merchants and the documents in the Engel Sluiter Historical Document Collection confirm that. In comparing the Anglo-American or Virginia's tobacco history and the history of tobacco cultivation and trade in Spanish America or Portuguese Brazil, Norton and Studnicki-Gizbert (2007) point to the fact that the take-off of tobacco as a staple good in the late sixteenth and early seventeenth centuries was made possible by multiple commercial partnerships emerging across the Atlantic involving traders and planters from both England and Spain-Portugal whereby Virginia was just an extension of existing relationships. In these relationships they mention Portuguese and English merchants engaged in the Atlantic trade networks but, oddly enough, they hardly mention Dutch merchants engaged in the supply trade and tobacco trade to and from *Tierra Firme* and later Virginia and the role Amsterdam Sephardic merchants played in the processing and distribution of tobacco in the Northern European market.

---

33 See, for instance, the case of Simon de Herrera!

34 Wim Klooster, "The Tobacco Nation: English Tobacco Dealers and Pipe-Makers in Rotterdam, 1620–1650," in Laura Cruz and Joel Mokyr (eds.), *The Birth of Modern Europe* (Brill, Leiden, Boston, 2010), pp. 17–34; and Marcy Norton and Daviken Studnicki-Gizbert, "The Multinational Commodification of Tobacco, 1492–1650: An Iberian Perspective," in Peter C. Mancall (ed.), *The Atlantic World and Virginia, 1550–1624* (University of North Carolina Press, Chapel Hill, 2007), pp. 251–273.

CONCLUSION 143

The roots of tobacco cultivation and trade among Amerindian communities and the role African-Caribbean and Creole coastal residents played in the commodification process and the spread of tobacco cultivation along the coast of *Tierra Firme* and in Hispaniola is another aspect of the multinational or multicultural nature of tobacco cultivation and trade.[35] With reference to various contemporary sources it has been suggested that some tobacco plantations had developed and that some commodification of the crop had occurred by the late 1590s.[36] In that process, Amerindian, Creoles and African-Caribbean populations played an important role and Portuguese resident merchants seem to have been the all important go-between. As evidence from Hispaniola, Trinidad, Cumana, and La Margarita Island from Sluiter's document collection shows, within a decade after tobacco plantation cultivation was introduced, the contraband trade had become a major concern among Spanish officials in *Tierra Firme* and on Hispaniola.[37] It is within a few decades thereafter that tobacco plantations sprung up across the islands of the Lesser Antilles including Barbados and St. Kitts; English colonies from where Amsterdam merchants (among them Sephardic merchants) alongside English merchants carried the tobacco to market.

Like in the case of the English merchants described by Norton and Studnicki-Gizbert (2007), Dutch merchants turned to Portuguese merchants

---

35 The first notice of tobacco exchange dates from the 1530s involving African slaves on Hispaniola and different Amerindian groups in *Tierra Firme*. See Norton and Studnicki-Gizbert (2007), "The Multinational Commodification of Tobacco, 1492–1650," p. 256, with reference to Oviedo y Valdes, *Historia General* [...] Apparently, the crop followed African and Creole slaves from Hispaniola (Santo Domingo) to Cuba, Panama and the Venezuelan coast. Among slaves in the pearl fisheries in the early seventeenth century, tobacco smoking is of common use and Norton and Studnicki-Gizbert (2007, p. 257) consider this example as first evidence of a consumer market. Sluiter's collection of documents shows evidence of this and confirms the case.
36 The first use of tobacco among mariners in Seville, London and Flanders is noted in the 1570s. Norton, *Sacred Gifts* (2007), Chapter 7, notes the transition of tobacco being a casual consumption good to becoming a commodity between 1590 and 1610. See also, Norton and Studnicki-Gizbert (2007, p. 258) with reference to Pablo E. Perez Mallaina, *Spain's Men of the Sea: Daily Life on the Indies Fleets in the Sixteenth Century*–translated by Carla Rahn Philips (Johns Hopkins University Press, Baltimore, 1998).
37 As documented and as the Sluiter collection for Cumana, La Margarita Island, and Trinidad illustrates, the first tobacco plantations were established near the mouth of the Orinoco River in the 1590s where previously, the Cumanagoto Indians had held tobacco fairs to which Dutch, English, and French mariners were drawn to barter or trade. See also Norton and Studnicki-Gizbert, "The Multinational Commodification of Tobacco," (2007), p. 260.

to conduct the contraband trade with Spanish America, a trade facilitated by the deep-rooted network relationships between Dutch and Portuguese merchants that developed when the colonial staple market transferred from Antwerp (in the Spanish or Southern Netherlands under Habsburg control) to Amsterdam in rebel territory. Like in the case of England, the Dutch tobacco contraband trade took place during a time of war which meant that merchants were often blocked in their efforts to bring goods to market and diverted cargo to other destinations. In the case of Amsterdam, this was Hamburg, London, or ports in France like Rouen, Nantes, La Rochelle, Bordeaux, or Bayonne. During this period when the *Treaty of Nonsuch* between the Dutch Republic and England was in effect from 1585 until 1604 the Dutch and English actively collaborated in their common cause against Spain.[38] As a result, English and Dutch merchants exchanged goods relatively freely among each other which, given the nature of the Caribbean contraband trade, involved Portuguese merchants in the Atlantic circuits in the slave trade and in trade of colonial wares. A common feature among English and Dutch merchants involved in trade with Portuguese merchants was bribery.

The case of Don Fernando de Berrio in Trinidad documented in the Sluiter collection, and the case of Nunes Lobo, discussed in Norton and Studnicki-Gizbert (2007) show a remarkable likeness.[39] In fact, during the first decade of the seventeenth century, Anglo-Portuguese and Dutch-Portuguese trade networks are strikingly similar and most likely connected through the Anglo-Dutch commercial bond at the time. In 1604, the Spanish and English agreed to a peace settlement in which the English Crown committed to halt the import of tobacco from the Caribbean region just as the Dutch Republic tried to settle affairs of war with the Spanish in advance of the Twelve Years' Truce. In neither case was the state successful to ban the tobacco contraband

---

38 Pauline Croft, "Trading with the Enemy 1585–1604," *The Historical Journal*, Vol. 32, No. 2, (June, 1989), pp. 281–302, confirms that free trade between the English and the Dutch took effect and that product exchange in both directions occurred.

39 Rodrigo Manuel Nunes Lobo had become the Governor of Trinidad. Nunes Lobo was a well-to-do Portuguese merchant who was the Governor of Trinidad at the time in the late 1590s. He had made his fortune in the sugar trade at Hispaniola and had purchased the governorship of Cumana prior to his bid to become governor of Trinidad. His trade relationships with Portuguese merchants included merchants involved with the slave trade originating in West Africa. Norton and Studnicki-Gizbert "The Multinational Commodification of Tobacco," (2007), 261, suggest that many of these ties carried over from his days in Cumana, a period that saw the small settlement turn into what one Spanish official called, "a bin of foreigners, traitors and other delinquents, all of whom are sheltered and provided for by the Governor (Nunes Lobo)."

trade as contraband trade between the Caribbean and respectively England and the Dutch Republic continued unabated. Norton and Studnicki-Gizbert (2007) conclude that: "[...] the ability of Portuguese and English merchants to bypass the official routes of the official trading system forced Madrid to attack the problem at the source and in 1606, the Council of the Indies imposed a ten-year ban on production of tobacco across the Caribbean." From what we have learned from the Sluiter Historical Documents Collection, not only English and Portuguese merchants prevailed in the tobacco trade but also Dutch and Portuguese merchants and, by extension Sephardic merchants in Amsterdam, profitted from the trade. Through the first decade of the seventeenth century the English and Dutch tobacco contraband trade continued and growing quantities of "Spanish" tobacco arrived in London and Amsterdam.[40]

5.3 Conclusion

Tobacco was one of the first global commodities in the early modern era spreading rapidly from the Americas and to the whole Eurasian continent both in production and consumption. As the Devil's Weed the diffusion of tobacco as a medicinal remedy or as a sacred gift is a remarkable story of entanglement linking the Atlantic world with the Mediterranean world and beyond. The various Portuguese and Sephardic trans-Atlantic merchant networks discussed here connected with other networks of the Portuguese Nation including Sephardic merchants in North Africa and the East Mediterranean. The early tobacco trade, in fact, provides a good example of informal trade networks operating outside and yet as a major part of the early nation states emerging in Europe and colonial ambitions fought for by rival empires. As the Devil's Weed was a threat to the integrity of the nation state, regulatory regimes were quickly set up to deal with the new consumer commodity. By the 1620s a growing number of European countries imposed state monopolies and tax systems to regulate production and consumption and to render fiscal benefits from the nuisance behavior. Beyond the scope of discussion here it suffices to point out that in the case of Spain, the Crown took the step to engage members of the Portuguese Nation to carry out the schemes. The same was true for Italy where Sephardic merchants were contracted in the 1620s and 1630s to collect and distribute tobacco as it came

---

40 Norton and Studnicki-Gizbert, "The Multinational Commodification of Tobacco," (2007), pp. 270–271 with reference to Chaunu et Chaunu, *Séville et l'Atlantique*, vol. IV, pp. 572–573.

to market and in the Italian city-states of Verona, Venice, and Genoa, Sephardic merchants were granted exclusive trading rights and freedom of religion to collect fees and revenues for the state.[41] Obviously, the complex commodity chain network among Portuguese merchants and their hosts was basic to handling supply and distribution markets from the Americas to Western Europe and the Mediterranean. Beyond, lay Persia and India, where Levantine Jewish merchants traded and distributed tobacco.

In the Atlantic tobacco trade of the early seventeenth century, trade relationships reached beyond Seville, Lisbon, London and Amsterdam and engaged merchants of the Portuguese Nation including Sephardic merchants from Amsterdam who were also part of a network of contacts in Northern and Eastern Europe and in the Mediterranean and managed to deliver the goods despite wars, embargoes, and pirates at sea. Merchants of the Nation engaged in the Atlantic tobacco trade in the early seventeenth century mostly circumvented the various checks and actions imposed by Spanish officials and other imperial masters as they tried to undermine the tobacco contraband trade. Over time, most European nations imposed their own rules and regulations (monopolies and tax measures) on the tobacco trade and consumption but not until English and French colonies were established in the Caribbean region and in North America and trade protections began to take effect.[42] The Dutch for the most part tried to maintain a free trade regime and except for a few attempts at control of territorial possession along the Wild Coast and in Portuguese Brazil, Dutch mariners were procurers rather than producers; merchants rather than cultivators. Dutch merchants established factors rather than colonists when they explored or exploited commercial opportunities. The factor, familiar with the trade of a particular product, would reside near the source of supply or traverse along the coast and procure available or desirable commodities and wait for vessels to arrive and bring provisions and supplies in demand in coastal communities with which they bartered or traded in exchange. In the case of the tobacco trade, the factors were Portuguese merchants who had their contact relationships in Europe and in the Atlantic world with the Portuguese Nation including Sephardic merchants who managed the supply and distribution networks before the imperial state took control over supply and demand and was able to enforce trade regulations as happened in the mid-seventeenth century.

---

41 The Tuscan free port of Livorno (Leghorn in Dutch) was a good example of how the "Vast Machine" worked beyond the Atlantic world.

42 Melissa N. Morris, "Cultivating Colonies: Tobacco and the Upstart Empires, 1580–1640," (PhD dissertation, Columbia University, 2017).

BIBLIOGRAPHIC NOTES[1]

The monograph introduces the reader to Amsterdam as the global marketplace for tobacco. In describing the seventeenth century, Simon Schama in *The Embarrassment of Riches: An Interpretation of Dutch Culture in the Golden Age* (Alfred A. Knopf, New York, 1987) sets the stage. The rise of Amsterdam and the emergence of the Dutch Republic as the premier Atlantic power in the seventeenth century is presented by Jonathan I. Israel, *Dutch Primacy in World Trade, 1585–1740* (Clarendon Press, Oxford, 1989), and Jan de Vries and Ad van der Woude, *The First Modern Economy: Success, Failure, and Perseverance of the Dutch Economy, 1500–1850* (Cambridge University Press, Cambridge, 1997). For detailed analyses of the circumstances and forces that explain the emergence and success see C. Lesger, *The Rise of the Amsterdam Market and Information Exchange* (Ashgate, Aldershot UK and Burlington VT, 2006) and the edited volume by C. Lesger and L. Noordegraaf, *Entrepreneurs and Entrepreneurship in Early Modern Times: Merchants and Industrialists within the Orbit of the Dutch Staple Market* (Hollandse Historische Reeks, the Hague, 1995). Johannes Postma and Victor Enthoven (eds.), *Riches from Atlantic Commerce: Dutch Transatlantic Trade and Shipping, 1585–1817* (Brill, Leiden, Boston, 2003) tie the success to Atlantic trade. Daniel M. Swetschinski, *Reluctant Cosmopolitans: The Portuguese Jews of Seventeenth-century Amsterdam* (The Littman Library of Jewish Civilization, London, Portland, 2000) describes and analyzes the role Portuguese Jewish or Sephardic merchants played in Amsterdam's rise to power.

Carl Ortwin Sauer, *The Early Spanish Main* (University of California Press, Berkeley and Los Angeles, 1966) lays the groundwork for our understanding of the Spanish conquest and early settlement of *Tierra Firme* and the Caribbean Islands. For the early Dutch explorations and trade in the Caribbean region see Cornelis C. Goslinga, *The Dutch in the Caribbean and on the Wild Coast, 1580–1680* (University of Florida Press, Gainesville, 1971). To understand the role Portuguese and Sephardic merchants played in early modern

---

1 Note: Included are only English language sources, no journal articles, and reference is made to edited volumes only when specifically addressing the relevant topic.

trade see Richard L. Kagan and Philip D. Morgan (eds.), *Atlantic Diasporas: Jews, New Christians, and Crypto-Jews in the Age of Mercantilism, 1500–1800* (Johns Hopkins University Press, Baltimore, 2009) and Jonathan I. Israel, *Empires and Entrepots: The Dutch, the Spanish Monarchy and the Jews, 1585–1713* (The Hambledon Press, London, 1990). See also, Daviken Studnicki-Gizbert, *A Nation Upon the Ocean Sea: Portugal's Atlantic Diaspora and the Crisis of the Spanish Empire, 1492–1640* (Oxford University Press, Oxford, New York, 2007) and Jessica Vance Roitman, *The Same but Different: Inter-Cultural Trade and the Sephardic, 1595–1640* (Brill, Leiden, 2011). The Atlantic circuit of trade and connections and the expansion of Europe overseas is skillfully presented with map illustrations by Donald W. Meinig, *The Shaping of America: A Geographical Perspective on 500 Years of History*; Volume 1: Atlantic America, 1492–1800 (Yale University Press, New Haven and London, 1986).

Significant contributions to our understanding of tobacco cultivation in the Caribbean region and trade with Europe include Marcy Norton, *Sacred Gifts, Profane Pleasures: A History of Tobacco and Chocolate in the Atlantic World* (Cornell University Press, Ithaca and London, 2008), and Melissa N. Morris, "Cultivating Colonies: Tobacco and the Upstart Empires, 1580–1640", (PhD dissertation, Columbia University, 2017). Our understanding of illicit trade and contraband trade in the later part of the seventeenth and the eighteenth centuries is illuminated by the works of Wim Klooster, *Illicit Riches: Dutch Trade in the Caribbean, 1648–1795* (KITLV Press, Leiden, 1998), Linda M. Rupert, *Creolization and Contraband: Curacao in the Early Modern Atlantic World* (The University of Georgia Press, Athens and London, 2012), and Jesse Cromwell, *The Smugglers' World: Illicit Trade and Atlantic Communities in Eighteenth-Century Venezuela* (University of North Carolina Press, Chapel Hill, 2018).

Rivalry between the Dutch Republic and Spanish America in the context of the Eighty Years' War (1568–1648) is discussed in detail by Jonathan I. Israel, *The Dutch Republic and the Hispanic World* (Oxford University Press, Oxford, 1982). The classic work on trade and navigation between Spain and its American colonies is Clarence Henry Haring, *Trade and Navigation between Spain and the Indies in the time of the Habsburgs* (Yale University Press, New Haven, 1917) and for an overview of more recently published research on specific topics on Spain and the Caribbean region see Ida Altman and David Wheat (eds.), *The Spanish Caribbean and the Atlantic World in the Long Sixteenth Century* (University of Nebraska Press, Lincoln, 2019). For information on specific Spanish colonial trade goods including tobacco see B. Aram and B. Yun-Casalilla (eds.), *Global Goods and the Spanish Empire, 1492–1824* (Palgrave Macmillan, London, 2014). Christopher Ebert, *Between Empires: Brazilian Sugar in the Early Atlantic Economy, 1550–1630* (Series: The Atlantic World, Volume 16, 2008) discusses how Portugal was drawn into the conflict between Habsburg Spain and the Dutch Republic.

On the Dutch and English colonization efforts see, Vincent T. Harlow (ed.), *Colonising Expeditions to the West Indies and Guiana, 1623–1667* (The Hakluyt Society, London, 1925) and Goslinga, *The Dutch in the Caribbean and on the Wild Coast* (University of Florida Press, Gainesville, 1971) which are the classic studies on English and Dutch explorations and expeditions along the *Tierra Firme* and Caribbean coasts. In *The Dutch Moment: War, Trade, and Settlement in the Seventeenth-Century Atlantic World* (Cornell University Press, Ithaca, 2016), Wim Klooster argues that by design the Dutch planned to unseat Portuguese and Spanish rule in Brazil and the Caribbean region. See also, Christian J. Koot, *Empire at the Periphery: British Colonists, Anglo-Dutch Trade, and the Development of the British Atlantic, 1621–1713* (New York University Press, New York and London, 2011) and L. H. Roper (ed.), *The Torrid Zone: Caribbean Colonization and Cultural Interaction in the Long Seventeenth Century* (University of South Carolina Press, 2018) which addresses, among other topics, the commercial relationships between British colonists and Dutch merchants. For discussions on westward expansion across the Atlantic see K. R. Andrews et.al., *The Westward Enterprise: English Activities in Ireland, the Atlantic, and America, 1480–1650* (Wayne State University Press, Detroit, 1979), Peter A. Coclanis (ed.), *The Atlantic Economy during the Seventeenth and Eighteenth Centuries* (The University of South Carolina Press, Columbia, 2005), Peter C. Mancall (ed.), *The Atlantic World and Virginia, 1550–1624* (University of North Carolina Press, Chapel Hill, 2007), and Laura Cruz and Joel Mokyr (eds.), *The Birth of Modern Europe* (Brill, Leiden and Boston, 2010).

Francesca Trivellato, *The Familiarity of Strangers: The Sephardic Diaspora, Livorno, and Cross-Cultural Trade in the Early Modern Period* (Yale University Press, New Haven, London, 2009), and Catia Antunes and Amerila Polonia (eds.), *Beyond Empires: Global, self-organizing, cross-imperial networks, 1500–1800* (Brill, Leiden, 2016) address the importance of merchant networks. See also Antunes and Polonia, *Seaports in the First Global Age: Portuguese Agents, Networks and Interactions (1500–1800)* (UPorto Edicoes, Porto, 2016). Jonathan I. Israel, *Diasporas within a Diaspora: Jews, Crypto-Jews, and the World Maritime Empires: 1540–1740* (Brill, Leiden, 2002) and *Empires and Entrepots: The Dutch, the Spanish Monarchy and the Jews, 1585–1713* (The Hambledon Press, London, 1990) addresses the role of Portuguese and Sephardic merchants in Atlantic trade networks more specifically. In a *World on the Move: The Portuguese in Africa, Asia, and America 1415–1808* (Carcenet, Manchester, 1992), Russell-Wood reminds us of the connections, interactions, and movement of goods and people in the early modern Atlantic world and Juan Ponce Vázquez, *Islanders and Empire: Smuggling and Political Defiance in Hispaniola, 1580–1690* (New York, Cambridge University Press, 2020) details how contraband trade came to define the political, economic and geographical situation in seventeenth-century Hispaniola.

INDEX

African slaves 25, 101
alcabala 36, 73, 74, 93
almojarifazo 93
Amsterdam 1n1, 3, 12, 18n40, 21, 23, 26, 28, 39, 43, 52, 54, 56, 95, 131–133, 136, 139, 140, 146
Andrews, K. R.
  The Westward Enterprise: English Activities in Ireland, the Atlantic, and America, 1480–1650 83n34, 128n4, 149
Anglo-Dutch trade 54n59
Anglo-Spanish War (1585–1603) 104
Antwerp 2, 3n5, 4, 7, 18n40, 54, 56, 95, 139, 144
Arawak Indians 91
Archivo General de Indias 67
Armada de Barlovento 68, 106
Arrendadores 58, 60
arribados 113, 114
Audiencia 33, 34, 42, 66, 76, 87, 92, 96, 101–104, 106, 110n33, 111, 113, 114, 119–123, 134
Aveiro 48, 73, 80

Baltic grain trade 3
Barbados 38
Batie, Robert C. 38n16
Bayonne 30, 56, 133, 136
Bernardo de Vargas Machua 84
African slaves 11, 41, 100, 113
Bloom, Herbert I.
  The Economic Activity of the Jews of Amsterdam 7n13, 17n37, 19n43, 20n47, 30n81
Bordeaux 56

Boyajian, James C.
  Portuguese Bankers at the Madrid Court, 1626–1650 59n76
Brabant 2
Brazil 18, 19, 29n78, 46, 65
Brongers, George A.
  Nicotiana Tabacum: The History of Tobacco and Tobacco Smoking in the Netherlands 7n12, 71

Cabildo 106, 119, 120
Canary Islands 15, 25, 29n79, 30, 36, 51, 54, 60, 70, 74, 75, 77–79, 96, 97, 99, 101, 115, 122, 131, 133
Cape Verde Islands 65, 72, 97
Caribbean islands 1, 4, 10, 14, 17, 18, 20, 29n80, 31, 37, 38n16, 41, 46, 50, 54, 55, 61, 63, 69, 97, 101, 105, 129n9, 132, 134, 137, 147
Caribs 72, 79, 90–92
Carrera de Indias 14n27, 56, 130, 131
Cartagena (Colombia) 103
Casa de Contratacion 33, 34, 67, 69, 77n24, 89, 92, 94, 113, 130
Cedula 74, 81n30, 82n33, 84, 93, 93n51, 94, 105–107, 109, 110, 118, 119, 123, 127, 128, 142
Charles V (1516–1556) 34, 35n5, 109
City Archives of Amsterdam 12n24, 19n44, 21, 22, 26, 27, 29n78, 63, 138
Columbus 101, 104, 105
Consejo de las Indias 53, 76, 85, 109–112, 120
Contaduria 41, 66, 73

Converso merchants 1n2, 14–17, 18n40, 20, 21n48, 23n56, 30, 31, 36n7, 48n42, 106n22
Count-Duke Olivares 23, 55, 59, 99
Croft, Pauline
  "Trading with the Enemy 1585–1604" 144n38
Cromwell, Jesse 96
  The Smugglers' World: Illicit Trade and Atlantic Communities in Eighteenth-Century Venezuela 2n4, 18n40, 20n45, 21n48, 29n79, 31n84, 40n21, 45n31, 49n45, 50n49, 65n4, 105n20, 129n9, 130n10, 134n19, 135n21, 148
crypto-Jewish merchants 50, 52, 105, 106n22, 123, 140
Cuba 20, 44, 106
Cumana 6
Cumanogote 86

de Alquica, Sancho 87, 90, 91
  Interrogatorio General 88
de Amaya, Suarez 75
de Aviles, Juan Valvarez 106
de Berrio, Antonio 82
de Berrio, Don Fernando 82, 87, 88, 128, 129, 136
de Castro, Baltazar Lopez 118
  Escribano de Camara de la Cancilleria 116, 117
de Fajardo, Luis 68, 71
de Haro, Juan 92
de Mancilla, Juan Diaz 92
de Muxica, Antonio 91
Devil's Weed 145
Don Juan Tostade 91, 92
Don Luis Fajardo 45, 76
Dutch Golden Age 1
Dutch mariners 6, 9, 20, 34, 42, 50, 52, 53, 64, 70, 78, 95, 124, 128, 138, 140, 146
Dutch merchants 1, 4, 6, 9, 28–30, 34, 38, 42, 50, 52, 54, 55, 63–65, 67, 70, 73, 80, 87, 96, 130–134, 138, 140, 142, 143, 149
Dutch Republic 2, 3, 10n18, 12, 13, 17n36, 18, 26, 28, 29, 30n80, 33, 43, 44, 4647, 48n42, 49n44, 51, 61, 63, 66, 71–73, 78, 80, 97, 102, 122, 124, 127, 131–133, 136, 140, 141, 144, 145, 148
Dutch ships 4, 44, 50, 53
Dutch trade 4, 22, 41, 46, 47, 53, 63, 66, 128, 132, 139, 140

Ebert, Christopher
  "Dutch Trade with Brazil before the Dutch West India Company, 1587–1817" 12n23
  Between Empires: Brazilian Sugar in the Early Atlantic Economy, 1550–1630 6n11, 148
Edmundson, George 38n38, 38n39
Eighty Years' War (1568–1648) 1, 2, 13, 16n34, 26, 31, 33–35, 40, 43n27, 44, 47, 48n42, 52, 53, 71n13, 104, 123, 132, 135n22, 148
Eighty Years' War (1609–1621) 22n52, 23n57, 55, 64, 65n3, 97
England 47n41, 77n25, 131, 144, 145
English mariners 128
English merchants 38, 50, 54, 71, 87, 130, 131, 142
European market 8, 10, 39, 46, 56, 57, 131

Flanders 2, 47, 143n36
France 47n41, 72, 77n25, 131
Frank, Andre G.
  Dependent Accumulation and Underdevelopment 8n15
Freire, Pedro 108
French merchants 38, 130, 131

Goslinga, Cornelis C.
  The Dutch in the Caribbean and on the Wild Coast, 1580–1680 4n8, 6n10, 20n45, 33n1, 38n15, 53n53, 53n57, 54, 147, 149
Guiana 83n34
Guyana 84, 87, 91, 93, 128n6

Habsburg Empire 15, 35, 59
Habsburg Spain 1, 63, 65n3, 132
Habsburg Spanish Empire 13
Hamburg 13, 18n40, 23, 30, 56, 133

Hamm, Brian
    "Between Acceptance and Exclusion: Spanish Responses to Portuguese Immigrants in the Sixteenth-Century Spanish Caribbean" 37n11
Haring, Clarence H.
    Trade and Navigation between Spain and the Indies in the time of the Habsburgs 16n33, 34n2, 34n3, 34n4, 35n5, 35n6, 36n7, 36n8, 36n9, 37n10, 101, 148
Harlow, Vincent T.
    Colonizing Expeditions to the West Indies and Guiana, 1623–1667 38n15, 149
Herrera, Simon 112n39
Hispaniola 6–8, 19, 20, 21n48, 33, 34, 36n7, 40, 44, 52, 67, 96, 99, 101, 102, 104–107, 112, 117, 121, 123, 124, 128, 129, 131, 134, 135, 138, 143
Holy Roman Empire 35
Hurtado y Vernal 79

Iberian Peninsula 13, 16, 22, 36, 47, 48, 54, 55, 128, 132, 133
Iberian-Baltic trade 2
illegal trade 63
interlopers 1
Israel, Jonathan I. 3n5
    "The Changing Role of the Dutch Sephardic in International Trade, 1595–1715" 65n3, 135n22, 141n32
    "A Conflict of Empires, Spain and the Netherlands, 1618–1648" 56n65, 65n3, 139n27
    Diasporas within a Diaspora: Jews, Crypto-Jews, and the World Maritime Empires: 1540–1740 26n67, 65n3, 72, 139n27, 165
    Dutch Primacy in World Trade, 1585–1740 3n5, 4n7, 4n9, 17n37, 27n70, 30, 50, 72n16, 80, 131n12, 143, 163
    The Dutch Republic and the Hispanic World 1606–1661 33n1, 164
    "The Economic Contribution of Dutch Sephardi Jewry to Holland's Golden Age, 1595–1713" 15n31, 17n35, 139n26
    Empires and Entrepots: The Dutch, the Spanish Monarchy and the Jews, 1585–1713 15n31, 72n16, 59n76, 60n81, 65n3, 72n16, 163
    "Jews and Crypto-Jews in the Atlantic World Systems, 1500–1800" 4n9, 9n16, 133n15
    "The Jews of Curacao, New Amsterdam and the Guyanas: A Caribbean and Trans-Atlantic Network, 1648–1740" 39n19
    "Sephardic Immigration into the Dutch Republic, 1595–1672" 16n32, 140n28, 140n29
    "Spain and the Dutch Sephardic, 1609–1660" 24n58, 43n27, 55n63, 72n16, 141n32

Jewish merchants 16, 17, 22, 24n58, 30, 52, 65, 102, 105, 107, 122–124, 133, 136, 139
Jimenez, Francisco 115
Judaism 2n2, 16, 24, 140
Junta de Guerra de Indias 78, 88

Klooster, Wim 65
    "Contraband Trade by Curacao Jews with Countries of Idolatry, 1660–1800" 39n19, 134n19
    The Dutch Moment: War, Trade, and Settlement in the Seventeenth-Century Atlantic World 38n16, 64n1
    Illicit Riches: Dutch Trade in the Caribbean, 1648–1795 2n4, 20n45, 53n55, 65n4, 130n10
    "The Tobacco Nation: English Traders and Pipe-Makers in Rotterdam, 1620–1650" 24n60, 96n54, 142n34
Koen, E. M.
    "The Earliest Sources Relating to the Portuguese Jews in the Municipal Archives of Amsterdam up to 1620" 22n52, 22n53
Koot, Christian J.
    Empire at the Periphery: British Colonists, Anglo-Dutch Trade, and the Development of the British Atlantic, 1621–1713 149

La Margarita Island 6, 74, 84, 90
Lesger, C.
 The Rise of the Amsterdam Market and Information Exchange 3n5, 16n33, 17n35, 48n42, 147
Lisbon 4n8, 12, 15, 55, 67, 71, 108, 122, 146
Lombardi, John V.
 People and Places in Colonial Venezuela 26n68
London 13, 18, 23, 27n71, 29, 30, 43, 54, 56, 71, 108n28, 121, 122, 133, 136, 140n28, 141, 143n36, 144–146
Lopez, Antonio 115
Lorenzo Lopez de Ycurrategui 93
Lorimer, Joyce
 "The English Contraband Tobacco Trade in Trinidad and Guiana, 1590–1617" 128n4
Luteranos 15n29, 105

Madsen, Arthus W.
 The State as Manufacturer and Trader: An Examination Based on the Commercial, Industrial and Fiscal Results Obtained from Government Tobacco Monopolies 57n69
Mancall, Peter C.
 The Atlantic World and Virginia, 1550–1624 11n20, 149
Maryland 7n14, 142
Mediterranean 3, 10, 11, 14, 19, 25, 26, 47, 48, 99, 145, 146
Meinig, Donald W.
 The Shaping of America: A Geographical Perspective on 500 Years of History 7, 148
Meneses, Simon de 112, 113
Mexico 107, 129
Morisco merchants 18n40
Morris, Melissa N.
 "Cultivating Colonies: Tobacco and the Upstart Empires, 1580–1640" 2n4, 26n66, 37n13, 146n42, 148

Nantes 56
Netherlanders 91, 92
Netherlands 1, 16, 35, 77n25, 135n22

New Christian merchants 1n2, 3, 4, 14, 17, 19, 23n57, 24n58, 25n63, 26, 28n76, 29n78, 40n22, 43, 46, 48–50, 52, 55n62, 55n63, 58–61, 66, 79, 81, 95, 99, 122, 125, 132, 133, 136–141
New Netherland Institute 40
Northern Europe 99, 131
Northern European market 47, 137, 142
Northern Netherlands 2, 3
Northwest European market 7
Norton, Marcy 10, 57
 Sacred Gifts, Profane Pleasures: A History of Tobacco and Chocolate in the Atlantic World 2n4, 10n18, 10n19, 12n24, 28n73, 31n84, 37n13, 56n66, 57n68, 58n72, 61n82, 71n13, 129n9, 134n19, 135n21, 143n36, 148
Notary Public records 12n24, 19n44, 20, 21, 26–30, 63, 132
Nuñez, Hector 108n28

Ocean Sea 124n62
Oficiales Reales 121
Oidores 110n33, 111
Old Christian merchants 25n65
Orinoco Delta region 6
Orinoco River 28
Osorio, Antonio 120, 122

Peace Treaty of Munster 47
pearl 11, 20, 31, 37, 42–44, 49, 64, 73n18, 115–117, 128, 136, 139
 fishery 53, 64, 73, 75, 86, 143n35
 fishing 37, 72, 84, 85, 93, 124
 industry 84, 89
 smuggling 70, 72, 97
 trade 73
Pedro Suarez Coronel 82, 86, 87, 89, 92
Perez, Christobal 115
Peru 107, 129
Philip II 35
Philip IV 23, 55, 99
Philips rulle (1556–1598) 36
Ponce Vázquez, Juan José
 Islanders and Empire: Smuggling and Political Defiance in Hispaniola, 1580–1690 100n4, 101n6

Portugal 3, 4n7, 29n78, 47, 64, 95, 97, 99, 131
Portuguese Brazil 12, 30, 37, 40, 41, 65, 133, 137, 140, 146
Portuguese mariners 52
Portuguese merchants 1, 3, 13, 20, 22, 28, 29, 40, 46, 50, 52, 53n53, 54, 73, 78, 80, 95–97, 99, 101, 105, 106, 123–125, 127, 129, 131, 132, 134, 136, 137, 139, 140, 142, 144, 149
and the "Nation" 121–123
Portuguese Nation 14, 15, 17, 18, 65–67, 76, 96, 99, 105, 124, 141, 145, 146
illegal tobacco trade 20–27
Vast Machine 131–145
Practico 105n20
Puerto Rico 107
Punta de Araya 6, 37, 43n27, 45, 46, 50, 51–53, 64, 70–74, 80, 95, 97, 123, 132, 136, 139

Roitman, Jessica Vance 20
The Same but Different: Inter-Cultural Trade and the Sephardic, 1595–1640 13n25, 18n40, 21n48, 55n62, 133n16, 148
Rojas, Andres de 70n12
Roper, L. H.
The Torrid Zone: Caribbean Colonization and Cultural Interaction in the Long Seventeenth Century 149
Royal Order 87, 128n6
Royal Spanish Treasury 59
Rupert, Linda M.
Creolization and Contraband: Curacao in the Early Modern Atlantic World 2n4, 20n45, 39n18, 39n19, 40n21, 65n4, 130n10, 135n22, 148
Russell-Wood, A. J. R.
A World on the Move: The Portuguese in Africa, Asia, and America 1415–1808 99, 100n3

salt 4, 43n27, 44, 47, 49, 64
hauling 44, 70–73, 80
mining 46, 72, 123
pans 39n18, 71, 86, 127, 136
shipments 45, 64, 72, 80
smuggling 45, 72

trade 43n27, 51, 52, 53n53, 55, 70, 72n16, 97, 139, 141
winning 64, 95, 123, 132
San Juan (Puerto Rico) 103
Santo Domingo 103, 117, 120
Sauer, Carl Ortwin
The Early Spanish Main 101n5, 147
Schama, Simon
The Embarrassment of Riches: An Interpretation of Dutch Culture in the Golden Age 1n1, 7n13, 147
Schreuder, Yda
Amsterdam's Sephardic Merchants and the Atlantic Sugar Trade in the Seventeenth Century 6n11, 9n16, 12n23, 19n42
Schwartz, Stuart B.
Sugar Plantations in the Formation of Brazilian Society, Bahia, 1550–1835 6n11
Sephardic merchants 1, 4, 9, 11, 12, 16, 17, 19, 22, 24–26, 28n76, 29n78, 31, 39, 43, 46, 48–50, 52, 54, 56–61, 65–67, 78, 80, 81, 96, 124, 132–134, 137, 139, 145, 146, 149
Sephardic/Sephardim 1n2
Setubal 48, 72, 73, 80
Seville 12, 15, 33, 34, 36, 41, 50, 55–57, 66, 67, 69, 106, 108, 143n36, 146
slave trade 14, 15, 24, 25, 37, 41, 42, 59, 100, 104, 125, 131, 134, 136, 137, 141, 144
Sluiter, Engel 44n30, 45n31, 45n32, 45n33, 46n35, 46n36, 47n38, 48n43, 49n45, 49n46, 50n49, 51n50, 51n51, 52n52, 53n57, 70n10, 127
"Dutch-Spanish Rivalry in the Caribbean Area, 1594–1609" 38, 47, 70, 95, 102, 127
Hispanic American Historical Review 105
Smith, David Grant
"The Mercantile Class of Portugal and Bahia in the Seventeenth Century: A Socio-Economic Study of the Merchants of Lisbon and Bahia, 1620–1690" 97n55
Southern Netherlands 2, 3, 53, 59, 141n31

Southwestern France 23, 43, 48, 56, 58, 60, 133
Spain 3, 4n7, 34, 47, 48n42, 64, 72, 73, 80, 99, 106, 121, 131, 140, 141
Spanish America 6, 12, 30, 37, 40, 41, 47, 65, 133, 140, 148
Spanish Crown 20, 37, 46, 101, 103, 107, 122, 131
Spanish Habsburg Empire 25, 48n42, 131
Spanish Habsburg regime 14, 31, 33
Spanish islands 41, 80, 106, 131
Spanish merchants 3
Strum, Daniel
   The Sugar Trade: Brazil, Portugal, and the Netherlands 1595–1630 6n11
Studnicki-Gizbert, Daviken 57
   "Vast Machine" of the Portuguese Nation 14, 141
   A Nation Upon the Ocean Sea: Portugal's Atlantic Diaspora and the Crisis of the Spanish Empire, 1492–1640 13n25, 14n26, 14n27, 15n28, 17n37, 21n48, 23n57, 24n61, 25n63, 25n64, 31n85, 43n26, 58n72, 59n77, 59n78, 95n52, 97n55, 99n2, 100n3, 103n15, 104n18, 124n62, 130n11, 131n13, 133n14, 134n17, 141, 148
sugar 4, 10, 25, 27, 131
   cultivation 6n11, 8, 38
   mills 110, 111
   plantations 15, 37, 131
   production 8, 9, 20, 92, 109
   refinery 7, 46
   refining 6, 30
   trade 1n2, 3, 6n11, 7, 9, 12, 17, 18n40, 19, 22n52, 24n58, 24n59, 26, 29n78, 48, 55n62, 65, 100, 102, 133, 137, 140, 144n39
Swetschinski, Daniel M. 12, 20
   "Conflict and Opportunity in "Europe's Other Sea": The Adventures of Caribbean Jewish Settlement" 21n50, 23n56, 23n57, 25n65, 26n68, 44n29, 50n48, 54n61, 55n63, 57n71
   Reluctant Cosmopolitans: The Portuguese Jews of Seventeenth-century Amsterdam 11n22, 17n37, 18n40, 19n42, 19n43, 20n45, 21n48, 21n49, 27n70, 30n82, 133n16, 134n17, 137, 147

Tazzara, Corey
   The Free Port of Livorno and the Transformation of the Mediterranean World, 1574–1790 11n21
Thirty Years' War (1618–1648) 23n57
Tierra Firme 4, 6–8, 14, 17–20, 21n48, 26n66, 28, 29, 31, 33, 36, 37, 38n16, 39n18, 40n21, 41, 44–46, 49–53, 55, 58, 63, 64, 66–69, 72, 73, 75, 77, 78, 80, 86, 89, 91, 94–97, 104, 106, 107, 123, 124, 127–129, 131, 132, 134, 135, 137, 138, 142, 143, 147, 149
tobacco 1, 9, 11, 12, 18, 20, 27–30, 37, 46, 52, 64, 87, 124, 131, 138
   consumption 1, 10, 54, 71, 146
   cultivation 2n4, 8, 10, 20, 26n66, 37n13, 44, 57, 72, 73, 79, 80, 84, 92–95, 124, 125, 127–129, 136, 138, 142, 143, 148
   leaf 7
   monopoly 57, 58, 59n79, 60
   plantations 15, 37, 53, 59, 82, 95, 128, 131, 142, 143n37
   shipments 27n71, 138
   smoking 9, 143n35
   smuggling 40, 43–45, 51, 66, 70, 72, 76, 82, 97, 122–125, 128, 136, 142
   trade 2n4, 3, 6–9, 10n19, 12, 17, 19, 20, 24, 26, 30, 37, 41, 55, 57, 65, 73, 80, 87, 91, 94, 95, 96n54, 105, 124, 128, 129, 132–134, 137, 140, 142, 143, 145, 146
Treaty of Nonsuch 144
Trinidad 6, 10, 28, 37n13, 38, 64, 82, 83n34, 84, 87, 88, 90, 91, 93, 96, 97, 128n6, 134, 142
Trivellato, Francesca
   The Familiarity of Strangers: The Sephardic Diaspora, Livorno, and Cross-Cultural Trade in the Early Modern Period 11n21, 13n25, 25, 67n7, 149

Twelve Years' Truce (1609–1621) 13, 22n52, 22n55, 28, 43n27, 45n34, 46, 55, 56, 63, 64, 72, 73, 80, 132, 139, 144

Usselincx, William 138n25

van den Hout, Julie
Listing to the Engel Sluiter Historical Documents Collection 40n23, 66n5

Vázquez, Juan Ponce
Islanders and Empire: Smuggling and Political Defiance in Hispaniola, 1580–1690 149

Virginia 7, 142

Wallerstein, Immanuel M.
The Modern World System 8n15

West India Company (WIC) 6, 24, 39, 46, 64

Western Europe 13, 146

WIC. *See* West India Company

Wild Coast 4, 146

Wilke, Carsten L.
"Contraband for the Catholic King: Jews of the French Pyrenees in the Tobacco Trade and Spanish State Finance" 23n56, 56n64, 58n72, 58n73, 60n80, 133n14

Williams, Eric E.
Capitalism and Slavery 8n5

www.ingramcontent.com/pod-product-compliance
Lightning Source LLC
Chambersburg PA
CBHW021144230426
43667CB00005B/242